QUEEN OF THIEVES

Also by J. North Conway:

Kings of Heists

The Big Policeman

Bag of Bones

Attack of the HMS Nimrod: Wareham and the War of 1812

The Weather Outside is Frightful

The Cape Cod Canal: Breaking Through the Bared and Bended Arm

Shipwrecks of New England

New England Visionaries

New England Women of Substance

American Literacy: Fifty Books That Define Our Culture and Ourselves

From Coup to Nuts: A Revolutionary Cookbook

QUEEN OF THIEVES

The True Story of "Marm" Mandelbaum and Her Gangs of New York

J. NORTH CONWAY

Skyhorse Publishing

Skyhorse Publishing books may be purchased in bulk at special discounts for sales promotion, corporate gifts, fund-raising, or educational purposes. Special editions can also be created to specifications. For details, contact the Special Sales Department, Skyhorse Publishing, 307 West 36th Street, 11th Floor, New York, NY 10018 or info@skyhorsepublishing.com.

Visit our website at www.skyhorsepublishing.com.

10 9 8 7 6 5 4 3 2 1

Library of Congress Cataloging-in-Publication Data is available on file.

Cover design by Anthony Morais
Cover photo credit Library of Congress

Print ISBN: 978-1-62914-435-1
Ebook ISBN: 978-1-63220-098-3

Printed in the United States of America

This book is dedicated to my wife, Julia, who is the real "Queen among Thieves" for stealing my heart so long ago.

A QUEEN AMONG THIEVES

MOTHER MANDELBAUM'S VAST BUSINESS.

BUYING STOLEN SILKS BY THE THOUSAND YARDS—
DEPOTS IN MANY CITIES—BLACKMAILING DETECTIVES.

IN NEW-YORK CITY there are not over eight or nine men and women who are known as professional receivers of stolen goods. First in the list and standing at the head of the country as the largest dealer was Mrs. Fredericka Mandelbaum . . .

—*New York Times,* July 24, 1884

CONTENTS

"Fredericka Mandelbaum achieved a significant level of power and success as a criminal entrepreneur and became an important figure in the contemporary narrative of crime. She achieved what she did *because* (not in spite) of the time and place in which she used her talents."

—Rona Holub, scholar and author, 2007

Introduction

A MINGLED YARN

"The web of our life is of a mingled yarn, good and ill together."
—William Shakespeare, *All's Well That Ends Well*

Fredericka Mandelbaum, a German-Jewish immigrant,became the most influential crime figure in New York City during the Gilded Age, accumulating more money and power than any woman of her era at a level inconceivable for any women engaged in any legitimate business. As the country's premier fence (receiver of stolen property), she became the head of one of the country's first organized crime rings. Hailed by the New York press as "Queen among Thieves" she was a driving force behind New York City's festering underworld for more than twenty-five years.

A July 1884 *New York Times*' article called her "the nucleus and center of the whole organization of crime in New York City." Her lengthy reign was enabled by both a corrupt New York City police department and an unscrupulous political and judicial system. But it was her cunning intellect and association with the best criminal minds in the city that allowed her to attain such prominence. The engine that drove her to the top of her criminal profession was fueled by her devotion to her family as well as the crime family she surrounded herself with: her own family because she loved and cherished them and her crime family because they were the source of her wealth and power. Her immersion into a life of crime, as opposed to one of legitimacy, was a backlash against the cruel treatment she and her husband had endured at the hands of German authorities before being forced to immigrate to America. That abuse and distrust of authority kept her on the wrong side of the law throughout her life. She also had the keen realization that a woman, no less a Jewish woman facing all the native prejudices of the era, could never find acceptability or the kind of wealth and power she attained in any legitimate business.

Mandelbaum immigrated to New York City from Germany in 1850 with her husband, who was a peddler, and her first child, after German authorities imposed a series of laws restricting travel and trade by those of the Jewish persuasion. She began her climb to the top of the crime world in America as a peddler on the rough-and-tumble, bustling streets of the city. Because of her height (she was close to six feet tall) and her massive girth (she weighed close to 300 pounds), she easily stood out among the throng of street vendors. But it was more than just her physical presence that drew people to her. She quickly established a reputation as a fair trader among legitimate customers as well as a trusted ally to criminals trying to sell their stolen wares. It was this latter quality that led her to become the most sought after fences in New York City and propelled her to a place of prominence among the criminal element. She was savvy enough to realize, even in the earliest phase of her climb to power, that she could not carry on her business without the support of the city's corrupt political powers, the police, from the cop on the beat to those in command and the judicial system. Knowing full well the power of the almighty dollar and how it fed the ongoing corruption at every level, she paid tribute to these three forces (politicians, police, and judges) religiously, which allowed her criminal operation to grow and thrive unabated throughout the years.

By 1864, her enterprise, buying stolen merchandise from criminals and reselling it at a profit, had become so successful, she was able to move off the streets and buy a three-story building at Clinton and Rivington Streets, where she opened a haberdashery shop on the ground floor. For decades, it served as a respectable front for the biggest fencing operation in the history of the country.

She bought and sold a variety of stolen goods including silk, securities, and diamonds. She was viewed as an "honest crook," one who made fair deals with her cadre of criminals. She was the person to see if you wanted to move stolen goods or needed protection from the law or money to finance a caper. Mandelbaum kept the prestigious law firm of Howe & Hummel on a $5,000-a-year retainer and whenever one of her gang got into trouble, she was there to back him up with her money and connections. Mandelbaum offered her criminal cohorts bail and legal defense if they needed it and bribed police and judges to fix cases. She ran a well-organized criminal enterprise, enlisting the services of an extensive network of criminals. At the height of her criminal career, every New York thief knew their best chance to realize a profit from their ill-gotten gains was to trust "Marm" Mandelbaum. She was also partial to helping young women get a foothold in the criminal world. She was once quoted as saying that she wanted to help any women who "are not wasting life being a housekeeper." Because of her efforts to help women find work, even if it was in the world of crime, some contemporary feminist historians view Mandelbaum as a Gilded Age heroine for her willingness to assist women finding work and helping them make more money than they could have as housekeepers, maids, seamstresses or factory workers.

Mandelbaum and her family, her husband, Wolf, sons Julius and Gustav, and daughters, Annie and Sarah,lived on the top two floors of the Clinton and Rivington Streets building she purchased. As her business flourished she was able to furnish the living quarter lavishly with expensive furniture, draperies, paintings, and silverware that had been stolen from some of the finest homes and mansions in New York City. Mandelbaum,though at first begrudgingly,was accepted in polite society, despite everyone's knowledge of her criminal enterprise. She held ostentatious dinner parties at her home where many of the country's most celebrated criminals mingled freely with countless of members of New York City's fashionable elite, including politicians, judges, police, and legitimate businessmen. Everyone who was anyone cherished the opportunity to be invited to one of her many soirées.

She opened a school for crime on Grand Street, where young boys and girls were taught the intricacies of the criminal trade by professional pickpockets, burglars, and sneak thieves. The school offered advanced courses in burglary, safe-cracking, blackmailing, and confidence schemes. She allegedly had to close the school when it was discovered that the son of one of the city's most prominent police officials was enrolled in it.

By 1880 she had become the premier receiver of stolen merchandise in the country and one of the most powerful figures within organized crime, amassing a personal fortune estimated at more than $1 million. She owned tenements in the city as well as warehouses in New Jersey and Brooklyn where she stored stolen merchandise that she openly bought and sold. Her exploits have been well documented in the press of the times. One of Mandelbaum's most infamous protégés, Sophie Lyons, became one of America's most successful confidence women. After Lyons retired from her criminal life in 1913, she published her memoirs called *Why Crime Doesn't Pay*. Mandelbaum also gave Lena Kleinschmidt, known as Black Lena, her start as a thief, pickpocket, and blackmailer. Kleinschmidt moved to fashionable Hackensack, New Jersey, where, posing as a wealthy widow, she threw elaborate parties, imitating Mandelbaum's style and opulence. Black Lena used the parties to size up her next victims.

Mandelbaum once paid to break her favorite piano player, the notorious safecracker Piano Charlie Bullard, out of jail since she missed the piano concertos he gave at her extravagant parties. She financed one of the greatest bank robberies in America by fronting the operations of George Leslie and his gang of burglars. Leslie, who became known as "The King of Bank Robbers," took three years to plan the heist of the Manhattan Savings Institution and in October 1878, the robbers broke into the bank and stole close to $3 million in cash and securities, comparable to approximately $50 million in today's currency.

Mandelbaum was a close friend and partner with Adam Worth, nicknamed "the Napoleon of Crime" by Scotland Yard detectives. He was reportedly the prototype for Arthur Conan Doyle's Professor Moriarity, the nemesis of Doyle's legendary literary character, Sherlock Holmes. In England, Worth stole a priceless Thomas Gainsborough painting from a London gallery and he stole more than $500,000 worth of uncut diamonds from a bank in South Africa.

In 1884, Mandelbaum's reign as the "Queen among Thieves" came to an abrupt and exacting end at the hands of some of the very people she had so steadfastly cultivated over the years for protection. Even several of her criminal protégés turned against her. Time had run out on her as the Gilded Age ended, tarnished by the greed of supposedly legitimate businessmen who came to be known as "robber barons," and as the inept and corrupt police and judicial system came under the harsh scrutiny of a new breed of law abiding citizens. Mandelbaum became a figurehead of everything that this new breed of New York City reformers detested.

The story of Fredericka Mandelbaum and her rise to power takes place during what has been named the Gilded Age. The term "the Gilded Age" comes from Mark Twain and Charles Dudley Warner's 1873 book by the same name. It refers to the ancient process of covering an object with a superficial layer of gold. In this case, it described an American society, from approximately 1870 to 1890, in which a small number of businessmen acquired great fortunes, put on outlandish and lavish displays of wealth, and built enormous, ostentatious mansions while the majority of Americans were poor, hungry and living in crime infested squalor.

Besides Mandelbaum, New York City during the Gilded Age was inhabited by a plethora of colorful criminals, all of whom worked for her. Among them was Piano Charlie Bullard, a handsome, raffish, classically educated, piano playing safecracker, who squandered his ill-gotten gains on wine, women, and gambling. After robbing $450,000 from the Boylston Bank in Boston, Bullard fled to London, where he married a beautiful seventeen-year-old Irish barmaid named Kitty Flynn. They moved to Paris where Bullard opened a popular expatriate bar called "The American Bar."

There was Adam Worth who was Piano Charlie Bullard's partner in crime. Worth was credited with stealing Thomas Gainsborough's famous painting, "Georgiana Cavendish, Duchess of Devonshire."

There was the well-dressed, international burglar and safecracker Max Shinburn who thought of himself as a European aristocrat and ultimately bought the title of Baron Shindell of Monaco with his illegal gains.

There was John "Traveling Mike" Grady, Mandelbaum's chief competitor in the fencing business. Grady was a frugal, penny-pinching man, despite being worth an estimated $4 million in stolen merchandise and property, who carried his money and wares in a wooden peddlers' box that he had slung over his shoulder.

There were Mandelbaum's notorious lawyers, William Howe and Abraham Hummel, two of the most devious and successful criminal lawyers the country has ever known. Howe was flamboyant and boisterous while Hummel was drab and quiet.

Two of the most corrupt and powerful politicians populated New York City during the era: Mayor Fernando Woods, considered the most corrupt mayor in the city's history and William Marcy "Boss" Tweed, the prototypical corrupt political boss.

Along with these criminals there were incorruptible reformers, like New York City's District Attorney Peter Olney, who was instrumental in ending Mandelbaum's career and the somewhat dubious Police Detective Thomas Byrnes, one of the department's most colorful, outspoken, and successful law enforcement officers.

All of these true-life characters were an integral part of the fiefdom within Fredericka Mandelbaum's sovereign criminal monarchy where she reigned for nearly 25 years as "Queen among Thieves" until her forced abdication in 1884.

——

Author's Note: I have included headlines and portions of newspaper articles from the period. These pieces are replicated exactly as they appeared. The typos and misspellings appear just as they were published in newspaper sources including *The New York Times*, the *Brooklyn Eagle*, and other period pieces.

PART I

MANDELBAUM'S RISE

1
PITY THE POOR IMMIGRANT

> "Ruined houses open to the street, whence, through wide gaps in the walls, other ruins loom upon the eye, as though the world of vice and misery had nothing else to show: hideous tenements which take their name from robbery and murder; all that is loathsome, drooping, and decayed is here."
>
> —Charles Dickens, 1842

The Mandelbaums' flight from Germany in 1850 was not a matter of choice but survival based on the potato blight, the failed German revolution, and growing anti-Semitism. A potato blight in 1840 left many like the Mandelbaums on the brink of starvation. Added to this was the failed revolution of 1848 that would have advanced more freedom to the poor and working classes of the country. Leading up to the revolution there had been intermittent hunger riots and violent disturbances but a concentrated insurrection did not come until early in 1848 predicated by the fall of the French king Louis-Philippe in Paris. Many of the rebellions against the German government were relatively minor although in the case of the Berlin uprising the fighting was harsh and gory. By the summer of 1849, the revolution was entirely extinguished. But it was the growing anti-Semitism that had its most dramatic impact on the Mandelbaums and other Jews like them.

Wolf Mandelbaum, Fredericka's husband, was a peddler, dealing primarily as a go-between with peasants who lived in the countryside. He bought and sold livestock, grain, vegetables, and wine grapes. Despite his hard work, the Mandelbaums remained impoverished because on top of the failing German economy and political upheaval, there was growing anti-Semitism. Jews had their right to work, settle and marry severely restricted. Without special letters of protection, they were prohibited from engaging in many different professions, and so often had to resort to jobs considered unrespectable, such as peddling to survive. A Jewish man who wanted to marry had to purchase a registration certificate, known as a *matrikel*, proving he was working in a respectable job. The certificates were expensive and often out of reach for most Jewish men and as a result, most Jewish men were not able to marry legally. Added to this, many Jews were extortionately taxed. As a result, many German Jews immigrated to America. The Mandelbaums were among them. In 1850, the Mandelbaums packed up what little belongings they had and immigrated to America, sailing on separate vessels. Wolf left first on the *Baltimore*, which arrived in New York in late July 1850. Fredericka and their infant daughter sailed on the *Erie* and arrived in New York in September 1850. Fredericka had given birth to the couple's first child, Bertha, nicknamed Bessie, in March 1849. Fredericka was just twenty-three years old.

Like her husband, Fredericka and Bessie traveled in steerage as third-class passengers. They were forced to endure the long, six-week journey below deck with the other lowly steerage passengers. It was an enormous physical burden for Fredericka who was nearly six feet tall and weighed close to 250 pounds. The space below deck consisted of a seven-foot-long passageway that was two feet wide with a ceiling of barely six feet. It meant that Fredericka spent most of her time hunched over in order to move around in what little space she was afforded. Provisions consisted of a daily small ration of water, hard bread, and salted meat. The close quarters below deck, along with the poor ventilation and lack of adequate waste disposal facilities frequently led to epidemics of typhus, cholera, dysentery, and other kinds of infectious diseases. Despite the torturous conditions, Fredericka and Bessie survived and arrived safely in the thriving port of New York City.

The New York City harbor was teeming with small ferries, barges, steamships, and schooners, and the East River was lined with vessels. By 1850, New York City was the largest and busiest port in America, bustling with people and goods being loaded and unloaded onto the congested wharfs. The narrow streets leading to and from the piers were also bustling, a hodgepodge of people—rich and poor, young and old, good and bad—coming and going. Men and women, couples, families, and young children navigated along muddy streets and cobblestone walkways. Some stopped to chat, exchange directions, offer help. Sometimes, if they had enough money to spare, they were able to buy roasted chestnuts from a street vendor. Peddlers of every type and variety hawked their wares along the streets, pulling their handcarts along behind them or carrying their goods on their backs, shoulders, and arms. Immigrants would stop and ask for directions, doing their best to make their intentions known, using the little English they knew. It was a cacophony of boisterous commotion. This was the all too human, dynamic city that Fredericka Mandelbaum and the other approximately two-million immigrants who landed in New York City in the 1850s found themselves—a world of endless possibilities.

And yet, the image of America as the land of opportunity and hope was shattered for most immigrant families as they tried to assimilate into the new world they had so unwittingly fled to. Fredericka Mandelbaum was one of them.

She, Wolf, and Bessie settled into Kleindeutschland (Little Germany) on New York City's Lower East Side where a contingent of German-Jewish immigrants like them had settled. When the Mandelbaums arrived in 1850, the population of New York City was a little over 500,000 with immigrants comprising more than half of that. German Jews made up 56,000 of that amount. In ten years, from 1850 to 1860, the population of New York City nearly doubled to approximately 800,000, with immigrants once again making up more than half of that number.

The Mandelbaums lived with relatives and friends in Kleindeutschland while they searched for a place of their own. This was the usual practice for newly landed immigrants to the city. In 1857, they settled into a tenement at 383 Eighth Street, in what is now the East Village, in the Eleventh Ward of Kleindeutschland. The neighborhood was bordered on the east side by the East River, on the west end by the Bowery, bounded on the north by 14th Street and the south by Division Street. At the time, more than 130,000 people lived in Kleindeutschland which was made up of the Tenth, Eleventh, Thirteenth, and Seventeenth wards. More than half of the people living in the neighborhood were German or Jewish. The next largest ethnic group living there were the Irish.

The Mandelbaums' Eighth Street home was an airless, lightless single room in a decrepit tenement that housed more than twenty families. The building was approximately twenty feet wide by seventy-five feet deep. There was no indoor plumbing or central heating. Wooden outhouses were located in the alley behind the house and water to be used for cooking, drinking, bathing, and washing had to be carried from hand pumps along the sidewalk up a narrow, dark flight of stairs. The city's infrastructure was crumbling. It was not able to keep up with the enormous population growth. Wharves and piers were falling apart, some sinking into New York Harbor, traffic caused gridlock in the downtown streets, increasing numbers of people needed to be housed, and all kinds of garbage from individuals, families, and businesses had no place for disposal. Communicable diseases, the by-products of crowded and unsanitary conditions, spread through communities. New York City of the 1850s was beleaguered with growing slums, overcrowding, disease and escalating crime.

In 1850, the city was made up of five separate boroughs. It wasn't until 1898 that these boroughs were incorporated into the single metropolis now known as New York City. Brooklyn and Queens made up the western portion of Long Island, while Staten Island and Manhattan remained on their own land mass. The Bronx, to the north, was attached to the New York State mainland. Within each of these boroughs there was a series of neighborhoods each given their own distinct name, each with their own distinct variety of crime. Five Points was known for its murder-for-hire. The Tenderloin district was the center of the city's prostitution rings. The Gas House was filled with opium dens. Hell's Kitchen was the hub of saloons and gambling houses. These notorious slums and dens of crime flourished just below the more fashionable apartments, homes, mansions, parks, stores, and banks of the well-dressed, high society residents living in the lap of luxury along Broadway and Fifth Avenue.

Thousands of impoverished immigrants like the Mandelbaums lived together in overcrowded unsanitary slums like Kleindeutschland. Thousands settled into this and other rat-infested, crime-ridden neighborhoods where garbage was discarded out of the windows and onto the streets, piling up so high that it surged over the tops of pedestrians' boots. Chamber pots were also emptied into the streets, producing pools of human excrement. The putrid stench filled the air. Half-starved and sickly immigrants dressed in rags, carrying everything they owned, gravitated to the cheap tenement housing. Many, like the Mandelbaums, were fortunate to have a single room to live in. Others lived in boardinghouses where dozens of people shared a single room and often slept on straw-covered floors. They were charged exorbitant rates and if they could not pay, their possessions were confiscated and they were thrown out onto the streets. Surviving in this environment meant that all members of the family had to find ways of earning a living by whatever means possible. Some were forced to resort to a life of crime or prostitution in order to survive. Alcoholism was rampant and frequently children were left to fend for themselves, roaming the streets, joining criminal gangs, all of them destined for a life of desolation. According to one report, "One aghast minister in 1866 estimated that the city's all-told population of 800,000 included '30,000 thieves, 20,000 prostitutes, 3,000 drinking houses and a further 2,000 houses dedicated to gambling.'"

Health department reports from the period indicated that nearly 75 percent of the children under the age of two died each year. Rampant strains of typhus, cholera, chicken pox, measles, and tuberculosis killed many of these poor immigrants and their children. Still others died from poor nutrition and unsanitary conditions. Sixty-five immigrant children died to every eight non-immigrant children.

TENEMENT HOUSES
FULL STATISTICS OF THEIR INMATES
HUMAN BEINGS CROWDED LIKE SHEEP INTO PENS
112 FAMILIES IN ONE HOUSE

A committee of the Legislature having been appointed to visit the City to make examination as to the propriety of legislation in the matter of tenement houses, they have applied to the Mayor for information wherein to base their calculations. The Mayor accordingly issued a general order to the Police, requiring a report of "the legality, and street, and number of houses, of the most populous tenement in each patrol, district or ward. The returns have been received at the Central Office, excepting only that from the Eleventh Ward ...... In the Fourth Ward there were reported 47, one of which, Capt. Ditchett remarks, (No. 38 Cherry street) when full has 112 families in it ...... In the Seventh District are 65 front and 10 rear tenement houses, containing in the aggregate 1,232 families, averaging 16 families in each house ...... Cherry-street has 233 families penned up in a dozen houses ...

—*The New York Times,* March 14, 1856

The dilapidated tenement on Eighth Street where the Mandelbaums lived was a whitewashed, wooden structure, six stories high, not including the dirt-floor basement, which also housed families. It was built to accommodate ten families. It housed double that amount. The apartments were reached by an unlighted, wooden staircase that ran through the center of the building. The rooms were darkened by the closeness of the tenements on either side. There was no toilet, no shower, no bath, and only a small stove to cook on. There was a small fireplace to heat the single room apartment. According to a *New York Times* article published in 1856, boxes of garbage were tossed out on the street and in the alleys and were "... composed of potato-peelings, oyster-shells, night-soil, rancid butter, dead dogs and cats ... one festering, rotting, loathsome, hellish mass of air poisoning, death-breeding filth, reeking in the fierce sunshine ..."

Sewage backed up in backyard privies and rats ran wild through the filthy muck. The unsanitary and overcrowded conditions characteristic of the tenement slums were the leading cause of outbreaks of disease in Little Germany and other congested ethnic neighborhoods. Most native-born New Yorkers from the middle and upper classes blamed the immigrants for bringing disease to America and endangering the well-being of their "innocent hosts." Whenever an epidemic broke out, the most convenient scapegoat was whatever immigrant group was the largest, most feared, and most visible at the time. It's no surprise, then, that tuberculosis became known as a "Jewish disease."

Sometime while the Mandelbaums were living on Eighth Street, Bessie, the child who had endured the long, hazardous journey in steerage with her mother to America, died. Bessie, like so many of the other poor, immigrant children had succumbed to one of the many diseases born out of the city's unsanitary conditions. Even after the Mandelbaums moved into a better home in the 1860s, a large building on the corner of Clinton and Rivington Streets, they were still not out of harm's way. That neighborhood had some of the highest rates of disease. However, the Mandelbaums were more fortunate this time around. Their second child, Julius, as well as two girls and another boy, all lived to adulthood.

The streets of the New York City slums were infested with "street-rats"—orphaned or abandoned children without any formal education, who lived on the streets, slept in alleyways, vacant buildings and warehouses, and plied their criminal trade on unsuspecting victims. Some worked, if they could, at menial jobs, sweeping sidewalks or selling newspapers, but mostly they survived by scavenging or turning to a life of crime. Picking pockets was a popular criminal endeavor for these children. They waited outside saloons, hotels, post offices, banks and the congested railway stations that were known as "pickpockets' paradise." The train stations were especially fertile grounds for these criminals in training since it was a literal playground of unsuspecting, naïve tourists. In 1860, New York City Police Chief George Matsell estimated that somewhere between 5,000 to 10,000 children, boys and girls both, lived on the streets and that a majority of them were engaged in some form of crime or vice. According to Matsell, "crime among boys and girls has become organized, as it never was previously. The bad times have driven a small army into our streets."

According to a report issued by the Children's Aid Society—an organization started in New York City in 1853 by the Presbyterian minister Charles Loring Brace to help the needy—street children ". . . gnawed away at the foundations of society undisturbed. In a country which identified geographic mobility and physical movement as freedom, the street kids represented the logical nightmare—the replacement of community, familial and even spiritual bonds with the rootless individualism of the nomad." *Harper's Weekly* claimed that the street children were the breeding grounds for more criminal activity: "Those who have once adopted the semi-savage and wandering mode of life in early youth seldom abandon it."

These children first gravitated toward petty crimes, picking pocketing and shoplifting. They later graduated to more serious crimes, including murder, bank robbery, and extortion. Girls as young as twelve years old worked as prostitutes in whorehouses, dance halls, and seedy dives. Many of these children, if they lived, often ended up with any number of the criminal gangs that inhabited the underbelly of the city. These children quickly became thugs, hoodlums, robbers, murderers, and ruffians who took refuge in the dark alleys and damp cellars of the gritty hovels. They lurked in halls, saloons, and darkened doorways preying on strangers with legitimate business to tend to in the tenement district along the waterfront and harassing and robbing tenement dwellers, poverty stricken immigrants, and sickly old men and women. Gang wars were deadly and frequent in the slums.

New Yorkers and tourists alike were warned against venturing into these dangerous sections of the city at night. Even the police assigned to these sordid areas patrolled the streets in pairs. Crime grew and spread in and among the squalor of the tenements, flop-houses, warehouses, old factories, seedy saloons, gambling dens, and houses of prostitution.

LIVING UNDERGROUND
VIEW OF CELLAR LIFE IN THE METROPOLIS
THE FOUL DENS AND THEIR INHABITANTS
THOROUGH CLEARING OUT BY THE HEALTH AUTHORITIES
SUNSHINE IN DARK PLACES

> Among the good works which the Board of Health has quietly but energetically pressed forward during the past year, has been the improvement of the homes of the cellar population of this Metropolis . . . It has been determined by an accurate census that there are about 2,000 basements or cellars used as residences in this City . . . the real underground residents, the troglodytes, were found associating themselves together in large numbers in a single room. No one can have even

> a remote idea of the filth, crime, drunkenness, debauchery and . . . During the day they leave their miserable loathsome dens and earn, beg or steal sufficient to eat . . .
>
> —*The New York Times*, December 5, 1869

One of the most notorious areas in New York City was the Gashouse District from 14th to 27th Street where the huge gas tanks loomed over the landscape blotting out the skyline. Built in 1842, rows of ugly giant tanks rose up in the neighborhood. The tanks leaked gas day and night filling the air with noxious fumes and dark clouds. The gashouse gangs, made up of dangerous, uneducated, out-of-work young men, terrorized the community and often plundered other unsuspecting neighborhoods.

If they were looking for trouble they would find it soon enough in Mulberry Bend, a one-block stretch that ran through Little Italy. The alleys between the rows of filthy tenements were barely wide enough for a person to walk through and nearly knee-deep in garbage. Many of these torturous paths led to dives and cellars where every sort criminal lurked. The crisscrossing, interconnecting alleyways with names like "the rat trap" or "bandit's roost" were safe havens for these criminals from the long arm of the law. Day and night, murder, rape and mayhem exploded in the Mulberry Bend alleys. *The New York Tribune* called it "New York's Black Hole of Calcutta."

Hell's Kitchen on the West Side was another spawning ground for gangs. It was filled with saloons, whorehouses,gambling dens, slaughterhouses, and dance halls crammed in among the rows upon rows of crumbling tenements. It ran from 23rd Street to 42nd Street, down Seventh Avenue to the Hudson River. A section of 28th Street was known as "The Tub of Blood" because of the explosive violence and murder that erupted there. It became known as the most lurid slum in America. The Hell's Kitchen gangs were mostly Irish thugs, often armed with brass knuckles. They were considered the toughest gangs that roamed through New York City slums.

The worst of all the slums was the villainous Five Points in the Lower East Side, a den of almost unspeakable gore and horror. It was the home to the city's most vicious criminals, robbers, prostitutes, and confidence men. Five Points derived its name from the crisscrossing intersection of Anthony, Cross, Mulberry, Orange, and Water Streets. There were no legitimate businesses in Five Points except for a very few grocery, dry goods, and clothing shops. It was filled with narrow streets and alleys running every which way, saloons, beer cellars, stables, slaughter houses and whorehouses. The nearly falling down tenements and sheds there housed hundreds of poor immigrants who were at the mercy of the gangs, many of which worked for absentee landlords collecting rents. Anyone who couldn't pay the high rents were physically tossed out and often beaten severely as a warning to those who could not come up with their weekly rent payment. Day or night Five Points was the scene of an uncontrolled abundance of murder, mayhem, robbery, and theft. No one, including the police, dared to venture into this den of thieves and murderers. And the police stood by and watched as crime rose in the slums and elsewhere. And for good reason—most of them were getting a piece of the action one way or another.

> "New York City in the mid-1860s was one of the most corrupt metropolises on earth. Its politicians were bribed, its constabulary paid off, and thieves, pickpockets, whores, gamblers and anyone else wanting life easy and fat and rich were prime clients. Graft was an accepted procedure and the golden key to finer clothing, tastier food and higher social standing. Crime raged and those who controlled it, many of the politicians and police chiefs, zealously fed it."
>
> —Joseph Geringer, "Adam Worth: The World in His Pocket"

Fredericka Mandelbaum began her life of crime as a peddler on the busy, crime-infested streets of Kleindeutschland. She hauled her goods, mostly bits of silk and other fabrics, on her back. At close to six feet tall and 250 pounds, she was a formidable presence. She was easy to pick out of any crowd. The Mandelbaums did not have enough money to purchase or rent a storefront or to buy a horse and cart which many peddlers used. Instead, Fredericka and her husband, Wolf, who also peddled on the streets, used the busy streets as their shop, moving through the crowds, hawking their wares. She became readily adept at peddling and used her experiences on the street as a tool to learn what she needed to know in order to find a better way to earn a living for herself and her family. Mandelbaum's work as a street peddler gave her and her husband an ongoing source of income, even during the most difficult economic downturns of the mid-to-late 1850s. In 1857, the country was hurled into a financial panic, the world's first economic crisis was caused by an over-extension of the country's economic expansion, fueled by an economic panic in England. Many once flourishing banks, investors, and businesses in America had over-invested and taken substantial risks with their money. When the markets began to fail, caused by the declining international economy, hundreds of businesses closed, banks failed, investors lost millions—the Ohio Life Insurance and Trust Company alone is reported to have lost $7 million—and tens of thousands of people lost their jobs, except for those like the Mandelbaums. In fact, the Mandelbaums' opportunities grew as more and more people became unemployed and were driven to the streets looking for work, bargains, and ways to feed their families. As a street peddler, Fredericka Mandelbaum came in constant contact with poor men, women, and children who rummaged the neighborhoods for what they could use or sell.

Mandelbaum's role as a street peddler was typical for many New York German-Jewish immigrants, more so than other ethnic groups. In Germany, many German-Jews had already gained experience as peddlers and later, just as the Mandelbaums did, as dry goods merchants and shopkeepers. The Mandelbaums began by peddling when they first arrived in New York City and later opened their own small dry goods shop on the corner of Clinton and Rivington Streets in the mid-1860s. The streets peddlers worked were often unpaved, muddy, and littered with garbage. Nonetheless, peddlers with carts and others like Mandelbaum, who carried their wares on their shoulders, filled the streets and byways, haggling old-world style with buyers, sellers, and each other. They called attention to themselves by ringing bells, blowing horns, singing, dancing, juggling, and even dressing their horses in outrageous costumes. Their voices rang out with, “Rags! Rags! Any old rags!” or “Hot corn! Get your lily white hot corn. Corn hot straight from the pot!” All of the activity created a carnival atmosphere. Fredericka Mandelbaum didn’t need any props or gimmicks to call attention to herself. Her height and weight made a distinct impression.

> “Chinese men sold candy and cigars. Men in general sold tobacco, socks, suspenders, hose yarn and gloves. Women sold most of the food . . . Boys sold ties, pocketbooks [and] pocketbook straps and photographs. Little girls sold matches, toothpicks, songs and flowers. Italians dispense ice cream; Germans dealt in sausages . . .”
>
> —*New York Magazine*, August 12, 1991

Garbage picking, scavenging, picking pockets, all manner of theft and robbery and shoplifting allowed the destitute street people to eke out a living with the help of keen-eyed peddlers like Mandelbaum, who knew a bargain when she saw it. She was always able to wring the most out of any deal. It was said that Mandelbaum never purchased anything for more than half its worth and always sold it for twice as much. She was also clever enough to know that buying merchandise meant you had to sell it and although she was particular about what she bought, she was even more particular about what she sold. She reportedly never bought anything for which she didn’t already have a buyer. Street savvy, smart, and a born entrepreneur, Fredericka Mandelbaum flourished on the streets of New York, constantly increasing her profits and her contacts. This shady street economy, with everyone in need of cash, gave Mandelbaum ample opportunities to ply her stock and trade, legally and illegally. She quickly became known on the streets as a useful and resourceful "middleman" when it came to the buying and selling of ill-gotten gains. She was always ready to buy the stolen merchandise criminals had to offer and just as ready and able to resell it to legitimate buyers looking for a bargain. Buyers and sellers could find just about anything they desired on the bustling streets.

The Mandelbaums' worked with an endless supply of unscrupulous sellers as well as an endless contingent of legitimate buyers, including dry goods merchants, and business people of all types who were on the constant lookout for a bargain. Their legitimate suppliers often charged twice as much for the same product they could buy at cost from the Mandelbaums.

Everyone was looking for a bargain—legitimate businessmen and women, street urchins, professional thieves, shoplifters, pickpockets, burglars, the cop on the beat, lawyers, politicians, and judges—and over time, Mandelbaum encountered, engaged, and wooed many of these divergent personas as part of her growing criminal enterprise. People of every ilk liked Marm Mandelbaum. Her prices were low and she didn't ask questions. Every criminal on the street knew or had heard of her. Slowly, she expanded her personal association with her shady street clientele to the upper echelons of New York society. She nurtured these relationships as readily as she nurtured her relations with criminals, and these relationships proved beneficial for her during her nearly twenty-five year reign as the "Queen among Thieves."

> "Mandelbaum negotiated with lawyers, bondsmen, police and prosecutors . . . Her Clinton Street dry-goods or haberdashery shop became a veritable clearing house for crimes and larceny, an underworld haven attracting the nation's most famous

criminals. George Walling sarcastically dubbed Mandelbaum's establishment the 'Bureau for the Prevention of Conviction.'"
—Timothy J. Gilfoyle, *A Pickpocket's Tale*, 2007

In 1860, the Mandelbaums moved to 141 6th Street in the Seventeenth Ward within Kleindeutchsland. Their eldest son, Julius, was born at that address in October 1860. By 1865, they lived in a clapboard house in the Thirteenth Ward, on the corner of Clinton and Rivington Streets. It was a highly industrialized six-block area that was home to more than 3,600 people as well as iron foundries, brick and sewing machine factories, and coal, lumber, stone, and lime yards. The houses and tenements were built close together, crowded next to the factories, shops, churches, synagogues, and schools. There were small retail and wholesale businesses run out of storefronts, small shops, and even out of some homes, along with more than a dozen hotels, inns, and taverns. It was a busy, growing community. The Mandelbaums were coming up in the world. Their new home was better than any of their previous ones and included a store and basement for storage. The family stayed there for the next twenty-five years in the heart of the expanding German immigrant wards. Besides Julius, Fredericka Mandelbaum had given birth to a daughter, Sarah, in 1862, another son, Gustav, in 1864, and another daughter, Anna, in 1867.

Despite her criminal activities, Mandelbaum remained a devoted and attentive mother. The sudden death of her first child, Bessie, made her overprotective and fawning. She never left her children out of her sight for long and she was known to call off a business deal if something of importance affecting her children, like an illness or school recitals, occurred. She doted on her four children and was close to all of them. She was very close to her oldest son, Julius, who eventually became an important part of her fencing business. Although he had a job outside the home by the time he was fourteen years old as an assistant with a local brewer, he continued to run errands for his mother at the store. Julius grew to become a devoted son who was always ready and able to do his mother's bidding. And like most parents, Mandelbaum wanted more for her children than she ever had and her life of crime was one of them. She did not allow her other children to become part of her criminal business enterprise, especially her two daughters.

At the Clinton and Rivington Street address Mandelbaum tended to her four children and grew her business. She looked after her husband who had become stricken with an undetermined affliction, most likely consumption, ran her legitimate dry goods store, and conducted her fencing operation, which entailed the buying and selling stolen merchandise out of the back of her store out of view of prying eyes. As she amassed her fortune, she filled her home with expensive furniture, paintings, draperies, silverware—the best of everything—stolen from some of the best homes, mansions, and businesses in New York City. Despite her growing wealth and notoriety she chose to stay in Kleindeutschland, where she was able to use the bustling crowded streets of the lower East Side to expand her fencing operations. As time went on she expanded her reach outside of New York City to places like Trenton and Newark, New Jersey, where she established relations with both wealthy, legitimate clientele as well as making contact with various New Jersey–based criminals. Her real estate holdings grew as well. By the 1880s, she reportedly owned several tenements in the city and warehouses where she stored the massive amounts of stolen merchandise. But the center of her operations remained the Clinton and Rivington Street address.

> "By 1864, she owned 79 Clinton St., a three-story building at the corner of Rivington Street. The family's haberdashery, managed by her husband Wolfe and their three children, had a back room for her real business: reselling pinched products to nominally legitimate businessmen across the city . . . A motley variety of ruffians, pickpockets, thieves and arsonists rounded

> out East Side Crime . . . Clinton Street's corpulent "Mother" Fredericka Mandelbaum operated a network of fences moving massive quantities of stolen goods around New York and the nation."
>
> —David Pietrusza, *Rothstein,* 2004

One can only imagine how the cunning Mandelbaum bartered with some enterprising criminal over a bit of stolen merchandise, ultimately buying it at a quarter of its worth and then selling it to a legitimate customer for twice or three times as much. But even then her prices would have been well below the going rate in the legitimate marketplace. She built her elaborate and successful business as a receiver of stolen property from the ground up, dealing with thieves and selling to legitimate customers, to bribing cops on the beat to look the other way when she engaged in some illicit transaction. Regardless of who she dealt with, everyone knew Mandelbaum was the person to go to if you had something to sell or something you wanted to buy at below cost. And she always had cash on hand to make a deal. There were three skills that made Fredericka Mandelbaum the success she became. First, she had learned to speak English almost as well as she did German, which made her a valuable interpreter. Secondly, her knowledge of silk and fabric and other precious goods gave her expertise in dry goods, which was an advantage over other "fences." And lastly and perhaps most importantly, her clients, both sellers and buyers, knew that this huge, dark-eyed, corpulent woman didn't question whether the merchandise she traded in was legitimately or illegitimately acquired. It was these three skills, along with her growing political connections as well as her beneficial association with the police, judges, and lawyers, which allowed her to grow and prosper for more than twenty-five years.

Mandelbaum was drawn to the criminal class for two reasons: First, as an outcast herself, both physically (her height and weight making her stand out) and ethnically, she had an affinity toward society's outcasts. And secondly, she was a savvy enough businesswoman to realize that by aligning herself with the criminal class, she would be able to grow her business. Criminals could provide her with an array of merchandise that she would otherwise not be able to get her hands on. Her synergetic relationship with the authorities grew out of her understanding that "one hand washes the other," and in her case, one hand washed the other with bribes, which allowed her to engage in her criminal activities untouched by the long arm of the law. Along with her personal affinity for society's outcasts and her ongoing relationship with the authorities, there was another driving force in Mandelbaum and that force was her desire for acceptance. As a Jew, a woman, and a criminal, and given her physical attributes, she already faced being ostracized and derided by polite society. The need to be accepted in the face of these impediments drove her to curry favor with New York City's high society. She soon discovered that those of the upper class had as much larceny in their hearts, however masked by their outward appearance and social standing, as her criminal cohorts. They were willing, although begrudgingly, to look the other way when it came to her criminal endeavors, in light of her accumulated wealth, power, and influence. Soon it was not Mandelbaum who needed to curry favor, but the other way around.

Mandelbaum was truly an American success story, ignoring of course, the fact that her enormous success was in the business of crime. She rose from the humble beginnings in the early 1850s as a lowly immigrant street peddler to become the greatest, most successful and notorious fence in the annals of New York City history. She ran her elaborate network of organized crime from a simple haberdashery shop on the Lower East Side for more than twenty-five years where she enlisted the services of an extensive group of criminals of every ilk, bribed police officials, politicians, and judges and stayed one step ahead of prosecution for much of her life. By the 1880s, it was reported she had amassed a fortune estimated at more than $1 million. According to the *New York*

Times, her operation was "the nucleus and center of the whole organization of crime in New York City . . . and is believed to have furnished the capital without which extensive enterprises even of theft cannot be carried on."

Along the way, Mandelbaum made both friends and enemies: Friends who helped her hone her skills in the fencing business and enemies who sought to end her reign. But it was the friends and her extended family of criminals that elevated her to her lofty position within the underworld. The enemies came later.

2

FENCES MAKE GOOD NEIGHBORS

"As by the fires of experience, so by commission of crime you learn real morals."

—Mark Twain, "On Being Morally Perfect," 1899

Mandelbaum's benefactors included some of the most notorious and successful fences in New York City, the upper echelons of New York City's criminal enterprises. Her mentors included "General" Abe Greenthal, who *The New York Times* called "one of the oldest and shrewdest criminals in this country"; Joe Erich, who, up and until Mandelbaum arrived, the New York press called the most "successful, adroit and daring fence known to the police annals of the city"; and Ephraim Snow, known as the "godfather" of fencing. Their desire to help her learn the ropes was predicated on their own need to pass along their life lessons to someone who would continue their dubious heritage. The fact that Mandelbaum was a fast learner, that she was also Jewish, like all of them, and that she paid them for their help worked to her advantage.

Together they taught Mandelbaum three important lessons about the fencing business. The first was to understand the old adage that in order to "play you had to pay," and that payment came in the form of bribes to both politicians and the police in order to keep them from shutting down her operation. Money talked and the politicians and police listened. The second thing they taught her was that although there was no honor among thieves, a fair honorarium (payment) to the criminals who worked for her would keep them coming back to her and provide her with an endless supply of merchandise she could sell. And lastly they taught her that she should only buy from her criminal vendors things that she already knew she could sell at a profit.

Receivers of stolen property had always been an integral part of the criminal underworld. Without them, thieves had no venue to sell their stolen merchandise. Abe Greenthal, who was described as having a stout build, gray hair, sandy beard, and prominent nose, was one of the country's most successful pickpockets and fences. His entire family was engaged in criminal enterprises. His sons, daughters, and in-laws were shoplifters and pickpockets. Greenthal, worked out of the city's Tenth Ward where he served as the boss of the "Sheeny Mob," a loosely knit collection of Jewish pickpockets who plied their trade throughout the city and beyond its boundaries. "Sheeny" was a derogatory word used to describe an untrustworthy Jew. At the time, all Jewish immigrants were viewed as conniving and untrustworthy. Greenthal had been known for many years for his fencing operations by the authorities, but his continued bribes to the politicians and police allowed him to go untouched by law enforcement.

> The Greenthals, for many years have been known to the police as professional thieves and receivers of stolen goods. The equally noted family of Hirsch Greenthal, alias Hirsch Harris, and the Mandelbaum family, also receivers of stolen goods, are near relatives of 'General' Greenthal's family.
>
> —*The New York Times*, November 24, 1874

Joe Erich operated his fencing business out of a shop on Maiden Lane in Manhattan's Financial District. For many years, he was the biggest dealer in stolen property in New York City and beyond, dealing in anything from the smallest article of stolen property, including brass or silver sewing thimbles, to large quantities of silks and other fabrics. By paying his criminal sources a fair and reasonable price for their stolen wares, he was the most sought after fence in the criminal underworld. His bribes to politicians and police also kept him out of jail for his entire fifteen-year career from 1850 to 1865.

Ephraim Snow ran a dry goods store on Grand and Allen Streets in Lower Manhattan that was a front for his fencing business. Snow, known to criminals and law enforcement authorities alike as "Old Snow," bought and sold a large and varied assortment of stolen merchandise at his tiny shop. The one rule he kept was that no matter what he bought from his endless stream of thieves, he already had a known buyer for the merchandise. In that way he was able to move the stolen merchandise quickly and at a profit, without having it stay in his shop long where prying eyes, including those of victims, might see and identify it. Old Snow dealt in anything and according to underworld legend, he once astounded his fellow criminal cohorts by buying and then disposing of an entire flock of sheep that had been stolen from a farm in upstate New York and then, according to Herbert Asbury's account in *The Gangs of New York,* the flock of sheep was brazenly herded "through the streets of the city to the shop of the fence." Despite his bribes to politicians and police, in 1875, Ephraim Snow was finally indicted for receiving stolen securities and a satchel of uncut diamonds. He was released on bail prior to his trial and fled to Canada, another lesson Mandelbaum took to heart. The authorities were unable to extradite Snow because there were no extradition agreements with that country at the time. The lessons Mandelbaum learned were put to good use over the years and she added several new twists to the fencing business. Over time, her operation far overshadowed those of her mentors.

There were other fences in New York City who were not as friendly and supportive of Mandelbaum, primarily because they saw her as a threat to their own business. John "Traveling Mike" Grady was one of them. Grady was what was referred to as a "walking fence." He carried a wooden peddler's box slung over his shoulder where he carried his cash and plunder. Unlike Mandelbaum, Grady traveled daily among his criminal cohorts. This gave him an advantage over Mandelbaum since if pickpockets, burglars or thieves happened to be in possession of any stolen loot, Grady was the first person in contact with them. He was almost always the first on the scene and as Edward Crapsey points out in his book, *The Nether Side of New York or the Vice, Crime, and Poverty of the Great Metropolis* (1872), "A thief is always impatient to turn his plunder into money, but he is doubly so when it is personal property that can be easily identified by the owner . . ."

Grady made no pretense to high society nor did he appear to care for it. He dressed in shabby clothes and kept less than $10,000 worth of property in his peddler's box or pockets as he made his daily rounds among his suppliers. He discovered it was more lucrative to deal directly and immediately with criminals where he could realize a profit of upwards of 200 percent on his shady dealings. He was an expert in diamonds and precious stones and focused his attention on these specific commodities.

Ironically, Grady's expertise was so well-known that even legitimate jewelers called on him to assess the value of some piece of jewelry. Even more ironic was the fact that in certain instances the piece of jewelry Grady might have assessed for a legitimate jeweler would end up as part of his plunder when one of his many associates stole the merchandise. Grady became known as "The Banker to Burglars." According to historical estimates, during his infamous career Grady handled more than $4 million worth of stolen property, cash, and securities.

Grady was not beyond playing both sides of the fence—quite literally—and this often paid off for him. He reportedly provided police with information on lesser criminals as a means of staying ahead of the law himself. In other words, he was a squealer. In 1874, while working with the notorious bank burglar Jimmy Brady trying to negotiate the sale of close to $500,000 in stolen securities that Brady had plundered, the two men were apprehended by the police. Grady surrendered to the officers but Brady tried to make an escape, jumping through a plate glass window in a fuselage of gunfire. Brady was shot in the thigh. Both Grady and Brady were tried but only Brady was sent to Sing Sing. Miraculously, and no doubt because of his snitching on other criminals, Grady was set free. That is not to say Grady didn't maintain some form of loyalty to his suppliers. In fact, Jimmy Brady later managed to break out of prison using tools that had been smuggled into him by "Traveling Mike."

Grady's operation was in direct competition with Mandelbaum. Although he peddled his fencing operation, he maintained a small second floor office on Broadway and Houston Streets, above a saloon he owned and operated. He began regularly fencing $10,000 a week in stolen goods. He was aggressive, employing the likes of Johnny "The Mick" Walsh, leader of the Bowery's Walsh Gang, as an enforcer and as protection against any moves that Mandelbaum might contemplate against his organization but that never became necessary. There was enough to go around for everyone. Although in direct competition he remained cordial to Mandelbaum for the sake of maintaining their profits in the stolen property market. An outright war between them would have only hampered both their businesses.

> "John D. Grady only did business with the most professional thieves. He financed some particularly lucrative robberies, and kept the city's police happy by informing on lesser thieves and burglars."
>
> —Michael Woodiwiss, *Organized Crime and American Power*, 2001

In order to operate her business Mandelbaum had to pay off politicians who controlled every aspect of city government. It was a symbiotic relationship. Because the political environment in New York City was already tainted by greed and corruption, and since the architects of the political machinery that drove this corrupt environment were the beneficiaries of much of the crime that churned unabated around them, it was unlikely that those in political power would seek to eliminate the successful workings of someone like Mandelbaum. The politicians profited from her endeavors one way or the other, either by receiving bribes to overlook her criminal activities or by relying on Mandelbaum to deliver the vote on election days. Mandelbaum and her cohorts, in fact a majority of criminals, could not have escaped prosecution if the political environment of New York City had not been rotten to the core to begin with.

The corrupt political climate that Mandelbaum thrived in was personified by two politicians—Mayor Fernando Wood and William Marcy "Boss" Tweed. In the early part of Mandelbaum's career, the city's political machinery was overseen by Wood. In 1854, he was elected mayor of New York City and reelected in 1860 after being ousted from office in 1857. During his first term, he was viewed as a reformer who put a clampdown on gambling dens, brothels, and saloons. Things changed, however, when Wood learned the financial and political benefits he could derive from tying himself to these various criminal enterprises. Ultimately Wood's mayoral administration was considered one of if not the most corrupt in New York City's history. Wood had his fingers in every illegal operation in the city from gambling dens to houses of prostitution, receiving a substantial cut of the profits for allowing these corrupt practices to continue unabated in the city. The bribes he received allowed Wood to live well beyond his means and gave him a substantial upper hand when it came to elective politics in the city: His criminal minions always managed to bring in the vote for him and his cronies on election day.

In 1857, the New York State Legislature, in an effort to reign in Wood's corrupt administration, passed legislation to do away with the Municipal Police Force, which was controlled by the mayor's office, and replace it with a state run Metropolitan Police Force. Wood refused to disband the department. When state officials were sent to arrest Wood at City Hall for ignoring the State Legislature's command, Wood's Municipal Police Department surrounded City Hall to protect him, and a riot broke out between the two competing police forces. After the militia was called in to quell the police riot, Wood was temporarily arrested. The Municipal Police Department was ultimately disbanded, and Wood was driven from office. Despite this, as a democrat, he was reelected in 1860 at the start of the Civil War because of his anti-Lincoln position and Lincoln's stance against slavery. Much of New York City's electorate was opposed to Lincoln's stance and solidly against the brewing war with the southern states. Wood's positions on the issue of slavery and the war were enough to get him reelected despite the vast number of charges of corruption that had been hurled at him during his first administration. Wood became a vocal Confederate sympathizer and advocated for New York City to secede from the Union and join the Southern cause. "With our aggrieved brethren of the slave states, we have friendly relations and a common sympathy," Wood told the press. Although Wood's corrupt administration left an indelible black mark on the city's political history, he is credited with at least one lasting contribution—he was a strong advocate for the development of Central Park and was instrumental in selecting its current location in the city.

Mandelbaum never expressed any political beliefs regarding President Lincoln, the issue or slavery or the pending civil war. Politics, at least electoral politics, was not part of the equation for her. She would have bribed whoever was mayor so that she could run her business unfettered. Despite the widespread acknowledgement of Mandelbaum's ongoing criminal activities, she was able to escape serious legal trouble for decades because of the elaborate network of political connections she had fostered over the years. The politicians controlled the police and the judicial system. The bribes she paid to them ensured that she was able to escape serious legal trouble for decades. If any of her criminal cronies were arrested, her political connections saw to it that the cases against them were dropped. Cases were fixed, juries bribed, and witnesses were convinced not to testify.

Mayor Fernando Wood's political clout was small potatoes compared to that of William Marcy "Boss" Tweed, and Mandelbaum saw to it that Tweed and his cronies at Tammany Hall, the New York City Democratic political organization, were all sufficiently taken care of. Although he held several elective offices including United States representative in 1852, New York County Board of Supervisors in 1858, and New York State Senator in 1867, his greatest influence and power came from being appointed to a number of New York City boards and commissions, especially as Commissioner of Public Works, a position he was appointed to in 1870.

In 1864 Tweed became the Grand Sachem of Tammany Hall and was referred to as "Boss." A huge, barrel-chested, pot-bellied man, he stood nearly six feet tall and weighed close to three hundred pounds. He had a large head, with a broad forehead, a bulbous nose, and a rosy complexion. He wore a neatly trimmed brown beard and had sparkling blue eyes. Tweed's appetites were not solely for money and power. He was known to gorge himself on huge, expensive meals that were prepared especially for him. Tweed was devoted to his wife and eight children, even though he was known to have kept two mistresses to whom he bestowed nearly $2 million for their upkeep. Not necessarily known for his tastes in high fashion, Tweed was nonetheless fond of expensive jewelry and always wore a large diamond stick pin on his usually starched, high-collared shirts. He was not a well-educated man, having dropped out of school when he was just fourteen years old, and his language was coarse and filled with profanities. He didn't smoke and although he'd once been a big drinker, he had given it up. He was a dog lover and breeder and had an affinity for flowers and caged birds. His offices were filled with fresh flowers and dozens of singing canaries were housed in elaborate gilded cages both there and at his home.

The son of a New York City chair maker, Tweed was the first politician in America to be called "Boss," a title that even today conjures up the image of power, money, greed, and corruption. He began his rise to power as a lowly bookkeeper and volunteer fireman. He was later elected alderman. By 1869, he was so powerful and had so many of his cronies, known as the "Tweed Ring," in political positions throughout the city that he was able to control practically everything, including the city treasury. It is estimated that between 1865 and 1871, Boss Tweed and his gang stole anywhere from $30 million to $200 million from the city. It was impossible to do anything in New York City, from holding political office to running a legitimate business, without the support of Boss Tweed and without Tweed receiving some form of kickback. Mandelbaum and every successful criminal paid off Tweed and his cronies for protection from the authorities. Graft and bribes to Tweed kept the police and prosecution at bay. It's no surprise then that Tweed himself was a frequent guest at the many dinner parties Mandelbaum threw at her Clinton and Rivington Streets home. Tweed and Mandelbaum had mutual admiration for each other. She admired his audacity, unapologetically plundering the city coffers at will and he admired her growing criminal operation, despite being a woman in a field dominated by men, not to mention she created for him another rich source of bribes.

The 52 Chambers Street courthouse building project was at the heart of Tweed's financial empire. Begun in 1861, the Criminal Courts Building was supposed to have cost the city $350,000. By 1869, it had cost the city nearly $11 million, with much of the difference lining the pockets of Boss Tweed and his cronies. From his headquarters, located on East 14th Street, Tweed orchestrated bribes and kickbacks that he demanded in exchange for city contracts. The County Courthouse project was mockingly referred to as Tweed's "Little Alaska," since the building ended up costing twice as much as the purchase of Alaska in 1867.

While Tweed was in power, Mandelbaum and others who regularly paid tribute to him were protected by Tweed's political control of the police and the judicial system. According to Alexander Callow's *The Tweed Ring,* "During the Tweed era 'covert crime,' practiced by confidence men, pickpockets, burglars, and sneak thieves increased enormously . . . At the same time there were about 30,000 professional thieves and 2000 gambling dens. In 1868 a total of 78,451 crimes were reported."

Prostitution was also a rich source of financial gain for the Tweed Ring. Within three miles of City Hall there were approximately four hundred brothels housing more than four thousand prostitutes. A police investigation conducted in 1873 uncovered "nine brothels, two saloons, a meeting place for professional thieves, and a public school with attendance of 1200 children. Behind the school were seven more brothels." According to reports, brothel owners paid upward of $600 per week to the police department for protection. The police in turn had to share their ill-gotten gains with politicians. In *The Dark Side of New York and Its Criminal Classes* written in 1873, Gustav Lening wrote that some brothels had established telegraphic communication with the police department who were summoned to help them in the event of a disturbance and to alert them of any pending raid.

The district attorney's office was also under the control of Tweed and became a sanctuary for known criminals. One word from Tammany Hall and cases simply disappeared from the docket. In 1868, more than 5,000 criminal cases were not prosecuted at the request of either the police or the district attorney's office on orders from Tweed and his cronies. According to a *New York Times* story on December 12, 1869, "a kind of languor steals over the proceedings; the case is never ready for trial, cases disappear, witnesses do not come forth and the culprit goes free." According to the same *Times* story, it was estimated that 10,000 indictments were quietly pigeonholed and never prosecuted.

Judges too were on the Tweed payroll so, even if by some strange happenstance the police arrested someone and the district attorney's office proceeded to prosecute, the Tweed Ring could always rely on corrupt judges to throw the case out. According to Richard Rovere's book, *Howe and Hummel*,Tammany Hall–appointed Judge Albert Cardozo was bribed on more than two hundred occasions to release clients.

Tweed appointed his cronies to high level positions, including commissioners and the superintendent, within the police department. Appointments to the police force were based on political connections or payoffs. Promotions within the force were also made based on politics rather than merit, and advancement within the department came at a price—quite literally. Police officers often had to pay up to $500 for an appointment to sergeant and upwards to $1000 for advancement to captain.

> "The police department was totally corrupt. There was no Civil Service. You paid to get on the job. You paid for promotions. You paid for your command. You had to go out and earn money to kick upstairs to your bosses and Tammany Hall."
>
> —Michael Bosak, quoted in the *New York Daily News*, July 3, 2011

The New York City Police Department was established in 1844. New York City's population at the time was approximately 320,000. It had been served by a police force made up of one night watch including 100 city marshals, thirty-one constables, and fifty-one municipal police officers. The New York legislature approved the proposal which authorized the creation of an 800 member police force on May 7, 1844. Under Mayor William Havemeyer, the force was reorganized on May 13, 1845, with the city divided into three districts, with courts, magistrates, and clerks, and station houses established. Havemeyer nominated George W. Matsell as Chief of Police. Matsell had served previously as a police magistrate in 1840.

The members of the newly formed police department didn't wear uniforms but sported eight-pointed stars as badges. The badge had the seal of the City in its center and was made out of copper. Although the newspapers referred to them as "The Star Police," the general public, taking note of their shiny copper badges began calling them "coppers," which later became shortened to "cops." Later in 1845, the police were issued uniforms to go along with their badges and were dubbed by Matsell and others as "the Finest."

Despite the bribery and corruption within the police department, it was just not equipped to meet the growing needs of the city's massive immigration. From 1865 to 1870, a mere five-year period, approximately 50,000 people a year immigrated to America and settled in New York City, bringing the total population of the city to over 940,000 people, according to the 9th United States Census. In 1870 there were 2,232 police officers in the city and only 1,700 were assigned foot patrols. There were more than four hundred and fifty miles of streets and piers to cover. Politicians and police were more concerned with maintaining control over the vast immigrant population than they were in the growth of organized crime. In fact, according to police arrest records most of the arrests during this period were for drunk and disorderly conduct than any other crimes.

> "There had been 4,927 arrests for petty larceny, 2,413 for grand larceny, 303 for picking pockets, 255 for receiving stolen goods, 630 for burglary, 132 for robbery and 78 for murder. But when these figures had been collated no progress had been made in determining the number of criminals in New York . . ."
>
> —Edward Crapsey, "Our Criminal Population," 1869

Mandelbaum saw to it that everyone from the officer on the beat to the captains of precincts were bought and paid for. The police benefitted from Mandelbaum's operation in other ways as well. In most instances, Mandelbaum's victims were more concerned about getting their property back than in prosecuting the criminal who had stolen it. Victims often sought police assistance in retrieving their stolen merchandise. This meant that the police had to deal with the likes of Mandelbaum and other receivers of stolen property. Because of this arrangement, the police became willing partners in crime. To get the property back, the police had to make deals with the fence and the fence in turn often offered the officers a kickback for their involvement.

Given that police officers, especially patrolmen, earned very little, the extra cash came in handy. It worked fairly simply. A criminal stole property worth $100. He took it to Mandelbaum who bought it for $20. The victim offered to pay the police whatever the property was worth to get it back. Mandelbaum offered to give back the property at full price: $100 with a $20 kickback to the police officer for mediating the return of the property. The victim paid the money and reclaimed his property. The police officer got a kickback of $20. The thief who stole it got paid $20. And Mandelbaum, received the largest portion of the dirty deal, $60, for her troubles and, of course, the knowledge that because the police officer was in on the deal, there was no way she would be prosecuted. It was a marvelous scheme, for everyone except the poor victim.

> "The *Herald* denounced a nameless group of police officers for extorting large rewards before they would return stolen property to victims of theft."
>
> —James Lardner and Thomas Reppetto, *NYPD*, 2001

Police Captain Alexander "Clubber" Williams was the epitome of police corruption. Williams became a police inspector in post–Civil War New York City. He obtained his notorious nickname "Clubber" because of his penchant for beating people with his night stick. In 1876, Williams was transferred to a precinct on West 13th Street. This seedy, high crime area, overflowing with gambling dens and brothels, was known as "Satan's Circus." Williams, however gave it a new name—The Tenderloin District. Remarking on his new position, Williams reportedly told an associate, "I have had chuck for a long time, and now I'm going to eat tenderloin," referring to the bribes and protection money he was likely to get from legitimate and illegal businesses located there, especially the many brothels, prostitutes, gambling operators, and illegal liquor shops. The name "tenderloin" stuck for this precinct and Williams became known as "The Czar of the Tenderloin" for his rough and ready crime-prevention tactics. Everyone had to pay to play in Clubber Williams's precinct. Max Schmittberger, a precinct sergeant, was Williams's bagman. He picked up the bribes from the various criminal enterprises and some legitimate ones as well that wanted protection, and delivered envelopes filled with money each month to Clubber's headquarters, Bernard Courtney's Saloon, that was located at 315 Seventh Avenue. According to David J. Krajicek, in his 2011 *New York Daily News* article,"The money flowed up through the ranks and into Tammany coffers, and everyone along the way took a share."

Although he was brought up on corruption and brutality charges several times over the years, Clubber Williams always somehow managed to beat the rap. Once, when charged with using excessive force, he reportedly said, "There is more law at the end of a policeman's nightstick than in a decision of the Supreme Court." According to Alexander Callow, author of *The Tweed Ring* (1966), "the police department was an independent kingdom where the Captain ruled, it was The Captain and his favorite subordinate often took exclusive control of cases, dropping cases as they saw fit, by divine right . . . The honest policeman was relegated to trivial cases . . ."

Not every police officer was corrupt. Although his career and rise to prominence within the department was dubious at best, Thomas Byrnes was never personally tainted with charges of corruption or receiving bribes from Mandelbaum or anyone else. Still, the question remained, in a department rife with corruption where kickbacks and bribes were the order of the day, how did Byrnes rise through the ranks to his lofty position of power? No one had an answer. Byrnes was one of the department's most highly respected and innovative police officers. He had come up through the ranks and had made a name for himself as a tough, ruthless, and successful detective, having helped solve a series of high profile cases, including the 1878 robbery of the Manhattan Savings Institution. He served as the head of the detective bureau from 1880 until 1895. Along with helping to solve many sensational cases, Byrnes was also instrumental in modernizing the New York City detective bureau. He made his detectives keep and submit detailed notes of all their activities, initiated the practice of photographing criminals when they were arrested, and archived criminal histories of known criminals. According to noted social reformer and newspaper reporter Jacob Riis, author of the groundbreaking social commentary about New York City's tenement crisis, *How the Other Half Lives: Studies Among the Tenements of New York* (1890), Byrnes was, ". . . a czar, with all the autocrat's irresponsible powers, and he exercised them as he saw fit. But he made the detective service great."

According to Riis, Byrnes ". . . shaped not just New York's Detective Bureau but the template for detective work as it would come to be organized and practiced in every modern American metropolis." Byrnes was a renowned investigator whose often brutal methods of interrogation popularized the term "the third degree," which he reportedly coined. The third degree as practiced by Byrnes included a combination of physical and psychological torture and led to the capture of some of New York City's most heinous criminals. Byrnes rose quickly through the ranks and served as the head of the detective bureau beginning in 1880. In 1892, he became the superintendent of the New York City police force. Byrnes was the "personification of the police department" and "a czar, with all the autocrat's irresponsible powers, and he exercised them as he saw fit. But he made the detective service great," Riis wrote. A master self-publicist, Byrnes published *Professional Criminals of America,* which became a law enforcement must-read for most police departments throughout the country.

Over his many years of service, Byrnes was able to gain wealthy and influential political support that allowed him to wield enormous and often unchecked power within the police force. He was considered a master psychologist who knew just the right approach with each criminal brought before him for interrogation. Backed by his uncanny detection abilities, his all-encompassing files, and his shadowy detective force, called "The Immortals," Byrnes always seemed to get his man, although the most well-known woman, Fredericka Mandelbaum, head of the largest criminal operation in New York City, somehow seemed to elude him.

A tireless self-promoter, Byrnes made sure his exploits in a series of sensational crimes were always front page news. Despite his many flaws and self-aggrandizement, Byrnes flourished as New York City's top cop, endearing himself to law and order minded citizens, especially wealthy bankers, merchants, and industrialists, whose money and valuables he pledged to protect—at a price. Byrnes was the first to open a police station on Wall Street in order to demonstrate his commitment to protect the fortunes of New York City's rich and well-to-do. Byrnes later became a central figure in the prosecution of Mandelbaum, although not in her arrest, when he was forced to defend the police department for allowing Mandelbaum to run her fencing operation in plain sight for nearly twenty-five years without prosecution.

With or without the likes of Thomas Byrnes, the Tweed Ring was able to consolidate its power by controlling every stage of criminal prosecution—the district attorney's office, judges, and the police department, but nothing lasts forever.

> Boss Tweed: "The fact is that New York politics were always dishonest —long before my time. There never was a time when you couldn't buy the board of aldermen. . . . This population is too hopelessly split up into races and factions to govern it

> under universal suffrage, except by the bribery of patronage or corruption."
>
> Elizabeth Kehoe, *The Titled Americans*, 2005

By the 1870s, a reform movement in New York City was bound and determined to get rid of Tweed and his cronies. The public attacks on Tweed were spearheaded by George Jones, the publisher of *The New York Times;* Samuel J. Tilden, New York City's district attorney; and *Harper's Weekly* cartoonist Thomas Nast. *Harper's* published Nast's scathing cartoons that depicted Tweed as thief, convict, and an enormous glutton. Tweed was so angry about the Nast attacks that he reportedly bellowed at Nast, "Stop them damned pictures. I don't care so much what the papers say about me. My constituents can't read. But, damn it, they can see pictures!"

The Tweed Ring was brought down in 1871 when *The New York Times* published an exposé on the graft and corruption of Tweed and his cohorts. In July 1871, two low-level city officials with a grudge against Tweed provided *The New York Times* with reams of documentation that detailed widespread city corruption by the Tweed Ring. The newspaper articles, coupled with Nast's political cartoons, created a public outcry and soon Tweed and many of his cronies were facing criminal charges and political oblivion. Questioned about the charges of corruption leveled at him by the *Times*, Tweed responded to a *Times* reporter, "What are you going to do about it?"

In 1871, New York City district attorney Samuel Tilden was named the head of a group of business and professional men to rid the city of Tweed and his cronies. Ultimately a grand jury handed down 120 indictments against Tweed. In December 1871, Tweed was arrested and held on $1 million bail. Tweed was bailed out by his friend and Wall Street financier Jay Gould.

A year later, Tweed was brought to trial but the case resulted in a hung jury and Tweed was set free, but not for long. Tilden believed that Tweed had bribed the jurors, so he retried the case in 1873. This time he assigned one police officer to guard each member of the jury, another police officer to watch his colleague, and a private detective to watch over all three. Tweed was found guilty at the end of the second trial and given a twelve-year prison sentence, which was reduced by a higher court. He served one year. When he was released in 1875, he was re-arrested on civil charges, sued by New York State for $6 million and held in debtor's prison until he could post $3 million bail. On December 4, 1875, Tweed escaped from authorities. While visiting his wife and children at their new home on Madison Avenue, and while accompanied by two guards and a warden of the jail, Tweed excused himself from the dinner table where the family, guards, and warden had all sat down to eat, and went upstairs to "freshen up" before being returned to his cell. After he was gone for an extended time, the jailers went upstairs and discovered that Tweed had fled out the back door. Tweed had reportedly paid $60,000 for help in making his escape. He hid out in an isolated farmhouse in New Jersey for several weeks where he altered his appearance by shaving off his beard, wearing a long gray wig, and donning eyeglasses. Going under the assumed name of "John Secor," Tweed took a schooner out of New York Harbor and landed in Florida where he hid out for a short time in a shack in the Everglades. From Florida he made his way to Cuba. By the time the authorities had traced his whereabouts to Santiago, Cuba, Tweed had escaped to Spain. Although never proved, it was long rumored that Mandelbaum had helped him escape by providing him with money and securing his safe passage to Spain. Mandelbaum's loyalty knew no bounds when it came to her criminal cohorts, even those like Tweed. For years she had paid Tweed off for protection from prosecution and Tweed had been good to his word. That alone in Mandelbaum's book was enough to merit loyalty.

United States Secretary of State Hamilton Fish requested that the Spanish authorities arrest and extradite Tweed to New York. Although Spain and the United States had no extradition treaty, Tweed was arrested and held until the United States Navy cruiser, *Franklin*, arrived to bring him back to the United States. Ironically, the Spanish authorities used a cartoon depicting the likeness of Tweed that was drawn by Thomas Nast and had appeared in *Harper's Weekly* to identify Tweed. Tweed could not escape the image of greed and corruption that Nast had forever ascribed to him in his drawings. Once the most powerful man in the most powerful city in the world, Tweed was returned to the Ludlow Street Jail.

Tweed was not the first corrupt politician to hold his sway over New York City, nor was he the last. Much like Mandelbaum, Tweed merely fine-tuned the corruption, just as Mandelbaum fine-tuned the criminal enterprise of receiving stolen property. After Tweed's downfall in 1871, "Honest" John Kelly was put in control of Tammany Hall but things didn't change dramatically. Police and judicial corruption continued unabated. When he retired in 1884, Kelly turned over the political control of Tammany Hall to one of his lieutenants, Richard Croker. Boss Croker became Grand Sachem and exerted massive authority over the workings of New York City government, including the police department. Although the faces changed at Tammany Hall the situation remained the same—New York City's district attorney's office, judges, and the police department remained under the control of political bosses and a cesspool of crime and corruption.

Even after Boss Tweed's downfall, Mandelbaum continued to bribe elected officials, judges, and members of the police department. Her operation flourished and she grew richer and more powerful. John Adams, the second President of the United States was quoted as saying America was "A government of laws, and not of men"; however, Mandelbaum discovered that if you paid the right men, then the law didn't apply, not to her. Despite her prosperity, she was not immune to personal tragedy and in 1870 she lost what was most near and dear to her.

3
EN GARDE

"The Gilded Age, the years immediately after the Civil War, saw numerous entrepreneurs—Vanderbilt, Gould, Fisk, Rockefeller—amass enormous wealth through ambiguous means. Marm was merely less ambiguous . . . "

—William Bryk, "The Scams of Grandma Fence," 2003

At the outbreak of the Civil War in 1861, legitimate businessmen used the war as an opportunity to make fortunes by selling inferior products to the military. War profiteering became the norm. These endeavors to make a profit at any price, including the life and safety of soldiers, found its way into the sale of inferior if not downright rotten food supplies, uniforms made of inferior fabric, and even war apparatuses like navy vessels that were outdated, substandard, and sold to the Union Navy at incredible profits by upstanding, wealthy industrialists like Cornelius Vanderbilt, who had sold off his steamship fleet to the Union Navy at the start of the war. He used the money to invest in the railroad industry which quickly made him a tycoon. Another "legitimate" businessman named Philip Armour made a fortune by selling pork to the Union forces at a huge profit and manipulating the stock market by selling pork futures short on the New York market. He then went to Chicago where he established the largest pork packing house in the country. War profiteering became one of the major ways that Gilded Age tycoons made their fortunes. Unscrupulous businessmen and government officials were all in it together. According to a *New York Times* article, "From the beginning, government representatives awarded contracts based not on the best product, or the fairest price, but on the highest bribe."

In 1861, Brooks Brothers was awarded a government contract for 12,000 Union uniforms for the New York State Volunteer regiment. Not only had the government contract been obtained through shady means, but many of the uniforms were ill-fitting, poorly sewn, and some were lacking buttons or even button holes. The uniforms, it was later discovered, had been made of old, shredded, decaying rags, glued together then ironed into what vaguely resembled cloth. The uniforms fell apart at the seams. The New York State Legislature paid $45,000 to replace the original order for uniforms, an amount comparable to nearly $11 million in today's currency. The new crop of war profiteering millionaires, their companies operating at outlandish profit margins by cheating the government, was given the dubious title of "The Shoddy Aristocracy." It was the sale of these inferior war supplies and soldier's equipment, from food to shoes—many government shoe suppliers made the soles of their army boots out of glued-together wood chips which fell apart after half an hour of marching—which gave rise to the word "shoddy." In 1861, *Harper's Weekly* coined the word, describing it as, "a villainous compound, the refuse stuff and sweepings of the shop, pounded, rolled, glued and smoothed to the external form and gloss of cloth." And according to an 1861 *New York Herald* story, "The world has seen its silver age, its golden age. . . . This is the age of shoddy. The new brown-stone palaces on Fifth Avenue . . . the new diamonds which dazzle unaccustomed eyes . . . the new people who live in the palaces and ride in the carriages and wear the diamonds and silk, are shoddy. . . . Six days in the week they are shoddy businessmen. On the seventh day they are shoddy Christians."

If the Civil War gave supposedly legitimate businessmen money-making prospects, then it also gave illegal enterprises, like Mandelbaum's, a multitude of opportunities to buy and sell stolen goods on the black market. It certainly goes without saying that a huge number of commodities from clothes to food stuffs were scarce and those who needed it could always find it through people like Mandelbaum and at a significantly lower price than if they had to purchase it through legitimate means. Most people who purchased goods from Mandelbaum were cognizant of why the merchandise they bought from her was cheaper, but it didn't prohibit them from taking advantage of Mandelbaum's many wares. It was simply and capitalistically what the market would bear, and during the Gilded Age it would bear a lot, both legitimately and illegally. All and all, Mandelbaum was engaged in the purest form of capitalism—supply and demand. It is impossible to pinpoint exactly how much money Mandelbaum made during the war and afterward since she kept no books, at least none anyone could locate, but suffice it to say, given the fact that she merely rented her Clinton and Rivington Street property at the start of the war and that she bought the property outright in 1873, it is fairly clear that she had made some substantial profit from her stolen property business.

COPY OF CERTIFICATE OF INSPECTORS FURNISHED TO BROOKS BROTHERS

I received from Brooks Brothers of New-York, 92 boxes containing uniforms for the Volunteer Militia of the State of York . . . said garments were badly cut and of unsuitable sizes and shapes, poorly sewed and many of them would become unfit for use upon being worn not over a week; that some of the garments received from Brooks Brothers were without buttons, had some buttons broken off and some of said garments so badly made that they soon would rip open on such garments being first tried on . . .

C.C. B. Walker
Assistant Quartermaster-General

—*The New York Times*, September 5, 1861

The *New York Tribune,* in 1861, described vultures as "human compared with monsters who furnish rotten blankets and rotten meat to the living in the camps." The practice of overpricing under-quality goods made fortunes for many of New York City's rich and powerful during the Gilded Age. Businessmen and politicians alike readily crossed the line between legitimate and illegitimate business practices, committing fraud and worse— all in the name of capitalism. Was it any wonder that Mandelbaum and criminals in general did not mimic their legitimate counterparts? If they were buying and selling stolen property, how much worse was it then selling tainted meat, appalling uniforms, and phony boots?

> If a Shoddy
> Meet a Shoddy
> A-raking of his "rye,"
> And a Shoddy
> Chokes a Shoddy
> Need anybody Cry.
>
> —*Vanity Fair*, November 1861

After the war, business only improved for Mandelbaum as the crime rates increased. Not only were there throngs of men returning from the war to an economy that was faltering, with no jobs or prospects in sight creating a ready-made pool of potential criminals, but with the growth of business and industry and the proliferation of new wealth as a by-product of industrialized growth, newer and more potentially lucrative criminal endeavors presented themselves. More wealth constituted more buying power by the rich. The more they bought—jewelry, clothing, paintings, silks—the more there was available to steal. It made perfect sense. And along with the influx of vast amounts of new money among the already rich and powerful, came the establishment of new banks, built to protect not only the cash and precious jewelry of the city's wealthy elite, but a greater number of securities, stocks, and bonds.

As industrialization and westward expansion got into full swing after the war, there were more profits to be made. This period saw the rise of the "robber barons" the likes of which included Jim Fisk, Jay Gould, Andrew Carnegie, the Astors, and the Vanderbilts, who made their fortunes in legal but questionable ways. This new class of wealthy Americans celebrated their newfound wealth in an ostentatious manner never before seen in this country. Nights at the opera and lavish dinner parties filled the social calendars of these industrialists and their families. Fifth Avenue above 50th Street was transformed into Millionaires' Row. Vast fortunes were poured into the palaces bordering the new Central Park. Yet even as these showy displays of newfound wealth began to flourish in New York City, with the establishment of elegant hotels and restaurants and one mansion after another, each ostentatiously designed to outdo its neighbors, the majority of New Yorkers lived in dire poverty and filth. The disparity between the pure gluttony of the rich and the pathetic straits of the poor was never more prevalent than during the Gilded Age in America. One noted restaurant catering to the rich hosted formal horseback dinners for the New York Riding Club. In one of the more outlandish and thoughtless displays of colossal wealth and conspicuous consumption, "Mamie" Fish, wife of Illinois Central Railroad magnate Stuyvesant Fish, held a dinner party to honor her dog, giving the mutt a $15,000 diamond collar. This, at a time when more than three-quarters of the country's population earned less than $1,200 a year. Fish, like many others of her social status, were seemingly oblivious to the dripping sarcasm with which Mark Twain, along with Charles Dudley Warner, coined the phrase "Gilded Age."

To say that the country's rich obtained their great fortunes legally is a stretch. They did it by whatever means possible and often with the complete sanctions of the government which they controlled. Laws that did not suit their ends were not merely broken, they were completely rewritten to serve their needs—something those of the lower and criminal class could not do. With business, industry, and manufacturing flourishing across the country, this progress and the vast profits connected to it enabled robber barons to freely engage in corrupt business practices, stock manipulations, and the establishment of monopolies. American businessmen moved forward with little restraint, and the nickname "robber barons" aptly described their methods.

This in no small way contributed to the public support of Mandelbaum and her ilk for being champions of the lower class, since they defied the laws—the laws that the rich broke for their own gain. Mandelbaum and her criminal cohorts generally stole their plunder from the institutions of the rich and powerful—banks, mansions, fancy restaurants, dry goods establishments, and jewelry stores. The poor practically cheered when they heard of another bank robbery or jewelry robbery. According to Edwin Burrows and Mike Wallace in their book *Gotham* (2000),when a gang of river pirates called "The Daybreak Boys" shot and killed a watchman during a robbery on board a ship and were caught, convicted, and sentenced to hang, they were "hailed as heroes by the Boweryrites. When they were hanged in January 1853, hundreds showed up at the Tombs courtyard to shake hands with the condemned men on the scaffold." There was a deep bond between those who defied authority and the poor and downtrodden. The poor saw these criminals as Robin Hoods, robbing from the rich and giving to the poor, since in fact, they themselves were the poor.

The Tombs was one of the most notorious prisons in New York City's Lower Manhattan. Its formal name was the New York Halls of Justice and House of Detention. The huge granite structure was built in 1838 on the site of a swamp that had been filled in. Only a few months after it was opened, the building began to sink into the swampland, making it even more inhospitable to inmates. It took up the square bounded by Centre, Elm, Franklin, and Leonard Streets. It was primarily a holding tank where defendants were confined until trial and sentencing. The jail was divided into sections based on the severity of the crimes the defendants were charged with. Those arrested for crimes like murder were kept on one floor of the jail, while those charged with lesser crimes like burglary or shoplifting were held on another floor. The Tombs were made up of three prisons, each several stories high. One of the prisons was exclusively for men, the other for boys, and the third for women. Approximately 50,000 prisoners were confined there annually.

As production increased and transportation by rail continued to expand at the hands of the country's robber barons, more goods flooded into the marketplace. The bulk of the nation's goods came and went through New York City. Luxury goods like diamonds and wine arrived daily in New York Harbor, while more than half of the country's imported textile goods came through the city. New York had already become the hub of the garment industry. More goods brought more opportunities for legal, as well as illegal, entrepreneurs. As these goods flooded into the marketplace, so too did the need to protect these goods from the likes of criminals like Mandelbaum, whose cohorts pilfered them at every turn. Mandelbaum in turn resold the stolen goods to a waiting and appreciative public who probably would not have been able to afford such commodities were they purchased through legitimate sources. But what New York City's citizenry hailed as business acumen in their robber barons, they detested in the likes of Mandelbaum, including her ostentatious dinner parties. They were tolerated but loathed.

But unlike their robber baron counterparts who were regaled for their show of wealth and fame, a criminal's outward display of wealth became a cause of concern for both reformers and newspapers. It was all right for robber barons like Carnegie and the Astors to give lavish parties, spend their vast profits on expensive frivolities, and snub their noses at the poor, but displays of wealth by criminals only served to ignite disgust and rage. How dare those who made their living stealing from the rich carry on in public in such an extravagant way? Mandelbaum kept a low profile, except for the dinner parties she and her husband held. Already an imposing physical presence, she kept her outward appearance unobtrusive. She was fond of saying, "It takes brains to be a real lady," and despite her criminal vocation and her height and girth, she took great pains to appear so in public. She was often stylishly dressed although always subdued in her choice of colors and material. She was partial to dark clothes—black, dark browns, and the customary deep blues of the period. Her dresses were made of satin and wool which were complimented with dark cloaks or long capes. She wore diamond earrings and sometimes a pearl encrusted pin on her collar. But even these few accessories were never ostentatious. The only flamboyant item of clothing was her signature hat, usually adorned with dark feathers or plumes, which she wore, perched on the very top of her head. It looked like a bird's nest resting in a sea of dark hair that she parted in the middle and wore pulled back tightly in a bun.

> "She was a huge woman weighing more than two hundred and fifty pounds and had a sharply curved mouth and extraordinarily fat cheeks, above which were small black eyes, heavy black brows and a high sloping forehead and a mass of tightly rolled black hair which was generally surmounted by a tiny bonnet with drooping feathers."
>
> —Herbert Asbury, *The Gangs of New York*, 1929

Despite her great wealth, she stayed in Little Germany and lived and worked in her ramshackle building on Clinton and Rivington Streets. For her, it was a matter of good taste as well as a good business strategy. She didn't want to arouse any more interest than there already was in her nefarious operation. The base of Mandelbaum's operations at the Clinton and Rivington Streets location was just one block from the Thirteenth Ward police station and only a few blocks from the Fifth District Court. Although living and working so closely to potential prosecutors might have seemed dangerous, even daring, it was in fact of great benefit to her. By having her stolen property operations so close to the authorities, it gave her the distinct advantage of developing relationships with law enforcement and judicial officials and she was able to keep abreast of the comings and goings of various authorities. The store provided a respectable cover for her criminal activities. It appeared, at least on the surface, to be a fairly busy and prosperous dry goods store. It was in the back of this tiny shop, far from the view of prying eyes and legitimate customers that the real business transpired. It was there that Mandelbaum trafficked in bolts of the finest silk stolen from some of the best homes and businesses on the East Coast. She dealt in just about anything that came her way—silk, lace, diamonds, horses, carriages, silverware, gold, silver, and bonds. A large portion of the property looted during the Chicago fire of 1871 ended up in her possession, which she subsequently sold for a sizable profit. She built an elaborate hiding apparatus within the store—a chimney with a fake back. Behind the fake back was a dumbwaiter that could be quickly raised or lowered with the pull of a secret lever. It allowed her to easily get rid of any loot if someone happened to pop into her store unexpectedly.

> "The house was rated as fourth class by the insurance company being possibly one-sixth brick and five-sixths wood. It was a straggling, ill-built yet curious looking building, more pretentious at its angle with Rivington Street than at any other. Sprawling away from this angle down Clinton Street was the actual business part of the establishment. This was a two-story, clapboarded wing, some twenty-five feet long. . ."
>
> —George Washington Walling, *Recollections of a New York Chief of Police*, 1887

Beneath her rough exterior and despite her disreputable business dealings, Mandelbaum tried to maintain an air of refinement and part of that refinement came in the form of her desire for social acceptance however tacit it might be. The only outward extravagance she and her husband engaged in was dinner parties that she threw for her colleagues from both sides of the tracks. Guests would receive stylish invitations sent from "The Honorable and Mrs. William Mandelbaum." The two floors above her store were filled with the most elegant furniture and draperies, mostly stolen property that had once decorated some of the finest homes or businesses in the city. A typical scene at one of Mandelbaum's dinner parties found her seated at the head of one of the many tables in her dining room, inevitably surrounded by her fawning protégés. She was too huge to fit comfortably into one of the dining room chairs, so she usually sat on an embroidered, cushioned bench. Her husband, Wolf, sat on one side of her, with her oldest son, Julius, on the other. Seated in close proximity around the table were her favorite protégés—Piano Charlie Bullard, George Leslie, Sophie Lyons, and Max Shinburn. Many of her soirées were attended by some of the most successful and notorious criminals in the country as well as a host of New York City's finest citizenry. Known burglars, sneak thieves, and swindlers mixed freely among judges, corrupt cops, businessmen, and politicians in the elegant rooms above her shabby haberdashery shop.

The dining room was spacious, elegant, and comfortable, with plush carpets of red and gold and an assortment of formal dining tables and chairs, as well as upholstered couches and high-back leather chairs. The room featured a coffered ceiling and hand-carved woodwork, including an ornate fireplace and bookcases. Huge pocket doors separated the two parlor sections. The windows were covered with luminously embroidered silk drapes along with carved wooden shutters that concealed guests from prying eyes. The ceilings rose nearly twelve feet high, while the cut-glass chandeliers were hung at a lower level so that extinguished candles could be easily replaced. More than sixty guests dined at the tastefully set Chippendale-style mahogany tables with matching chairs, each of which had a shaped crest with an acanthus carving.

The tables were covered with linen tablecloths and lighted with gold candelabras. The walls were covered with paintings, some framed, some not. The elaborate decor of the dining room was abundant with Victorian elegance and whimsy, all of it stolen from some of the best homes and offices throughout the city and country. Mandelbaum had exquisite taste in home décor, food, and music. Guests dined on the finest cuts of lamb and ham. Piano Charlie Bullard entertained her guests on the piano, perched on a stool in front of the white, baby grand piano that graced Mandelbaum's lavish dining room. Mandelbaum was by all accounts a charming woman, easily able to curry favor with influential criminals, legitimate business people, as well as police, judges, politicians, and prosecutors.

Everyone knew she was a fence and that she had made a fortune being one. It had been long established that without the likes of Mandelbaum and other receivers of stolen property, the criminal world of New York City would have been diminished considerably if not altogether. But eliminating fence operations like the one Mandelbaum ran would prove to be near impossible for law enforcement. In his 1886 book, *Professional Criminals of America,* Thomas Byrnes made it clear that although the elimination of fencing operations would endanger criminals of every ilk, closing down these operations was unlikely. "Without a safe market for his ill-gotten property the avocation of the rogue would be unprofitable. The buying of stolen goods is therefore not a crime of recent origin, but dates back to the very beginning of thievery. It is really the root of evil but the suppression of receivers of stolen goods in the State of New York owing to existing laws, has been made almost an impossibility . . ." Byrnes wrote.

Mandelbaum's enterprise was a beneficial outlet for the many criminals she had working for her. She secured the stolen merchandise, removed any identifying marks, and resold it back into the marketplace. By taking the stolen property off their hands, her business operation helped those who made their living from stealing by making sure merchandise could not be traced back to them and by giving money to the thieves in exchange for the goods. It worked out for everyone, except of course the poor souls whose merchandise had been stolen. She generally paid between 10 and 20 percent of the value of the merchandise brought to her. She could then resell it at half the cost of retail and still make a substantial profit, or she could sell it back to the owner for the full retail price. She reportedly paid approximately 65 cents per yard for silks that usually wholesaled for $3 a yard.

She gained a reputation as a respected partner among her criminal followers. She was smart enough to realize that as her business grew she had to reinvest in it. For her, reinvestment meant more bribes to higher authorities as well as adding new benefits to her employees—her cadre of elite criminals. In order to maintain her business, she needed her pickpockets, thieves, and burglars out on the streets so she set up expense accounts for them to cover bail, legal representation, living expenses, and financial backing. The services she provided to criminals was no less similar to what any legitimate businessman might do—investing money to make money. It was the American way.

Crime was not new to New York City. Loosely organized gangs had always been involved in petty crimes like pickpocketing, extortion, burglaries, and even bank robberies. Mandelbaum was one of the first to try to organize this loosely knit group of law breakers by developing a mutually beneficial arrangement that kept the criminals dependent on each other, out of jail and beholden to her. Up until Mandelbaum's emergence as the center of criminal activity within the city, these gangs undertook their illegal enterprises in a disorganized flurry. Sometimes they were successful, but often times not. Petty thieves, burglars, and pickpockets were often apprehended by police. Without the police protection, legal defense, and bail money that Mandelbaum offered to those who worked for her, many of these criminals found themselves serving time in Sing Sing or worse—headed for the city morgue. According to the *Brooklyn Eagle*, she was no mere receiver of stolen goods, but the person who "first put crime in America on a syndicated basis."

BOLD ATTEMPT AT BURGLARY—A GANG OF THIEVES ATTEMPT TO ENTER A HOUSE ON CONEY ISLAND ROAD—THE ATTEMPT FRUSTRATED AND TWO MEN SHOT—CAPTURE OF THE THIEVES

> It seems that these men, who are Russian Jews and whose names are Udell Coburn, Eziut Bloom, Mark Goldwater and Esadore Shey had been often to the house of Mr. Stryker . . . [Stryker] fired at them and Mark Goldwater received the contents of the barrel in his hand. He fired again and this time Issac Goldman, was shot in the hand and the shot just grazed his lips. The thieves had come well prepared to carry out their burglarious intentions, having with them a diamond to cut glass, knives, skeleton keys, meat to silence the dogs, and large bags to carry their plunder.
>
> —*Brooklyn Eagle*, February 29, 1868

In 1870, in her continued effort to cultivate a plethora of current and future criminals, all of whom would be indebted to her, Mandelbaum established a school for crime on Grand Street in Lower Manhattan. The school offered young street urchins, like Sophie Lyons, and up-and-coming thieves, like Adam Worth, courses in burglary, safe-cracking, blackmailing, and confidence games. Amazingly, the school was not far from police headquarters. Children of all ages and either gender could learn from professional pickpockets and thieves. Students might advance to taking courses in burglary and safe blowing; the "doctoral" level offered training in confidence schemes and blackmail. Advanced classes in safecracking, burglary, blackmail, and con artistry were free of initial charge for astute students. The Grand Street school became the most highly esteemed institution for young criminals in the United States. The best and brightest graduates were offered salaried positions with Mandelbaum, but they had to turn over everything they stole directly to her and no one else. The school only operated for six years. It thrived until Mandelbaum discovered that the son of a prominent police official had enrolled in the school. Mandelbaum knew this was too dangerous and she closed the school.

Mandelbaum's fencing operation benefited legitimate business people as well. Police reported that hundreds of well-known men and women, who were upstanding members of their community, often frequented Mandelbaum's haberdashery shop along with the usual assortment of criminal types. She cultivated relationships with these businesspeople in and around Little Germany as well as with uptown merchants and business owners. For example, George Rettinger, the wealthy owner of the Passaic Hotel in New Jersey, was a frequent client of Mandelbaum's and visited her shop often to purchase silverware, tablecloths, cotton napkins, sheets, and blankets for his hotel at half the price it would have cost him to purchase these items from legitimate retailers.

She provided jobs for people, helped struggling business people by providing goods they needed at less than wholesale, and generously donated to various charities and her neighborhood synagogue. She hired a network of associates, from artisan engravers to jewelers and even carriage drivers to help with hasty getaways. She was one of the earliest equal-opportunity employers. The German-Jewish community of Kleindeutschland provided her with a vast and endless pool of talent including many skilled artisans who she hired to melt down gold and silver, reset diamonds and other precious stones, or remove identifying marks from silks and fabrics. Her biggest expenditure was hiring the legal firm of Howe and Hummel, the most notorious, successful, and crooked legal firm in the city. Mandelbaum reportedly paid "Big Bill" Howe and "Little Abe" Hummel an annual retainer of $5,000 to represent her interests. Her neighbors were devoted to her, even those who were fully aware of her nefarious occupation. In a roundabout way, Mandelbaum was strengthening the American economy with her fencing operation. She was putting people to work—the criminals who stole the goods. She was circulating capital—by buying and then reselling the stolen goods. And she was, in her own small way, redistributing the wealth and merchandise to those who couldn't otherwise purchase certain commodities.

> "By 1880, Marm was inarguably the most successful fence in the United States, selling to dealers in every major city along the East Coast and Canada. Over the course of her career, she handled an estimated $5 million to $10 million in stolen property. Dozens of preeminent bank robbers and thieves sought her business, and she mentored those who displayed exceptional cunning."
>
> —"The Life and Crimes of 'Old Mother' Mandelbaum," 2011

At the height of her career, in addition to her base of operations at Clinton and Rivington Streets, she maintained warehouses chock-a-block full of stolen property. The scope of her fencing operations far exceeded the boundaries of the city as she received stolen property from all over the country. Hers was a well-oiled, million-dollar enterprise and according to Chief of Police George Washington Walling, Mandelbaum, as a receiver of stolen property, had "no peer in the United States." As her sphere of influence and her business operations grew, like any good businesswoman, she invested in real estate. She needed more space to accommodate the larger parcels of plunder that were coming her way. The ownership of real estate was a huge part of the American dream of success and Mandelbaum was no exception. She was able to realize financial success very much in the same way her legitimate counterparts did. Growing her business, diversifying her services, accumulating real estate—all of this represented her business acumen. She bought warehouses as well as tenements. In the warehouses throughout the city and in nearby New Jersey she stored vast amounts of stolen property. She collected rents from her tenement investments. She was the epitome of the American businesswoman.

With a well-oiled operation like Mandelbaum's, she didn't have to fear prosecution. If she did, she might have found herself facing the sparest of punishments and fines. The laws concerning stolen property stipulated that the receivers could not be prosecuted unless they were connected to the theft itself. It wasn't enough just to buy the hot merchandise; the fence had to either have ordered the theft or bought the property knowing of its illegal origins. The receiver could not be prosecuted unless the thief or thieves had been convicted. Receivers, if caught, could be charged with either a lesser charge of a misdemeanor or a felony depending upon the scale and worth of the stolen property.

POLICE REPORTS
A NOTORIOUS RECEIVER OF STOLEN GOODS
ARRESTED IN CANADA

> New York policemen will be glad to know that Samuel Sprince, the well-known receiver of stolen goods, who was convicted of that offence in this City about a year ago, and fined six cents by Judge Russell has been arrested in Canada, charged with burglary..."
>
> —*The New York Times*, February 20, 1861

Mandelbaum and other receivers of stolen property seldom faced capture and conviction, however, but even in those rare cases where they did, judges often handed down lighter sentences that did not hinder their ongoing business, primarily because they were either on the take or they had other more important crimes to deal with.

As each new wave of immigrants flooded into New York City, each ethnic group became threatened. Gangs of immigrants, made up of poor young men and women, disenfranchised from societies' mainstream began to roam the streets seeking to defend what little turf they had. This lead to gang fights and riots, most notably the New York City Draft Riots of 1863 when bands of

Irish rioters, protesting President Lincoln's call for a draft, killed at least 120 civilians, injured more than two thousand, lynched eleven African Americans, and caused nearly three million dollars in property damage. They were followed by the Orange Riots in 1870 and 1871, when Irish Protestants and Irish Catholics clashed on the streets of New York City causing the death of sixty people, including three militia men sent to quell the riot, injuring close to two hundred people and causing close to one million dollars in property damage. Because of these and other violent battles, the police and judges were more concerned about dealing with civil unrest and violent crimes than with stopping the growing organized crime problem.

> **THE MOB IN NEW-YORK**
> **RESISTANCE TO THE DRAFT—RIOTING AND BLOODSHED. CONSCRIPTION OFFICES SACKED AND BURNED. PRIVATE DWELLINGS PILLAGED AND FIRED. AN ARMORY AND HOTEL DESTROYED. COLORED PEOPLE ASSAULTED—UNOFFENDING BLACK MAN HUNG. THE TRIBUNE OFFICE ATTACKED—THE COLORED ORPHAN ASYLUM RANSACKED AND BURNED—OTHER OUTRAGES AND INCIDENTS. A DAY OF INFAMY AND DISGRACE**
>
> —headlines from *The New York Times*, July 14, 1863

All of Mandelbaum's success and all her accumulated wealth were not able to forestall the single most tragic event in her life—the death of her husband, Wolf. He was her husband, the father of her children, and her closest confidant. She looked to him for advice and counsel both in personal as well as business matters. In early 1870, he was stricken with a serious and terminal disease, more than likely tuberculosis. Bedridden for the next five years, he was dutifully cared for by Fredericka and the children. Although he did some peddling when they first came to America, he was not involved, at least not visibly, in the evolution of his wife's criminal empire. He was listed as a peddler in the city directories and census records until the 1860s; after that, both he and Fredericka are listed separately as dry goods store proprietors at 79 Clinton and 163 Rivington Streets. Much of the reliable information available concerning Wolf Mandelbaum's involvement in his wife's criminal empire indicates that he had little or no input in the real family business of receiving stolen property. It is hard to believe he didn't know what was going on right under his nose, but there remains no sufficient evidence to show he personally engaged in the illegal activities of his wife, aside from offering her advice. New York City Police Chief George Washington Walling called him "a nonentity," while others who knew him referred to him as a silent partner who never involved himself in his wife's dealings. The success of the whole operation from start to finish belonged to her. He died in March 1875. According to the New York City Board of Health, his death certificate stated he was fifty-one years and six months old when he died. The primary cause of death was listed as encephalitis gravura sometimes referred to in those days as "brain fever." The secondary cause was identified simply as "the wasting away disease." Mandelbaum was devastated and mourned for nearly a year, neglecting much of her business endeavors. He was buried in the family plot in Union Fields Cemetery of Congregation Rodeph Sholom in Queens, New York. She saw to it that fresh flowers were placed at his grave every day.

Following her husband's death, Mandelbaum came to rely heavily on her son, Julius, and a man named Herman Stoude when she once again resumed the reins of the business. Stoude, a burly, blond German of few words, was devoted to Mandelbaum and although he was supposedly merely a store clerk, he was later identified in court documents as Mandelbaum's constant companion, loyal confidante, and able bodyguard. He could, however, never take the place of her husband, Wolf. Stoude became such an integral part of Mandelbaum's illegal activities that when Mandelbaum was ultimately brought to justice, he was charged with grand larceny along with her and Julius. He was the only person outside her family who Mandelbaum kept in her complete confidence. He was allegedly always with her when she ventured out to examine stolen merchandise outside the confines of her shop. It was Stoude who would carry off the merchandise if Mandelbaum bought it, taking it to one of her many warehouses or to the back of her store. How he came into Mandelbaum's confidence remains a mystery. However, shortly after his wife died in 1876, he began working for Mandelbaum, doing odd jobs. By then Mandelbaum herself had been a widow for almost a year. Some people, although certainly not to their faces and especially not in earshot of Mandelbaum herself, referred to them as a couple. More than anything else, Stoude appeared to have acted as Mandelbaum's eyes and ears outside the shop, keeping track of rumors and scuttlebutt and reporting directly back to her on matters of interest whether generated within the criminal community or among the police, politicians, and legitimate businessmen. Aside from Mandelbaum, who had every confidence in him, Stoude was not well-liked by any of her associates and they tried to keep him at a distance because of his reputation as a stool pigeon. Although he remained close to her in every way and always looked out for her best interests, he was not involved in any aspect of the control of Mandelbaum's criminal business empire. Like Julius, Stoude was at the beck and call of the Queen.

The biggest move she made after her husband's death was to expand her operations to include not only receiving and selling stolen merchandise, but to planning and financing major crimes, including bank robberies. The most notable was the infamous Manhattan Savings Institution robbery in 1878 in which Mandelbaum invested approximately $2,500 so that the bank robbers could purchase the most modern tools to carry out the heist. The burglars absconded with approximately $3 million in cash and securities of which, had the robbery panned out as it should have, her take was estimated at fifty percent.

For Mandelbaum these bank heists became one-stop shopping, or, more aptly, one-stop stealing. Instead of having to rob individuals one at a time for single pieces of merchandise—a gold pocket watch, a diamond necklace, an emerald ring, a bolt of silk—she was able to peripherally engage in robberies in which her minions could get away with large hauls in one single take. She concentrated most of her efforts on making the big haul whether through banks or from larger merchandising concerns. But even as the world was changing for Mandelbaum's operations, so too was the world changing in other socioeconomic areas. The rich and powerful who had earned their wealth even under unscrupulous means, were not about to let it be taken from them. The rich and powerful depended on the banks to keep their money, securities and jewelry safe. What Mandelbaum was doing by facilitating bank robberies was striking at the very heart of that security.

In order to expand her criminal empire, Mandelbaum had to enlist the talents of not just mere pickpockets, petty thieves and burglars, but bank robbers and safecrackers. Among those that she drew into her inner circle were Max Shinburn, Piano Charlie Bullard, Adam Worth, and the "King of Bank Robbers," George Leslie—the cream of the criminal crop.

> "Marm was an established legend and arguably the most influential criminal in America."
>
> —Ben Macintyre, *The Napoleon of Crime, 2011*

PART II

MANDELBAUM'S MOB

4 HER LITTLE CHICKS

> "They call me Ma because I give them money and horses and diamonds."
>
> —Fredericka Mandelbaum, 1869

If Mandelbaum was going to expand her operations to include bank robberies she only wanted the best bank robbers and safecrackers in her organization and that's exactly what she got, starting with international burglar and safecracker Max Shinburn. She called her new cadre of criminals her "little chicks." They called her "Marm" which was short for "mother," because like a mother hen, she hovered over them, guiding and nurturing their notorious careers.

Shinburn, who wore expensive clothes, sometimes donning a full-length ermine cape, called himself "The Baron." He often complained he was at heart an aristocrat and that he detested the crooks with whom he was compelled to associate. His biggest heist while in Mandelbaum's employ was the robbery of the Ocean Street Bank in New York City in June 1869, where he, along with fellow bank burglar George Leslie, made off with close to $800,000 in cash and securities, making it the biggest haul ever up and until that time. Mandelbaum received her customary share—fifty percent.

Despite his extravagant clothes, he lived frugally and invested all his ill-gotten gains in foreign money orders payable to relatives in Prussia. He eventually retired from his life of crime in America and sailed to Europe, where, by the judicious expenditure of part of his fortune, he bought the title of Baron Shindel of Monaco. Although he was able to live royally and aristocratically for a time, Shinburn ultimately squandered all his wealth and was forced back into a life of crime. He was ultimately apprehended in Belgium during a bungled bank robbery and sent to prison. While incarcerated there he informed on a fellow American inmate, the international burglar and art thief, Adam Worth, in an attempt to have his sentence reduced. Following his release he returned to America to once again ply his trade as a bank robber. He was sixty-two years old and no longer the same wily, talented bank robber he used to be. While trying to rob a bank in Middleburg, New York, he was caught by Pinkerton detectives and sent to prison where he spent the next fourteen years of his life. He was finally released in April 1908. He wrote a history of safecracking, *Safe Burglary: Its Beginnings and Progress*, that was deemed so instructive for novice criminals that it was never published and remains to this day in the Pinkerton Detective Agency archives. He died in 1916 at the John Howard Home for Reformed Prisoners in Boston at the age of seventy-seven years old.

SHINBURN AGAIN CAUGHT
THE MOST EXPERT BANK BURGLAR KNOWN
ARRESTED IN THIS CITY A CAREER IN CRIME
OF MANY YEARS ACCUSED NOW OF ROBBING
A NATIONAL BANK IN MIDDLEBURG, N.Y.—SUSPECTED
OF OTHER RECENT ROBBERIES

> Maximillian Shinburn, alias Max Shinburn, alias Mark Shinburn, alias "Count" Shinburn, alias M. H. Baker, alias M. H. Zimmerman, alias "The Dutchman," was arrested Friday by Pinkerton detectives for the robbery of the First National Bank of Middleburg, N.Y. He is supposed to have been connected with other recent robberies . . . Shinburn saved a fortune from 1860 to 1869 when he was obliged to flee from the United States . . . Just before he left the United States on a lucky turn in the market, he cleared

> about half a million dollars. He went first to Brussels where he remained a few years. He finally purchased an estate, an interest in a large silk mill and the title of "count" . . .
>
> —*The New York Times*, June 30, 1895

Mandelbaum was always obsessed with social acceptance through association, and no association was more in keeping with this obsession than her relationship with the Boston-bred, boarding-school educated and classically trained Charlie Bullard, whose ancestors reached all the way back to *The Mayflower*. Although Bullard had already given himself over to his worst angels—wine, women and crime—he was an expert safecracker, and burglar, he still carried an air of pedigree about him, something that Mandelbaum could never truly attain. He was everything she was not and everything her children, despite all her money, could never be.

Bullard was one of her favorite "little chicks." The handsome and raffish Bullard came from a wealthy family in Milford, Massachusetts. He was the lucky recipient of a large inheritance from his businessman father, and was fluent in English, French, and German. With his long nimble fingers, he was able to play the piano like a professional. His favorite selections were sonatas that, when he played them, "could reduce the hardest criminal to tears and lure the most chaste woman into bed," according to Ben Macintyre, author of *The Napoleon of Crime: The Life and Times of Adam Worth, Master Thief.* His musical talents earned him the nickname of "Piano Charlie."

Bullard had squandered his inheritance on his three favorite things—wine, women, and gambling. He had tried his hand at becoming a butcher before turning to crime. Because of his constant piano playing, Bullard developed not only his musical talent but an extraordinary sense of touch, so much so that it was rumored he was able to discern the combination of any safe simply by turning the tumblers a few times. Under Mandelbaum's tutelage, Bullard became one of New York City's most skilled and daring burglars, pulling off a string of successful bank and train robberies including the theft of $100,000 from the Hudson River Railway Express. With all he had going for him, how could someone of Bullard's social standing end up in the White Plains jail? The answer was easy. He was caught.

On April 30, 1868, Bullard and an accomplice, Ike Marsh, robbed $100,000 in cash and securities from the Merchant's Union Express Company. They bribed a train guard named Putnam Brown and concealed themselves inside the baggage car of the Hudson River Railroad as it made its way from Buffalo, New York, to Grand Central Station in New York City. Bullard and Marsh broke into the safe, stuffed the cash and securities into carpet bags and then leapt off the train as it slowed somewhere near Yonkers.

The authorities discovered the theft when the train pulled into the station. They found the guard named Putnam Brown bound and gagged inside the baggage car with foam dripping from his mouth. The foam made it appear that he'd been tied up for a long time but he hadn't been. Not only had soap been put in his mouth to produce the foam, but he had been tied up with ropes loose enough to slip out of. Police immediately arrested Brown, and he subsequently confessed, naming Bullard and Marsh as the culprits. Pinkerton detectives were called in and Bullard and Marsh were tracked down and apprehended. They were held in the White Plains jail to await trial.

THE EXPRESS ROBBERY
EXAMINATION OF THE ALLEGED ROBBERS OF THE MERCHANTS' UNION EXPRESS COMPANY

The examination of ISSAC MARSH alias ISSAC MORTON, and CHARLES BULLARD alias CHARLES E. THOMPSON for the alleged robbery near Yonkers of a car belonging to the Merchants Union Express Company was, after several adjournments because of the absence of Mr. WILLIAM

> T. HOWE, the counsel for the prisoners, this morning resumed before Justice FERRIS in the Grand Jury room in the Courthouse at White Plains . . .
>
> —*The New York Times*, January 9, 1869

When "Marm" heard the news of his arrest and subsequent incarceration, she wasn't about to let one of her favorite "little chicks" languish in jail. She needed him, in more ways than one. Bullard would draw on his skills as a butcher and provide the best cuts of meat for the lavish dinner parties she threw at her Clinton and Rivington Streets home. Bullard also entertained Marm's dinner guests, playing anything from Beethoven's "Sonata in C sharp minor" to "Little Brown Jug," one of the most popular songs of the times, on the white, baby grand piano that adorned Marm's extravagant dining room. Besides that, it was men like Piano Charlie Bullard and Ike Marsh who kept her in business bringing her an assortment of stolen goods that she would purchase from them and then resell at a profit.

When she discovered Bullard had been arrested, she first tried to get him out using the usual legal means. She sent her legal counsel, William Howe and Abraham Hummel, whom she kept on a reported $5,000-a-year retainer, to defend them. Howe and Hummel had made a lucrative career out of successfully defending many of New York City's most infamous criminals. Since it didn't appear that her notorious lawyers could get Bullard off, she decided to use other means.

She called together several of her protégés, including Max Shinburn, George Leslie, Billy Forrester, and Adam Worth, and had them break Piano Charlie out of jail. The gang was led by Shinburn. He acquired the necessary tools and hired a get-away carriage. George Leslie, who would go on to surpass Shinburn and become known as "King of the Bank Robbers," was sent to visit Bullard in jail. Because of his photographic memory and his background as a trained architect, Leslie memorized the layout of the building. Adam Worth went about renting office space in a vacant building next door to the jail. And Billy Forrester located several underpaid prison guards who wanted to make some extra cash by looking the other way. The gang rented an office next door to the jail and hung a sign out advertising appraisals. They blacked out the windows putting up another sign stating that the offices were under construction and would soon open. The blacked out windows kept prying eyes from seeing what was really going on inside the empty office space. The gang easily dug through the walls of the office into the White Plains jail and Bullard and Marsh escaped, returning once again to the streets. No one was hurt and not a shot was fired. The plan had worked to perfection.

MYSTERIOUS ESCAPE OF EXPRESS ROBBERS FROM THE WHITE PLAINS JAIL

> WHITE PLAINS, N.Y. Monday, April 5—The two express robbers MORTON and THOMPSON (Bullard) with two other prisoners, committed for theft, escaped from jail last night, leaving no trace by which the authorities can capture them. They are supposed to have taken a carriage and driven away. The affair is involved in great mystery.
>
> —*The New York Times,* April 6, 1869

According to author Ben Macintyre, "the crooks promptly returned to New York City for a long, and in Bullard's case, staggeringly bibulous, celebration." Marm held a celebration party and invited Bullard to once again entertain her guest by playing the piano. Everyone that was anyone in the underworld came. Besides freeing Bullard from jail, the incident cemented Bullard's relationship with Adam Worth, a fledgling bank robber, and they went into partnership. A few short months after the jail-break, Bullard and Worth robbed the Boylston Bank on Washington Street in Boston of approximately $450,000 in cash bonds and securities. Even Mandelbaum was hesitant to "fence" such a large amount of stolen loot. Normally, Bullard and Worth would have been able to sell the stolen bonds back to the bank for a percentage of their worth, but under the circumstances, such a large haul made it impossible for the time being. Besides, such a large bank heist attracted the attention of Pinkerton detectives who were immediately hired by the bank and were on Bullard and Worth's trail, tracing them from Boston back to New York City.

"Those damn detectives will get on us in a week. I don't want to be playing the piano in Ludlow Street jail," Bullard reportedly told Worth.

There was no use sticking around. They hid the bonds and securities, making plans to have an intermediary, most likely Mandelbaum, sell them back to the bank in a few months, once things cooled down. They packed up their cash and sailed for Liverpool, England, but not before Bullard gave one last private recital for Marm Mandelbaum. Mandelbaum may have lost one of her favorite and most productive criminal associates, but there would be others to take his place. There always was.

While Mandelbaum was busy solidifying her reputation as the "Queen among Thieves," Bullard and Worth were trying to make a name for themselves as well, although not as successfully. They had taken with them approximately $100,000 in cash and settled into a luxurious hotel in Liverpool under the assumed names of Wells (Bullard) and Raymond (Worth). Although well-known criminals in New York City, they were unknown in England and elsewhere on the continent. In Liverpool they met a seventeen-year-old Irish barmaid named Kitty Flynn who was working at the hotel bar. Flynn was a beautiful girl with blonde hair, big blue eyes, and a shapely figure. Both men fell in love with her and each tried to win her over. Bullard represented himself to Flynn as a rich oil man. Worth told her he was a wealthy New York financier. Flynn, who had run away from home to escape growing up as the wife of a poor Irish farmer, had set her sights on seeing the world preferably on the arm of a wealthy, sophisticated man.

Both Bullard and Worth fit the bill. They both wined and dined her, bringing her expensive gifts, taking her out to dinner at the best restaurants, and accompanying her to plays and musicals. Flynn was dazzled by the attention they showered on her and both Bullard and Worth were mesmerized by Flynn's exquisite and alluring beauty. They both wanted to marry her. Going after the same girl didn't weaken their friendship. Rather, pursuing her became a game but sooner or later one man had to win. During the course of this whirlwind courtship by both men, Flynn learned the truth that they were not in fact wealthy businessmen but criminals on the lam. It didn't make a difference to Flynn. Whether businessmen or criminals they had what she was after—money and lots of it, at least for the time being. Although she became intimate with both men, she finally accepted Bullard's proposal of marriage. It broke Worth's heart, but he soldiered on with his partner Bullard. All three moved to London where they bought a three-story building near the Paris Opera House and turned it into a popular expatriate bar called "The American Bar."

The bar provided both legal and illegal entertainment from gambling to prostitution. On the second floor of the bar were several lavishly decorated private dining rooms and bedrooms where customers could entertain their guests or paramours. The bar did a fine business and life seemed good, but Bullard, despite his marriage and newfound respectability was unwilling to give up his wanton ways. He gambled. He drank. He womanized. While Bullard was out carousing for days and nights on end, Kitty Bullard found comfort in the arms of Worth. It was during this period, the early to mid-1870s, that Kitty gave birth to two children: Lucy and Katherine. But not even children slowed Charlie Bullard down. Kitty might have stuck it out, even with Charlie's callous ways, but when she discovered that her husband was a bigamist, with another wife in New York, she threw him out. In an alcoholic daze, Bullard left for New York City where he thought he might regain his former stature as a premier safecracker, but his once nimble fingers were gone. His hands shook and his concentration had abandoned him. He couldn't even play the piano anymore. He ended up robbing pawnshops and flophouses for pocket change.

Adam Worth, on the other hand, and on the other continent, sold the American Bar in Paris and with the profits moved to London, where he continued his guise as a wealthy American businessman. He kept the assumed name of Henry J. Raymond. Kitty Bullard went with him and stayed for a time, making Worth, who was still deeply in love with her, the happiest man on earth. But his happiness was short lived. Despite the fact that he bought her a 110-foot yacht, christened *Shamrock,* Kitty became restless. Worth might have loved her deeply but Kitty's heart still belonged to her estranged husband despite all that he had done to betray her. Eventually Kitty Bullard left Worth and London and returned to America with her two daughters. Worth generously and gallantly split the proceeds from the sale of the American Bar with her. In London, Worth continued his illicit undertakings, committing every sort of crime including forgery, safecracking, burglary, swindling, diamond theft, and bank robberies. Maintaining his pretext as a socially mobile American businessman required money and lots of it. Worth's criminal endeavors substantially provided it.

In 1876, Worth fell in love with two women—one was living and the other a painting. While staying in a luxurious bachelor flat in a London hotel, he became enamored with the much younger daughter of the owner of the hotel. He courted her with abandon even though she was barely out of her teens and finally asked her to marry him. Louise Margaret Boljahn agreed to become Mrs. Henry J. Raymond. She had no idea of her husband's true identity. Worth became a faithful husband and when his wife gave birth to their two children, Harry, in 1888, and a daughter, Constance, in 1891, he became a doting father as well, yet all the while plying his dishonest trade.

During the same period that he met and fell in love with his wife, Worth also became enamored with another woman, "Georgiana

Cavendish, Duchess of Devonshire," a painting done by the much celebrated Thomas Gainsborough in the late 1780s. It went up for sale at Christie's auction house in London in 1876, and the art dealer William Agnew purchased it for the astronomical price of $60,000 which would be equal to approximately $600,000 by today's currency. It went on display at the Thomas Agnew & Sons Gallery. The alluring painting of the beautiful duchess became the sensation of all London. Hundreds came out to view it. Adam Worth was one of them and he fell immediately in love with it.

Three weeks after it went on display, in a daring night time robbery, Worth broke into the gallery and stole the painting. Not even Marm Mandelbaum back in New York City would be able to fence this prize. But Worth had no intention of selling it. He loved it so much he kept it, often hiding it beneath his bed or, if traveling, in the false bottom of a trunk. He could not bear to part with it. Scotland Yard was called in to solve the case but not even England's much heralded detective agency could solve the theft. It wasn't until nearly a quarter century later that the authorities would discover it had been Adam Worth who stole this famous painting.

Things began to change in London for Worth after William Pinkerton, the son of the noted detective and founder of the Pinkerton Detective Agency, Allan Pinkerton, arrived in London to help Scotland Yard in their attempts to find the Gainsborough robber. William Pinkerton was someone to be reckoned with. He had been on the trail of Worth and Bullard since the 1869 Boylston Bank robbery. Feeling that the law might be closing in on him, Worth told his wife he had to leave on business and set off for Cape Town, South Africa, with his precious painting hidden in the false bottom of his steamer trunk. In Cape Town, Worth pulled off another stunning robbery, stealing $500,000 worth of diamonds from a post office safe where they had been stored for safe keeping. With Worth around, nothing was safe. He ultimately returned to London to be with his wife and children where he settled into an anonymous and nondescript routine until he received word about Charlie Bullard's arrest in Belgium.

Things had gone from bad to worse for Piano Charlie Bullard back in the United States. After leaving Kitty Flynn in London, he was unable to make a living using his once delicate and finely tuned fingers. He spent much of his time in a drunken haze. Not only had he lost his abilities, he was emaciated from hard drinking and his once handsome features were decimated. Hoping to make one last big score, Bullard teamed up with another former associate of Mandelbaum's, the illustrious Max Shinburn, who had also fallen on hard times and together they planned to rob a bank in Belgium. The robbery failed and the two men were arrested, tried, and sentenced to twelve years in the Prison de Louvain near Liege.

In September 1892, after receiving word of Bullard's confinement in the prison in Liege, Worth decided to try to free his old friend. Taking a page out of his old mentor's book—he had learned from Mandelbaum that just about anybody could be bribed—he decided to make a trip to Liege to see if he could bribe a judge or politician to get his friend Bullard released. Explaining he had another important business trip to make, he said goodbye to his wife and children for the last time and left for France. Traveling by train from Calais to Belgium, he received the news that his oldest friend and partner, Charlie Bullard had died in prison. He was devastated.

Although grieving over the loss of his good friend, Worth decided that since he was already there he might as well make the visit profitable. On October 5, 1892, Worth and two other men he had conspired with, tried to rob a small bank. The robbery went awry and although his accomplices managed to escape, Worth was apprehended by the police. Although being held by the Belgium authorities, Worth refused to divulge any information about who he and his accomplices were to the officers who interrogated him. Police only knew that the man they were holding was New York City businessman, Henry J. Raymond.

The Belgium authorities sent a photo of Worth to the New York City Police department and Scotland Yard. The New York police identified the man in the photo as the notorious bank robber and sneak thief Adam Worth, who was wanted in connection with any number of crimes, including the robbery of the Boylston Bank in Boston. Suspicions mounted. Scotland Yard identified him as the man wanted for questioning in connection with the theft of the famous Gainsborough painting. Also working against him was Max Shinburn, who had been incarcerated with Bullard. In an attempt to have his own sentence reduced, Shinburn informed authorities that the man they held in custody was the notorious bank robber, Adam Worth. The jig was up.

In March 1893, Worth was tried and sentenced to seven years in prison in the very same prison that had held Bullard. News of Worth's arrest and imprisonment reached his wife in London. Louise was unable to deal with the knowledge of her husband's true character. Suddenly ostracized by London's high society she began drinking, taking laudanum, and ultimately sank into insanity. When she was found wandering the streets of London in an incoherent daze she was committed to a London asylum. The two children, Harry, age five, and Constance, age two, were sent to live with Adam's brother, John, in New York. The news crushed Worth, who was languishing in the Belgium prison unable to help his poor wife or children.

The only ray of hope for Worth during this darkest of times came from Kitty Flynn. After leaving London she had moved to America where she married a Wall Street banker named Juan Terry. He died unexpectedly leaving Kitty a very wealthy widow. Hearing of her old friend and sometime lover's plight, she contacted him and sent him money for his defense and his appeals. Although all the money in the world wasn't enough to free Worth, his renewed relationship with Kitty was the one bright spot in his torturous life.

In the fall of 1897, after having completed four of the seven years of his prison term, Worth was released. He was fifty-three years old. Prison had taken its toll on his body and spirit. He returned to London where, either for money or to put his life of crime finally to rest, he arranged to sell back the famous Gainsborough painting to its original owner. Using an intermediary to keep his identity secret, Worth sold the painting back for the hefty sum of $25,000. He spent the remainder of his life getting reacquainted with his two children who were now back in London living with him.

Marm Mandelbaum mourned the loss of Bullard and the incarceration of Shinburn and Adam Worth, both personally and professionally. They had all been vital sources of income for her. But she had another heir apparent in the dashing George Leslie. Leslie came to Mandelbaum from Cinnicinati, Ohio in 1865, an unknown commodity, having never robbed a bank before, but he became her biggest asset by revolutionizing the bank robbery business.

5

A SENSATIONAL BANK ROBBERY, BY GEORGE

> "It was at one such soirée in 1869 that she met George Leonidas Leslie, the future star of the Manhattan Savings Institution robbery. . . . Leslie was the son of a wealthy Cincinnati brewer—he was charming, handsome, well-educated and had moved to New York with the express purpose of becoming a bank robber. . . . Marm Mandelbaum was charmed by Leslie and impressed with his approach to bank robbery . . . "
>
> —"Bank Heist"

Fredericka Mandelbaum took an immediate liking to George Leslie. Perhaps it was his good looks or his exquisite good manners. More likely it was because she prided herself on being a good judge of character and she sensed that the handsome, well-mannered gentleman from Cincinnati was someone special. He was. Leslie was a tall and handsome and was always impeccably dressed. Like many men of the period, he had a fashionable moustache that he kept groomed and waxed. With his dashing good looks, stylish suits, flawless manners, and outgoing personality, Leslie had no problem ingratiating himself into New York City's upper echelon, or for that matter, the city's seedy underworld. There was an air of preeminence that sprang from him. Since arriving in New York City from his hometown of Cincinnati, Ohio, following the close of the Civil War in 1865, Leslie became a fixture at Mandelbaum's side. He was one of her favored protégés, and became her most productive and profitable criminal associate. Although Mandelbaum had already surrounded herself with many of the country's top bank burglars, Leslie ultimately became the brightest jewel in Mandelbaum's criminal crown.

Leslie had taken flight from his hometown of Cincinnati, Ohio, driven to the anonymity of the bustling metropolis of New York City by the lingering spectra of the Civil War that hung around his neck like an albatross. The bloodiest conflict in the country's history just over, deep wounds in the North and South were still fresh. Wounded veterans, physically and emotionally scarred by the ravages of war, returned to their homes and families. Cincinnati was no different. Families had been torn apart leaving a trail of widows and orphans. More than a quarter-million men and boys from Ohio had enlisted or were drafted into the Union army. George Leslie, however, hadn't joined them either voluntarily or otherwise, despite the fact that Leslie, who was twenty-one years old and eligible for the draft. President Lincoln's Union Conscription Act of 1863 ordered all able-bodied males between the ages of twenty and forty-five to be drafted into military service. But it also included a loophole, letting potential draftees pay as sum of $300 to buy their way out of military service. They could also pay someone to take their place in the draft. Leslie's father, a wealthy brewer with a business in Toledo, took advantage of the provision and paid for his son to escape the draft. Although it was a perfectly legal tactic, and one that many wealthy men like the elder Leslie took advantage of, it was a highly controversial and unpopular step. After the war, many people did not forgive or forget those who had shirked their duty by buying out of the draft. Young men like George Leslie, through no fault of their own, except for having wealthy fathers, were considered worse than deserters and were shunned by many. It was no different for George Leslie. He had graduated from Cincinnati University with a degree in architecture and set up his own architectural firm in Cincinnati after graduation. Despite his upbringing, wealth and education, he was ostracized by many Cincinnati families and former friends who did serve in the war. The resentment he faced in his hometown was too much to bear for him and so he decided to start over in a place where no one knew him or his background. After his parents died, he sold the family home and his father's business in Toledo, closed his own firm in Cincinnati and moved to New York City. Leslie told several friends that the move to New York was predicated on his desire to make what he referred to as "easy money." No one could suspect at the time that the so-called "easy money" would come to him from robbing banks.

Besides all of his other attributes—good looks and manners, his intelligence, and his architectural background—Leslie had a keen mechanical ability. As he dove headlong into a life of crime, he fabricated a new burglary tool called "the little joker." Although a simple device consisting of a small tin wheel with a wire attached to it, it transformed the bank robbing business forever. Leslie's little joker fit inside the combination dial of any bank safe. By surreptitiously placing the device inside the combination dial of a safe, when the combination was used to open the safe, the little joker would record where the tumblers stopped by making a series of deep cuts in the tin wheel. The deepest cuts in the wheel would show the actual numerical placement of the combination. Although it couldn't record the order in which the numbers to the combination were used, through a series of trial and error, trying different combination settings based on the deep cuts in the tin wheel it wouldn't take long to open any safe. Although keenly inventive, it did require a robber to break into a bank twice—once to place the little joker inside the dial of the safe and a second time to retrieve it and actually open the vault. Clearly, it took a very special person with nerves of steel, a keen aptitude and incredible patience to perform such a complicated undertaking. George Leslie was that person. It didn't take long for Marm Mandelbaum to realize it.

Up and until George Leslie's arrival on the bank robbery scene, robbers had engaged in an often dangerous and laborious effort to break into bank safes. Many used dynamite to blow open a vault. It was dangerous, noisy, and often did not accomplish the desired results. There was the chance a robber could blow himself up, maiming or even killing himself or his cohorts. The blast always alerted the police and often resulted in a failed robbery attempt. And often robbers not only blew up the bank vault, but all the valuables inside it as well. Leslie's little joker also removed the tedious and time-consuming process of safecracking: turning the safe dial to different numbers and listening with a stethoscope to determine the right order of the combination clicks. Safecracking took hours and it wasn't foolproof. Leslie's little joker did away with these two previously dubious bank robbery methods.

Mandelbaum knew that she had to diversify her fencing business and venture into other criminal initiatives like robbing banks but she didn't want to invest in uncertain outcomes by financing heists that produced little or no results. When she made the acquaintance of George Leslie, all that changed for Mandelbaum. Leslie's first major heist was in June 1869. With the help and guidance of Max Shinburn, he broke into and robbed $800,000 from the New York City Ocean National Bank. Considered the largest haul in the city's history up to then, they had pulled off the caper without using dynamite or the usual safecracking techniques. Leslie let the little joker do all the work. Even the city newspapers gave credit to the unidentified culprits. The *New York Herald* called it "A masterful bank job pulled off by one very special bank robber." Even New York City's political kingpin, Boss Tweed was impressed with the finesse of the robbery. "I couldn't have done better myself," Tweed reportedly said.

Mandelbaum financed Leslie and Shinburn's Ocean National bank heist and it was the start of an almost ten-year symbiotic relationship. "The King of Bank Robbers," a name later given to Leslie by both his associates, as well as police and newspapers, always worked closely with Mandelbaum, paying her a percentage of the profits he made from every bank job or laundering stolen securities and other valuables through her.

HEAVY BANK ROBBERY
THE SAFES OF THE OCEAN BANK OF NEW YORK CITY
OPENED AND ROBBED OF THEIR CONTENTS
HOW AN ENTRANCE WAS EFFECTED
THE PROBABLE LOSS-RUMORS, ETC.

> Between the hours of six o'clock Saturday evening and eight o'clock this morning, the Ocean National Bank of New York City, situated on the corner of Fulton and Greenwich streets, was robbed to a heavy cost . . . The police say that the tools discovered in the Bank were the finest that have ever been used by burglars in New York.
>
> —*The New York Times*, October, 1869

Leslie and his handpicked gang pulled off a series of profitable bank robberies including the robbery of the South Kensington National Bank in Pennsylvania, the Third National Bank of Baltimore, the Wellsboro Bank in Chicago, and the Saratoga County Bank in New York. It was reported that this string of robberies netted him approximately ten million dollars. But not only did Leslie rob banks, he also offered his services to other bank robbers, collecting $20,000 for helping them to plan their robberies. He was considered a criminal mastermind. His reputation spread beyond New York City all the way to the West Coast where his special talents were always in demand. And despite his lengthy series of fruitful bank robberies, he skillfully managed to avoid arrest. In fact, he never served a single day in jail for any of his many exploits.

Leslie continued to keep up his appearance as a well-respected gentleman in New York society. He became a patron of the arts and a collector of literature. His clothes were made by the most fashionable tailors. He slipped seamlessly through the many layers of New York City high society with no one ever suspecting he was the same man responsible for 80 percent of the great bank robberies in the country during the early part of America's Gilded Age.

All of his robberies made headlines:

ANOTHER BANK ROBBERY
THE AUBURN CITY BANK ROBBED OF $31,000

AUBURN, N.Y., April 26—The Auburn City National Bank was robbed today, between the hours of 12 and 1 o'clock, of $31,000 in greenbacks . . .

—*The New York Times,* April, 1870

BOLD BANK ROBBERY AT SCRANTON, PENN.
$30,000 IN CURRENCY STOLEN

SCRANTON, Penn., Aug. 1—The banking house of JOHN HANDLEY & CO. was robbed of $30,000 in currency at 10 o'clock this morning by parties entering the vault from the rear of the bank . . . The plan was boldly and adroitly accomplished. There is no clue to the robbers . . .

—*The New York Times,* August, 1870

HEAVY BANK ROBBERY
THE THIRD NATIONAL BANK OF BALTIMORE ROBBED OF MORE THAN $234,000—LIST OF THE STOCKS, BONDS AND OTHER VALUABLES

BALTIMORE, Aug. 19—The provincial City of Baltimore has had an unusual sensation today in the shape of a wholesale bank robbery, the amount being stolen being variously estimated at from $200,000 to $250,000 in money, stocks and securities. . . These scamps proved to be experienced bank robbers . . .

—*The New York Times,* August, 1872

In order to guard his reputation as a member of good standing in New York City's elite society, Leslie refused to openly associate with other members of the criminal class whom he did regular business with, except Mandelbaum. Like Shinburn before him, Leslie was scornful of most criminals, even members of his own gang. He regarded most of them as too unsophisticated to make crime pay. He was often right. A bungled bank robbery in Northampton, Massachusetts, in 1876 was an example.

Although Leslie planned the Northampton bank robbery, he did not oversee it. The badly bungled job spelled the beginning of the end of Leslie's unprecedented run of successful bank heists. He turned the Northampton Bank robbery over to a gang of experienced criminals, headed by Robert C. Scott and James Dunlap, two Illinois penitentiary ex-convicts, and Billy Connors, a well-known New York City criminal. Dunlap enlisted the help of several of Leslie's trusted partners in crime including Red Leary, Billy Porter, Johnny Irving, Shang Draper, and Gilbert Yost. Although the gang was able to rob the bank of a record $1.6 million, considered one of the largest heists in the country, breaking even Leslie's Ocean National Bank record, much of the loot was in nonnegotiable bonds, which made the heist useless. Scott and Dunlap were almost immediately apprehended after they tried to sell the nonnegotiable bonds back to the bank. Their arrest placed Leslie in jeopardy, since he had planned the heist and since there was no telling what Scott and Dunlap might tell the authorities to save their own necks. Leslie never excused himself for not going on the robbery and promised he would never let it happen again. He decided he would plan and lead the next bank heist. But even his participation in his next bank robbery in 1877, the robbery of the Dexter Bank in Maine, was no guarantee of success.

THE NORTHAMPTON BANK ROBBERY

BOSTON, Mass., Jan. 27—The table of the securities taken shows a total of $670,000. Of course, much of this is nonnegotiable, so that it is difficult to estimate the real loss to the bank and depositors.

—*Brooklyn Eagle,* January 27, 1876

In the winter of 1878, Leslie drew up plans to rob the Dexter Savings Bank in Maine. It should have been an easy score but it turned out to be a worse debacle than the Northampton robbery. The entire Dexter Bank heist was bankrolled by Mandelbaum. She fronted Leslie $30,000 to cover the cost of the job. According to Leslie, her return on her investment would be substantial, since, based on his best estimates, there would be approximately $800,000 in the Dexter Bank vault and she would get her usual cut of 50 percent. Leslie would take the largest portion of the remaining cash and securities and would then divide up the remainder evenly among the rest of the gang. Leslie and his cohorts made their way to Dexter, Maine, in February, each of them taking separate routes. Leslie had already bribed a bank employee, James Wilson Barron, who agreed to work as an inside man on the bank heist for a portion of the take. Barron had agreed to let Leslie and his gang sneak into the bank undetected by unlocking the door from the inside and providing Leslie with the key to the vault. It seemed like a perfect plan.

Johnny Irving was the get-away driver. He had a horse-drawn sleigh hidden in a lane along the side of the Dexter Bank. Because the streets were covered with snow, the sleigh seemed like the perfect get-away vehicle. The way the plan was designed, once the gang had broken into the vault and had the loot, they would hide it in several trunks that would then be shipped back to New York from the Dexter railway station. In that way, even if one of the gang were caught for any reason, they wouldn't have any of the stolen loot in their possession. Even while the authorities were looking for the money, it would be sitting safe and sound and undetected right there in the Dexter train station waiting to be shipped to New York.

Leslie and his gang, including Red Leary, Billy Porter, Johnny Irving, Shang Draper, and Gilbert Yost stayed at various boarding houses in Dexter, keeping their distance from one another so as not to be seen in public together. Because Leslie had rehearsed the heist with them all so many times, each of the men knew exactly what their role was in the upcoming robbery.

On the night of February 23, 1878, Leslie and his gang met in the back of the Dexter Bank. The weather was frigid and the wind made it seem even colder than it was.

According to the plan, Leslie knocked on the side door of the bank. He and Barron had agreed that when he knocked, Barron would unlock the door and let them inside, but despite the knock, no one came to the door. Leslie knocked again but still Barron didn't come to the door. Finally, frustrated that Barron had abandoned him, Leslie had Red Leary put his shoulder to the door and forced it open. When the gang slipped inside they found Barron waiting for them. He immediately blurted out that he had changed his mind and that he wasn't going to help them rob the place. It infuriated Leslie who had depended on Barron to provide him with the key to the bank vault. Barron refused to give up the key. All hell broke out. Red Leary and Shang Draper grabbed Barron. Leslie tried to stop them but he was no match for the two men. Barron struggled but it was no use. Leary and Draper threatened to beat the location of the vault key out of him but still Barron refused to give it up. Leslie wanted to call the whole thing off. The other would have none of it. Draper pulled out a handgun and hit Barron across the head several times. Blood streamed from Barron's wound and he fell to his knees. It was only then that Barron confessed that the key to the vault wouldn't do them any good. The vault was on a timer and couldn't be opened until the morning. Leary and Draper tied Barron's hands behind his back and gagged him. They dragged him to the vault where they stuffed him in between the inner and outer doors leading to the vault and pushed the two heavy doors shut, trapping Barron inside between the two doors. Refusing to leave empty handed despite Barron's change of heart, Leary and Draper stole $100 from one of the bank cash drawers and another $500 from Barron himself. Aside from the mere $600 Leary and Draper stole, the gang slipped out of the bank empty-handed.

They climbed into the horse-drawn sleigh waiting for them in the alleyway beside the bank and Johnny Irving drove away. Leslie was furious, not about the money, or even Barron's refusal to help. What bothered him was the violence. Hurting Barron could only make things worse. Neither Leary nor Draper cared. Barron deserved everything he got for backing out.

> "The operations of the Leslie gang—composed of men bound by the strongest of ties to 'Marm' Mandelbaum—in nine years, in this city alone, amounted to a round half million dollars. Throughout the United States their plundering cannot have been less than $7,000,000, comprising 80 percent of all the bank robberies perpetrated . . ."
>
> —George Washington Walling, *Recollections of a New York Chief of Police,* 1887

Back in New York, Leslie found out from a newspaper article about the bungled Dexter Bank robbery that James Barron, the bank cashier, had died. The police discovered him stuffed between the vault doors. The newspaper account reported that Barron had died a hero for discovering the robbers inside the bank and refusing to give up the key to the vault. Although there was no description of the robbers, Pinkerton detectives had been hired by the bank to track down the criminals who had killed Barron. After reading the newspaper account, Leslie decided to go into hiding. Bank robbery was one thing. Murder was another. He could face hanging if he was caught and convicted of Barron's murder, even as an accomplice to it. While he was in hiding Leslie made a momentous decision: It was time to get out of the bank robbery business. All he wanted was one last big haul. He set his sights on the Manhattan Savings Institution, the biggest, wealthiest, and best protected bank in New York City.

It took Leslie nearly three years to plot the Manhattan Savings Institution heist and on October 27, 1878, his gang broke in and stole nearly three million dollars in cash and securities.

It was reported in the newspaper, based on statements from the bank examiners and the authorities, the exact amount stolen by the bank robbers was $2,747,700, most of it, $2,500,700, in registered, nonnegotiable securities. The gang also absconded with another $11,000 in cash. Despite the bulk of the loot being nonnegotiable securities that the gang couldn't cash, the robbery was hailed by the press as the most astonishing bank heists in the history of bank robberies. Based on today's currency standards, the robbers' haul would equal approximately fifty million dollars.

A GREAT BANK ROBBERY
THE MANHATTAN SAVINGS INSTITUTION ROBBED
THREE MILLION AND A HALF IN CASH AND SECURITIES STOLEN FROM THE VAULT—THE JANITOR HANDCUFFED AND COMPELLED TO GIVE UP THE SAFE KEYS AND TELL THE COMBINATION—THE AUDACITY OF THE ROBBERS

The Manhattan Savings Institution on the north-east corner of Broadway and Bleecker-street was the victim yesterday of one of the most daring and successful burglaries ever perpetrated. It is estimated that fully $3,500,000 in cash and securities were carried off and beyond mere suspicion, it is believed that the police have no clue to the robbers.

—*The New York Times,* October 28, 1878

THE RESPONSIBILITY FOR YESTERDAY'S BANK ROBBERY

The daring robbery of the Manhattan Savings Institution . . . will probably be remembered as the most sensational in the history of bank robberies in this country. The sum of money represented by the securities stolen, namely $73,000 in negotiable and $2,506,700 in registered securities, together with $11,000 cash, makes this haul the largest yet recorded . . .

—*Brooklyn Eagle*, October 28, 1878

The Manhattan Savings Institution was the Fort Knox of banks. It kept for safekeeping the cash, jewels, bonds, and other precious valuables of many of the wealthiest inhabitants of New York City. Valuables were kept in an enormous vault constructed of solid concrete and steel, and safeguarded by three iron doors, each with its own separate combination. It was an impenetrable network of combination locks and security defenses; however, despite its massive security provisions, nothing was ever safe from George Leslie.

Once again, just like with the bungled Dexter Bank heist, Leslie bribed a night watchman named Pat Shevlin, who would let them into the bank through the apartment of Louis Werckle, who was the bank's janitor, and lived in an upstairs apartment over the bank. Leslie also bribed a police officer, John Nugent. Nugent would be on duty the night of the heist and on foot patrol along a beat that covered the Manhattan Savings Institution. The robbers easily gained entrance into the janitor's apartment thanks to Pat Shelvin where they held Werckle and his family hostage while they broke in and robbed the bank. This time, the robbery was not carried out with the expert finesse that Leslie usually integrated into his bank jobs. The gang used hammers and chisels to break into the vault.

The steel doors leading into the vault were ripped from their hinges. The brute force used to get into the bank vault caused a noisy commotion, but it didn't matter. The only one outside who could possibly hear it was John Nugent, the police officer they had bribed. He was the only police officer on duty outside the bank and besides, it was the weekend and the streets were empty.

Inside the vault, the gang went to work breaking into the array of steel security boxes, often ripping off the tops of them and taking the valuables inside. The empty boxes were thrown haphazardly to the floor. Although there were twenty-five steel deposit boxes in the vault, the gang only managed to open fifteen of them. The other ten were discovered intact. In their fury to break into the steel security deposit boxes, the gang missed taking an additional two million in cash that was stored in the vault and lying inside canvas money sacks on the floor of the vault. After the gang made a clean getaway with the loot, Werckle and his family were set free, unharmed.

George Leslie had hoped that the robbery of the Manhattan Savings Institution would be his greatest and last bank heist. He planned to use the money from the robbery to move out west with his wife, Molly, and begin a new life. Tension had been growing between Leslie and Shang Draper ever since the bungled Dexter Bank robbery. The Pinkerton detectives were still searching for the robbers who had broken into the Dexter Bank and killed James Barron. With a potential murder rap hanging over their heads, everyone in the gang was on edge. Draper was convinced that Leslie would sell out the rest of the gang to the authorities to save his own life and he persuaded the others in the gang that Leslie wasn't to be trusted. But it was more than just the Barron murder that got under Draper's skin. It was more personal. For months he had heard rumors that his beautiful wife, Babe, had been carrying on an affair with Leslie behind his back. Although he couldn't prove it, he was certain that Leslie harbored certain affection for Babe and she for him. It was enough to drive him over the edge.

Although the gang had successfully robbed the most significant bank in New York City, it didn't have any of the trademarks of George Leslie's usual finesse, because in fact, George Leslie didn't take part in the robbery. He was dead by the time the gang broke into the bank. Career criminal Jimmy Hope took over as the leader of the gang following Leslie's murder.

In late May 1878, some five months before the robbery, Leslie stopped into his favorite saloon, Murphy's Saloon in Brooklyn. He was handed a note that he read quickly. The handwriting appeared to belong to Babe Draper, the woman he had been carrying on an affair with behind Shang Draper's back. The note said that she wanted to meet him and gave him directions to a place where they would rendezvous. Leslie left the saloon, hailed a carriage and headed off to meet Babe. It was the last time anyone ever saw him alive.

George Leslie's body was discovered at the foot of Tramp's Rock, in Mott's Woods, three miles from Yonkers on June 4, 1878. He had been shot twice: once in the heart and another in the head. His body was badly decomposed by the time it was discovered. A small pearl-handled pistol was found near his body and was later identified as the murder weapon. Leslie was forty years old when he was killed. It fell to Marm Mandelbaum to go to the morgue and identify Leslie's body. Word had gotten to her that he was dead but that someone had to come and identify and claim the body. Mandelbaum immediately contacted Leslie's wife, Molly, who was in Philadelphia. Mandelbaum paid the costs of her train trip back to New York City, as well as Leslie's funeral and burial costs at Cypress Hills Cemetery. The once King of Bank Robbers, the man authorities held responsible for stealing millions of dollars, ended up being buried in a ten-dollar plot. Draper, Irving, Porter, Yost, Grady, Walsh, and a crowd of other notorious gangland figures attended Leslie's funeral. Molly Leslie fainted and had to be carried from the service.

> "Mrs. Leslie was advised of the death of her husband by 'Marm' Mandelbaum. She came to New York to the funeral (the expenses of which were borne by the noted receiver), was entertained by that lady, given a small sum of money and sent back to Philadelphia . . ."
>
> —George Washington Walling, *Recollections of a New York Chief of Police*, 1887

George Leslie's murder was never solved. The authorities speculated that he had been killed by one or several of his criminal associates who had a grudge against him. Even though his body had been found at Tramp Rock, evidence indicated that he had been killed elsewhere and dumped in Yonkers. Additional police work led authorities to believe that in all likelihood, Leslie was lured to his death. They were able to establish that the last time he was seen was at Murphy's Saloon in Brooklyn. They were able to learn, based on an anonymous tip, that Leslie was given a note by someone at the bar and after reading it, left the saloon in a hurry. He didn't tell anyone where he was going and the note was never found. The police were able to track down the carriage driver who had picked Leslie up that night and after questioning him, discovered that he had been dropped off on Halsey Street, in Brooklyn. Shang and Babe Draper lived on Halsey Street at the time. The police question Draper, since they knew he was an associate of Leslie, but Draper had nothing of importance to say. His wife, Babe, was nearly hysterical when the police questioned her. When they asked her about the supposed note Leslie was given at Murphy's Saloon, she broke down in tears. Still there was nothing to connect either Shang or Babe Draper to the murder of George Leslie.

A *New York Times* article, dated June 10, 1878, described the funeral as such: "The funeral of George Howard [Leslie], the burglar, who was found murdered in Mott's Woods, on Palmer-avenue, Yonkers, took place at noon yesterday from the establishment of J. J. Diehl, undertaker. . ." The article went on to say that not only was Leslie's widow present at the funeral, but there was also an elderly woman, whose name was not given in the article. It was assumed the woman was Mandelbaum since the article indicated that she was well known to the police.

Another article appearing in the *Brooklyn Eagle* on March 10, 1879, speculated as to how he had been killed. According to the article, "If the alleged clues are true, it would seem that Shang Draper, Billy Porter, Johnny Irving, John Dobbs, and a burglar named Perris are all implicated in his death, although it is not stated which one of them, if any, fired the fatal shot . . ." The article called him "a man of refinement and culture," and said, "he was enabled to live with almost princely extravagance..."

> "Leslie was no ordinary villain. Born in Ohio to a more than respectable family, he was cultured and genteel, a reader of good books, a lover of good food, a patron of the arts, and a boon companion in a number of prestigious men's clubs. He might also have been the best bank robber in history."
>
> —Cait Murphy, *Scoundrels in Law*, 2010

The tireless work of New York police detective Thomas Byrnes led him to Pat Shevlin, the night watchman. Shevlin was only paid $1,200 for his part in the robbery although he had been promised much more. Shevlin was not a career criminal like the others associated with the robbery and Byrnes knew he could break him. Using his special kind of interrogation techniques, that included isolating Shevlin in a cell for several days and reportedly beating him, Byrnes was able to get a confession out of him. Although he could face up to twenty years in prison for his role in the bank heist, Byrnes promised Shevlin that if he confessed, he would see to it that Shevlin would never serve any time in prison. Shevlin gave Byrnes the names of the gang members.

Byrnes was able to apprehend some of the Manhattan Savings Institution bank robbers, although he was unable to link Mandelbaum to the crime. Red Leary, Shang Draper, Johnny Irving, Billy Porter, and Gilbert Yost had all been arrested on other charges and were awaiting trial. Gang member Johnny Dobbs managed to escape arrest by Byrnes, but he was later apprehended on other charges and sent to prison. Dobbs died in the alcoholic ward of Bellevue Hospital in 1892. In 1879, police officer Nugent was arrested but was found not guilty when his case went to trial. One of the jurors in the trial reportedly had been bribed by Nugent, although it was never proved. Nugent subsequently ended up in prison several years later when he was arrested and convicted of highway robbery.

Red Leary was arrested in 1879, charged with robbing the Northampton, Massachusetts, bank. Although sent to the

Ludlow Street Jail, he managed to escape with the help of his wife Kate. She and several friends of Leary dug a tunnel beneath the jailhouse and he escaped. He was able to escape capture for several years before finally being apprehended by Pinkerton detectives in 1881. He was sent to Massachusetts to stand trial for the Northampton Bank robbery. Shang Draper was also arrested and charged with robbing the Massachusetts bank. Although both men went to trial they were ultimately acquitted due to of lack of evidence.

Billy Porter and Johnny Irving were arrested for breaking in and robbing a grain store. The jury failed to agree on a verdict in Porter's first trial, but the authorities tried him again, and this time he he was sentenced to five years in prison. Johnny Irving was tried and found guilty. He was sentenced to five years in prison. Neither Porter nor Irving was officially charged in the Manhattan bank robbery. Although both men managed to escape from prison, Porter was recaptured immediately, sent back to prison, and served his full sentence. He was released from prison in 1883. Johnny Irving eluded capture for almost a year but was finally arrested during a failed robbery attempt in Philadelphia. He was tried, convicted, and sentenced to four years in prison. After he completed his sentence in Philadelphia, Irving was returned to New York to complete his prison sentence there. He was discharged by the New York courts based on the time he served in Philadelphia.

Gilbert Yost, who had been arrested on charges other than the Manhattan bank heist, had a mental breakdown. After attacking a guard he was placed in solitary confinement, where he refused to eat and began ranting and raving. He was declared insane by the courts and sent to a mental hospital in Auburn, New York, where he spent five years. After his release, he committed another burglary, was apprehended, and sent to prison where he spent the rest of his life.

Shang Draper renounced his former criminal life after he was acquitted of the Northampton bank robbery in Massachusetts.

He ran a saloon on Sixth Avenue until 1883, and later began a successful sporting goods business.

Johnny Irving was killed in 1883. He died in a gun fight at Shang Draper's Sixth Avenue saloon. Underworld figure Johnny "The Mick" Walsh was at the saloon when Irving and Billy Porter came into the place. Walsh and Irving had some personal scores to settle. Walsh confronted Irving, who was drunk. Irving became belligerent. They began to fight. Walsh took out a gun and shot and killed Irving. Billy Porter then drew a pistol and shot and killed Walsh. Porter was never charged by the police who conveniently concluded that Irving and Walsh killed each other simultaneously.

Jimmy Hope had been arrested on other bank robbery charges and was sent to Sing Sing prison. He managed to escape by jumping off a bridge while on a prison work detail. Although Hope was pursued by the authorities they never managed to catch him. It was after he had escaped from Sing Sing that Hope joined up with the gang to rob the Manhattan Savings Institution, where he became the leader of the gang after Leslie's murder.

In July 1879, Johnny Hope, the son of the ringleader, Jimmy Hope, was arrested for his involvement in the Manhattan bank robbery. He was found guilty and sentenced to twenty years in the state prison. Also arrested and charged in the Manhattan robbery was Billy Kelley who was convicted and sentenced to ten years. Peter Ellis and Abe Coakley were apprehended but were never officially charged in the Manhattan bank heist. Only Johnny Hope and Billy Kelley were ever convicted for the Manhattan Savings Institution bank robbery. Shevlin, the night watchman, was granted immunity for testifying against the robbers. Nugent, the corrupt police officer, went to trial but wasn't convicted. And Jimmy Hope, the leader of the gang, was never apprehended or charged for his involvement in the heist. In 1880, Hope was already serving time a prison sentence in San Francisco for a bungled bank robbery in California. After his release from the California prison, he was returned to New York to complete a previous prison term there. He was finally released from prison in 1889. He died in New York City in 1905.

In the end, the police were able to recover most of the stolen securities taken in the Manhattan Savings Institution robbery. The securities were nonnegotiable except by the person whose name was listed on them, which meant the robbers couldn't cash them in. Most of the criminals involved in what *The New York Times* called, "the most sensational bank robbery in the country," were either dead or in prison. Marm Mandelbaum once again escaped from the long arm of the law, at least for the time being.

> ". . . her self-conscious connection to women supports the notion that she was a proto-feminist, in her own way. . . . She apparently thought that women ought to have their own lives, be involved in something for themselves outside of the home, and not depend on men for their financial well-being.
>
> —Rona Holub, "Frederika 'Marm' Mandelbaum 'Queen of the Fences'"

It wasn't just men that Mandelbaum drew into her inner circle. She always had a soft spot in her heart for female crooks and was the friend and patron of such famous criminals as Big Mary, Ellen Clegg, Queen Liz, Little Annie, Old Mother Hubbard, and Kid Glove Rosey, all sneak thieves, pickpockets, and blackmailers who worked for her. Mandelbaum took a special interest in women who were starting out in their criminal careers and readily and anxiously helped them. She nurtured the criminal career of the glamorous jewel thief, Lena Kleinschmidt, known simply as "Black Lena." But her favorite was sixteen-year-old Sophie Lyons, who, under Mandelbaum's tutelage, became a criminal celebrity in her own right but who ultimately betrayed her.

6
SOPHIE'S CHOICES

"Mother Mandelbaum. Alas ! I knew her well—too well."
—Sophie Lyons, *Why Crime Does Not Pay*, 1913

Mandelbaum remained a staunch advocate for working women throughout her life—although her idea of working meant engaging in nefarious business. Still, her lifelong support and mentoring of women criminals points to the impression that Mandelbaum may have been one of the earliest advocates for women's rights. Some might find this assertion a stretch but clearly Mandelbaum believed that intelligence in a woman was an important attribute that should and could be used in more profitable ways than merely menial work. The changing social, political, and economic trends of the Gilded Age produced newfound opportunities for women. In 1878, a Woman Suffrage Amendment was introduced in the United States Congress and by the 1880s, women were making great strides in professional, legal, and educational equality. The 1890 United States Census reported that women were represented in 360 occupations out of 369; however, most worked in textile factories where the average weekly wage was $5.68. Or they could do household work as maids and nannies. Was it any wonder some women turned to the more lucrative life of crime?

> "The percentage of women who worked outside the home steadily increased throughout the Gilded Age: 15 percent in 1870, 16 percent in 1880, 19 percent in 1890 . . . The typical female worker was young, urban, single and either an immigrant or the daughter of immigrants . . . The job she was

> most likely to hold was that of domestic servant . . . Female brothel owners could make great sums of money . . . Married women sometimes engaged in prostitution, with or without the knowledge of their husbands, to add to the family income."
>
> —Stacy A. Cordey, "Women in Industrializing America"

Accordingly, might not Mandelbaum have been influenced by this changing role of women in American society? Since she was a woman and enormously successful at what she did, especially in a milieu controlled by men, in both legitimate and illegitimate business enterprises, it seemed logical for her to further the careers, however illicit, of women. Given the economic circumstances of the times and the dichotomy between the rich and poor where the richest 2 percent of the country controlled one-third of its wealth, it is logical that the poor and disadvantaged, with no real road to advancement, would turn to crime. And turning to a life of crime in New York City meant an association with Mandelbaum.

Mandelbaum offered women alternatives to prostitution even though petty theft, pickpocketing, or confidence scams did not conform to the standards of normal, middle class propriety. Most working class women had to make hard choices outside their family circle. Women like Mandelbaum worked hard in order to survive. The plight of women was mostly ignored by polite society. Lower class women did what they had to in order to survive and provide an income for their family. If they engaged in criminal activities, so be it.

Most working class women suffered from low wages and labored long hours, averaging approximately ten to twelve hours a day, and still had the responsibility of raising their children and maintaining homes. Unlike what some may have claimed, that crime doesn't pay, to many women, crime paid far more than legitimate work. It was because of her success that Mandelbaum fostered the ambitions of other women who would not or could not make any significant strides within the legitimate world of work.

Many of the women Mandelbaum helped rose to great heights within the criminal world, and in doing so, gained a certain status and respect for their abilities, skills, and achievements. According to crime reports of the period, women made up at least 50 percent of all shoplifters in New York City. Women shoplifters worked in pairs, as they also did in confidence schemes and when picking someone's pocket. The female companion served as a lookout while the other woman stuffed merchandise into her dress. They could serve as helpless decoys while the other deftly picked the pocket of some good Samaritan absorbed in the decoy's sad story of woe. And in confidence schemes they could serve as both a witness to whatever debauchery the other woman might manage to engage some poor sap into as well as a person who could handle all the exchanges of money. Mandelbaum saw to it that her shoplifting "chicks" only traversed the highest class stores in their quest for goods and when it came to stolen merchandise, Mandelbaum directed them to concentrate their talents and attentions on merchandise that could readily and easily be turned into cash—cashmere, silk, shawls, jewelry, and sealskin bags—anything valuable that could be stuffed into large pockets that were beneath their wide skirts and dresses. They in turn would receive a percentage of the profits. Following Mandelbaum's advice made many a young girl if not wealthy, at least financially solvent. Lena Kleinschmidt, Black Lena, was one of them.

The elaborate dinner parties Mandelbaum threw provided opportunities for her criminal cohorts to consort with New York City's social elite. Black Lena was always among the invited guests. The parties were perhaps one of the earliest forms of social networking. For Mandelbaum, it was an opportunity to cultivate relationships that inevitably helped her ongoing fencing operations. In a rough profession not noted for generosity, Mandelbaum was an exception, retaining a soft spot in her heart for female crooks and others who might need a helping hand up the criminal ladder. She was an equal opportunity employer. She was a stalwart believer that gender was no barrier to criminal success. She herself stood as a living example of that enlightened view. However, although she encouraged and nurtured women who had chosen a life of crime, she could not tolerate competition from them. Black Lena, one of her protégés, fine-tuned her confidence and pickpocketing skills under Mandelbaum's tutelage and she would have been one of Mandelbaum's greatest success stories had it not been for the fact that Lena became greedy and worse, she decided to challenge Mandelbaum's lofty position within the criminal community. When Black Lena pulled up stakes, moved to Hackensack, New Jersey, Mandelbaum became furious. Lena began modeling herself after Mandelbaum—throwing dinner parties and climbing the Hackensack social ladder. Lena had made massive amounts of money through her association with Mandelbaum and was like all those in her employ forced to pay Mandelbaum a hefty percentage of her earnings. When Lena moved to New Jersey, she cut her ties with Mandelbaum, no longer paying her benefactor and mentor anything. This too did not go over well with Mandelbaum.

In New Jersey, Black Lena posed as the wealthy widow of a South American mining engineer. Her soirées became an immediate hit among Hackensack's high society. She quickly became known as the "Queen of Hackensack." Despite her newfound notoriety she still spent two days a week in New York City plying her trade and enhancing her wealth outside of Mandelbaum's control. Lena was ultimately exposed when she showed up at one of her own dinner parties sporting a diamond ring that one of her guests recognized as having been stolen from her handbag. The woman whose ring had been stolen was the wife of a prominent New Jersey judge. Lena was immediately arrested, her house searched, and a vast amount of stolen merchandise was discovered in her possession. She was sent to prison and died in 1886.

The debacle with Black Lena made Mandelbaum cautious of her tutelage of young women. However, when it came to the young and beautiful Sophie Lyons, she treated her like a daughter, for many reasons other than Lyons's many illicit talents. Mandelbaum saw in the young and beautiful Lyons the image of how she wished she had been. Mandelbaum, tall, fat, and unattractive was drawn to the waif-like beauty of Lyons. And since Mandelbaum had forbade her own daughters from engaging in the fencing business, she desired to have someone, a woman in particular, learn the ropes from her. Lyons was the one.

In 1853, Lyons stole her first purse before she was six years old and was first arrested when she was twelve. It would not be until she was twenty-five years old that she would learn to read and write. She went on to learn to speak four languages fluently. Lyons came from criminal pedigree. She was born in 1848 in New York City as Sophie Levy. Her father, Sam, was a notorious burglar. Her mother, also named Sophie (Elkins) was a renowned pickpocket and shoplifter. Both her parents served jail terms which at times left Sophie to fend for herself. Her grandfather James Elkins was a notorious burglar in England. Sophie learned most of what she knew from her mother and later her stepmother. It was when her parents were serving simultaneous prison terms that the sixteen-year old Lyons came under the tutelage of Mandelbaum. Sophie was sent to Mandelbaum's school for little criminals on Grand Street and quickly became Mandelbaum's star pupil.

An attractive young girl when she first met Mandelbaum, in later life, Lyons maintained that it had been Mandelbaum who had encouraged her to use her good looks in a series of immoral and criminal endeavors. Lyons portrayed herself as a victim—an abused child, victimized first by her abusive parents and then by Mandelbaum. Lyons had met Mandelbaum when she was a teenager and was molded by her claims of compassion and concern into a criminal extraordinaire. According to Lyons, Mandelbaum's compassion and concern were predicated on her desire to create a high-class crook she could manipulate and depend on to carry out her wishes. Sophie Lyons fit the bill.

"I shall never forget the atmosphere of 'Mother' Mandelbaum's place on the corner of Clinton and Rivington Streets. In the front was the general store, innocent enough in appearance; and, in fact, the real business of buying and selling stolen merchandise went on in the rear of the place," Lyons claimed.

Lyons knew more than most what went on at Mandelbaum's establishment since she was, like Piano Charlie Bullard, one of Mandebaum's favorites. "I was very happy because I was petted and rewarded," Lyons said. "My wretched stepmother patted my curly head, gave me a bag of candy and said I was a good girl." But when little Sophie failed to bring home the required number of stolen pocketbooks, she was beaten. She claimed her stepmother burned her arm once as punishment for not bringing home the bacon.

During the 1860s and 1870s Lyons was part of the inner circle of Marm Mandelbaum's cadre of pickpockets, thieves, burglars, and confidence men. According to Herbert Asbury's seminal work, *The Gangs of New York*, Sophie Lyons was "perhaps the most notorious confidence woman America has ever produced." A confidence man or woman, as in Lyons' case, engaged in defrauding people by gaining their trust and promising them some significant financial gain for placing their trust in them. The enterprise is often referred to as a "con game," "scam," "flim-flam," "swindle," or "grift." The victims of a con game are known as "marks." And the person behind the con game is known as a "con man" or "grifter." When an accomplice is used in the scam, they are known as "shills."

The phrase itself became part of the lexicon of the English language in 1849, when the *New York Herald* coined the term "confidence man" in reference to the American criminal William Thompson who was arrested for swindling people out of their watches. The elegantly dressed Thompson approached upper-class gentlemen and pretending to know them, would strike up a conversation. After gaining their trust, he would ask to borrow their watch for an appointment, promising to return it immediately. He reportedly said to his victims, "Have you confidence in me to trust me with your watch until tomorrow?" The victim, usually too polite to say no to a former acquaintance, would hand over the watch, and Thompson would disappear with it never to be seen again. Herman Melville's 1857 novel *The Confidence Man* was based on Thompson. The con game can run the gamut from simple tricks to elaborate constructions. Among notable conmen was George Parker who managed to win the confidence of unsuspecting victims to whom he famously sold the Brooklyn Bridge, twice a week, for several years, before being caught. One of the most famous con men was Charles Ponzi, whose get-rich-quick scheme—the Ponzi Scheme—bears his name.

New York Police detective Thomas Byrnes described the confidence game in his book *Professional Criminals in America* (1886) as "the safest, pleasantest and most amusing way for a shrewd thief to make his living." Byrnes also described Sophie Lyons as a "notorious shoplifter, pickpocket, and blackmailer."

> "She was beautiful when young, and the traces never quite rubbed off . . . Her features were regular and chiseled into a well-shaped oval face. Her eyes were an indeterminate gray-blue, and her almost-blond hair was piled on top of her head. She was a consummate actress, could be demure when it best fitted the circumstances, or she could assume the grand and lofty manner. She could weep or smile, as she chose. She wore dresses trimmed in laces and rich embroideries."
>
> —Richard Bak, "From Rogue to Reformer," 2009

Lyons made her debut as a blackmailer in Boston sometime in the late 1870s. After being released from prison on a larceny charge in 1876, Lyons went to Boston with her partner, Kate Leary, who was another known confidence woman. There, using her good looks and ample charms, she lured a wealthy businessman up to her hotel room. While the unsuspecting "mark" was undressing in the bathroom, she took his clothes and threatened to expose him if he did not make out a check in the amount of $10,000 and give it to Leary, who was just outside the door. Not wanting to be caught in such an indelicate situation, he wrote out the check as Lyons asked. Leary took the check immediately to the bank to cash it but when the check bounced she was held by the police. During questioning, she revealed the whereabouts of Lyons and her captive. The police went to the hotel where they arrested Lyons and released the embarrassed businessman. The man refused to appear in court to press charges against Lyons or Leary for obvious reasons, and they were released from custody. Although his money was saved, his reputation and his marriage were ruined.

Sophie Lyons was irresistible to men because of her beauty, charm, and intelligence. She was ultimately married four times. She was first married in 1864 at the age of sixteen to Maury Harris, a professional pickpocket, who claimed to be the best in the business. Harris, however, was not as good as he thought. On their honeymoon, the police caught him red-handed trying to steal a wallet. He was arrested and sentenced to New York State Prison for two years.

While Harris was in prison, Sophie took up with Edward "Ned" Lyons, a notorious bank burglar. He was a big, strong man, eleven years her senior, with long reddish hair and a drooping red moustache. He combed his hair over his ears to hide where the top of his left ear had been bitten off in a drunken barroom brawl.

Sophie met Ned at one of Mandelbaum's dinner parties. At the party, she deftly stole a gold watch and diamond stick pin from "Sheeny" Mike Kurtz, one of the most talented sneak thieves and burglars of the times, and gave them as gifts to Ned. When Kurtz finally realized what had happened, everyone at the get-together had a laugh at Sheeny's expense. It was an intriguing way to introduce herself to Lyons and obviously it made the right impression on him, since they were married shortly thereafter.

It is not known whether Sophie obtained a legal divorce from Maury Harris before marrying Ned. It didn't matter since there was no way Harris would go up against someone as powerful and dangerous as Lyons.

> "Lyons was then an uncommonly good looking rascal, not yet thirty years old, and his bride, Sophie, is described by those who knew her as an exceedingly beautiful girl with brilliant dark eyes and auburn hair that flowed to her feet when shaken from its coils."
>
> —Benjamin Eldridge and William Watts, *Our Rival, The Rascal*, 1897

After they were married, Ned Lyons bought a home for Sophie on Long Island and demanded that she give up her life of crime and dedicate herself to being a wife and mother. Initially, Sophie embraced her new life of domesticity. She became pregnant and gave birth to her first child, George. For a time she adapted to her newfound familial role. It didn't last long. She missed the action. When George was only a few months old, she resumed her former vocation.

While Ned was occupied in one robbery or another, Sophie would go to Manhattan where she would ply her chosen trades—shoplifting or picking pockets—and take her stolen loot to Mandelbaum in exchange for cash.

> "Lyons married a young Jewess named Sophie Elkins, alias Levy a protégée of Mrs. Mandelbaum. Her mania for stealing was so strong that when in Ned's company in public she plied her vocation unknown to him and would surprise him with watches, etc. which she had stolen Ned expostulated, pleaded with and threatened her but without avail . . ."
>
> —Thomas Byrnes, *Professional Criminals in America,* 1886

In 1870, Sophie was convicted of shoplifting and sent to jail on Blackwell's Island. Blackwell's was the women's prison located in the middle of New York City's East River. Not only a prison for women, it served as an asylum for the insane, the poor, and the infirm. The ferry that carried Lyons and other women to the grim, inhospitable prison, which housed some seven thousand unwanted or convicted people, was known as "the ferry of despair." Shortly after arriving at Blackwell's, Sophie's husband was arrested and sent to nearby Sing Sing. While serving her time on Blackwell's, she began to have second thoughts about continuing her life of crime. Still, when she was finally released she returned to her life of thievery. She was again caught trying to steal several diamonds from a jewelry shop and was sent this time to Sing Sing where she was reunited with Ned. In 1871, using her feminine wiles, she was able to get her hands on a prison pass from one of the guards, along with a change of clothes and was able to help her husband break out of jail. Once on the outside, Ned Lyons was quick to break his wife out by secreting a key he had made from a wax mold he'd managed to make while in Sing Sing. The couple fled to Canada. By then they had five children. In 1876, the couple were again arrested and sent back to Sing Sing to serve out their terms. This time there was no escape for either of them. She was released first. While Ned was still serving out the rest of his prison term, Sophie decided to divorce him.

THE ROGUE'S GALLERY
SKETCHES OF PROMINENT CRIMINAL

The difference between romance and reality is no other way so easily perceived as by an inspection of the collection of photographs at Police headquarters popularly known as the Rogues Gallery . . . The picture numbered 334 is that of Sophie Levy, a thief from her very infancy. Her father was a receiver of stolen goods and her mother a pickpocket . . . Every member of the family has been in state prison . . . She there married Ned Lyons, and accomplished pickpocket and burglar . . . Ned Lyons last year escaped and then devoted

Mulberry Street was located in the notorious Five Points section of New York City. During the Gilded Age, it was considered one of the most crime-ridden parts of all New York City. Shoppers could buy virtually anything they wanted legally or illegally. (Courtesy of The Library of Congress)

Peddlers sold their wares along the busy streets of New York City using hand drawn carts or carts driven by a single horse. Some, like Mandelbaum, carried their wares on their shoulders. (Courtesy of The Library of Congress)

Sophie Lyons was another Mandelbaum protégé known for her extraordinary cons. She was given the dubious title "The Princess of Crime." (Courtesy of The Smithsonian)

Lena Kleimschmidt (a.k.a. "Black Lena") was one of Mandelbaum's protégés who made a massive amount of money through blackmail, thievery, and pickpocketing. (Courtesy of the Pinkerton Photo Gallery)

Fredericka Mandelbaum was a German-Jewish immigrant who became the driving force behind New York City's festering underworld. (Illustration courtesy of The Smithsonian)

Red Leary was one of New York City's most notorious bank robbers of the 1870s, frequently pairing with other known criminals to pull off spectacular bank robberies. (Courtesy of The Crime Library)

Max Shinburn was an international burglar and safecracker. With his ill-gotten gains, he bought himself the title of Baron Shindell of Monaco. Shinburn later became a police informant. (Courtesy of The Crime Library)

Piano Charlie Bullard was an educated, piano playing safecracker. After robbing $450,000 from the Boylston Bank in Boston, Bullard fled to London. (Courtesy of The Crime Library)

"Georgiana Cavendish, Duchess of Devonshire" was painted by Thomas Gainsborough in the late 1780s. It went up for sale at Christie's auction house in London in 1876 and sold for $60,000. It went on display at the Thomas Agnew & Sons Gallery and became the sensation of London. In a daring night time robbery, Adam Worth broke into the gallery and stole the painting. (Courtesy of the Devonshire Collection)

Adam Worth became known as "The Napoleon of Crime" in Europe. In Europe, Worth's partner in crime, Piano Charlie Bullard, ran afoul of the law and fled back to the United States. On his own, Worth stole the famous Gainsborough painting, "Georgiana Cavendish, Duchess of Devonshire," and kept it until the last days of his life. (Courtesy of Jewish American Society for Historic Preservation)

Kitty Flynn was an object of desire for both Adam Worth and Piano Charlie Bullard. After Bullard deserted her in London she moved to America where she married a Wall Street banker. (Courtesy of The Crime Library)

George Leonidas Leslie was dubbed "The King of Bank Robbers." He planned and executed more than a hundred robberies and stole between seven and twelve million dollars, including the theft of three million dollars from the Manhattan Savings Institution in 1878. A comic book depicting Leslie's exploits appeared in *Clue Comics* in March 1947 with drawings by Jack Kirby. (Courtesy of The Jack Kirby Museum)

Boss Tweed and his gang stole between $30 million and $200 million from the New York City coffers between 1865 and 1871. For criminals like Mandelbaum, bribes to Tweed kept the police and prosecution at bay. Tweed was a frequent guest at Mandelbaum's parties. (Courtesy of The Library of Congress)

Mandelbaum's parties provided an opportunity for her to consort with New York City's social elite as well as her criminal cohorts. (Courtesy of The Crime Library)

This illustration from *Puck* magazine makes the humorous claim that perhaps there was a vaccine that could be given to criminals to stop them from their thieving enterprises. Mandelbaum is depicted in the lower right. (Courtesy of The Library of the Smithsonian)

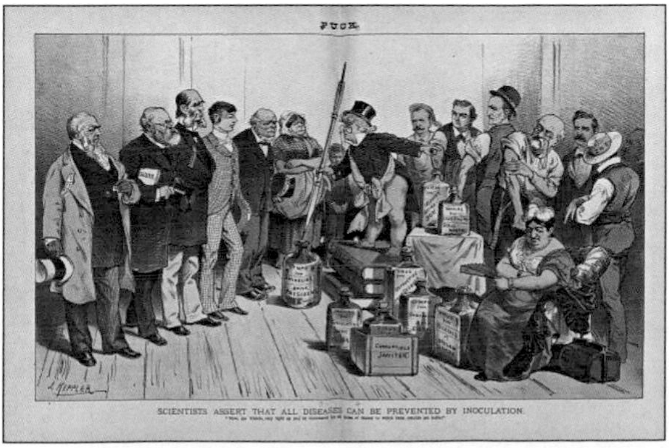

Brothers Robert and William Pinkerton took over their father's famous detective agency. It was Robert's undercover detective, Gustav Frank, who finally apprehended Mandelbaum. William Pinkerton was instrumental in the capture of Adam Worth and the return of the famous Gainsborough painting. (Courtesy of The Library of Congress)

William Howe was half of the notorious criminal defense team of Howe and Hummel. He was eloquent, humorous, and his profound knowledge of the law and the works of Shakespeare gave him an advantage over his opponents. (Courtesy of the Widener Library, Harvard University)

Abraham Hummel was a dour, quiet man who sat beside his flamboyant partner, William Howe, during courtroom proceedings. Mandelbaum reportedly paid Howe and Hummel an annual retainer of $5,000 to represent her criminal interests. (Courtesy of the Widener Library, Harvard University)

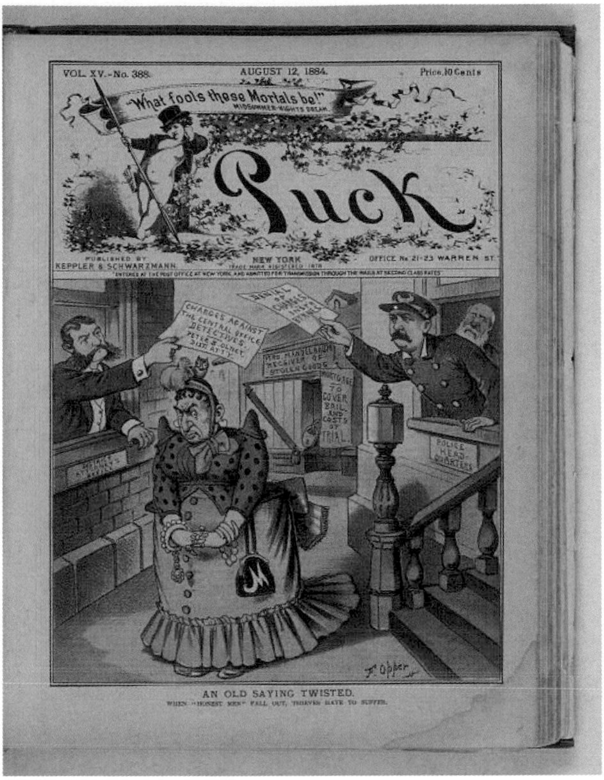

This *Puck* magazine cover shows Mandelbaum caught in the middle of the ongoing fight between the district attorney's office and the police department. (Courtesy of The Smithsonian)

Thomas Byrnes was the most celebrated police officer in New York City's history. District Attorney Peter B. Olney claimed the police had protected Mandelbaum for years, while Byrnes claimed the district attorney's office was looking for a scapegoat. (Courtesy of The National Night Stick)

This *Puck* cover from 1885 shows a defiant Mandelbaum thumbing her nose at American authorities who were unable to extradite her from Canada. "When the strong arm of the United States law reaches after the thieves, Canada leans gently over the boundary line and says, 'I have them and you can't get them.'" (Courtesy of The Library of Congress)

> all his energies to affect the escape of Sophie. This was accomplished about eight months ago . . . Sophie Levy is a very handsome woman of the Jewish type of beauty . . .
>
> —*The New York Times*, June 27, 1875

In 1895, Sophie Lyons was credited with being the first defendant to use the "kleptomaniac" defense before a jury. Arrested for shoplifting, her attorney, William Howe, who had been on retainer for years with Mandelbaum, advised Lyons to break into sobs when she recounted for the jury how her compulsive thievery was the result of her abusive upbringing at the hands of a family of criminals. The jury bought Sophie's alligator tears and her poor, abused child routine and set her free.

Beautiful, daring, and smart, Sophie managed to elude arrest on many occasions. During one incident when she was caught stealing red-handed by police who were beside themselves that they had finally apprehended the notorious Sophie Lyons, she managed to talk the police out of arresting her by claiming that the real Sophie Lyons would have been too smart to have been caught by such inept police officers. She reportedly told police, "Sophie Lyons is a hardened criminal, and too smart to be caught like this." It worked. She wasn't arrested but was summarily escorted out of town based on her denial.

According to an 1897 *National Police Gazette* article written by none other than the illustrious William Howe, who had represented Sophie on many occasions at Mandelbaum's behest, she had "stolen more money than any other woman in the world." But everything she accomplished she owed to Mandelbaum, who guided and nurtured her long and successful career. While Ned Lyons was still in prison, Sophie hooked up with a much younger, more handsome thief named Billie Burke. She and her new husband entered into a new phase of crime—bank robbery. They made a fabulous team. Sophie would act as a decoy distracting bank clerks or guards while Billie snuck inside and cleaned out the cash drawers. Their partnership became so successful that she and Burke were able to afford a home in Manhattan, a villa on the Riviera, and even a ranch out West.

> "Wife and sweetheart of bandits, bank robbers and gunmen, Sophie robbed on two continents with a flair that enabled her to rub elbows with royalty and top social figures."
>
> —Joseph McNamara, *The Justice Story*, 2000

The couple moved to Paris where they hobnobbed with royalty and society's upper crust.

It was rumored that she and her husband had even been guests of the Prince of Wales.

Sophie hired tutors to help her learn languages, art, music, and history, allowing her to pass herself off as a cultured lady of exquisite taste and upbringing. She assumed the nom de plume of Madame de Varney. While engaged in their social climbing, Billie and Sophie kept busy with their criminal transactions. Using their many high society connections they were able to engage in a slew of robberies undetected or suspected. They once managed to steal $500,000 in jewelry and cash in one night's haul. Lyons was quoted as telling her Parisian friends, "I have a very expensive family and my tastes require artistic gratification. I am accustomed to the best art, music and literature. One cannot live without the good things of life."

> She tricked the nobility of Paris out of three hundred thousand dollars by sheer audacity, her beauty of face and figure and her magnetic smile enabling her literally to hypnotize her victims. It was said that she never approached a man in vain.
>
> —Mary Francis, "Fair Financiers Who Have Fleeced Cautious Capitalists," 1908

When Ned Lyons was finally released from prison, in a jealous rage he attempted to kill Billie Burke. Lyons got the worst of it and was shot twice in the chest but survived. Burke was unharmed.

Lyons was never able to assume his former place among New York City's criminal elite. He was arrested several more times and finally died in prison. But his wife Sophie became so famous for her criminal exploits that she was parodied in a popular song written in 1919 by Edgar Leslie, Bert Kalmar, and Pete Wendling:

> "Oh! what a gal is Sophie.
> Oh! what a pal is she."

After ultimately being exposed as a charlatan in Paris and elsewhere in Europe, having been caught trying to lift a diamond necklace from a host's bedroom during a gala party, Lyons and Burke were sent packing for America. Rather than settling back in New York City, they moved their base of operations to Detroit. One of Detroit's many attractions, especially for criminals like Sophie, was that it wasn't far from Canada, which did not have an extradition treaty with the United States. Criminals in danger of being caught in America could easily cross the border into Canada without fear of being sent back. Sophie and Billie Burke plied their trade in Detroit for a time but finally in early 1883, Sophie was arrested and sentenced to three years in the Detroit House of Correction for larceny. When she was finally released in 1886, after more than twenty years in crime, she made a life-changing decision—she decided to go legit.

She decided she had become too well known, she was getting older and she could not rely on her former beauty to slip out of trouble. Now in her early forties, she had spent almost a quarter of her life behind bars. Most of her family, including two of her sons, had been in and out of prison. At one time or another all of her children (she claimed she had nine children in all, by five different fathers) had been placed into orphanages or convents. Sadly and perhaps inevitably, her first born, George, who had turned to a life of crime and spent much of his young life in and out of jail, died in prison. Her daughters were luckier than her sons. One daughter, Lotta, became a noted opera singer in Paris.

Another lived in London. Perhaps the saddest relationship of all was between Sophie and her youngest daughter, Florence, who lived in Detroit. She had spent most of her childhood in a convent and changed her last name because of her mother's notoriety. Florence was married but after her husband died she was forced to becoming a beggar on the streets of Detroit. According to one anecdotal report, Sophie once passed her impoverished daughter on the street, ignoring her completely. In the end, Florence wound up as the major beneficiary of Sophie's will, making her a very wealthy woman.

In 1897, Sophie Lyons, once the "Princess of Crime," turned over a new leaf. She became one of the first society gossip columnists in the country, writing for the *New York World*, and a Detroit real estate magnate, making a small fortune buying and selling homes and businesses in the city. But that wasn't her transformation in its entirety. She dedicated the rest of her life and fortune to funding prison libraries and orphanages. She was credited with spending thousands of dollars on food and clothing for the families of prisoners. She tried to help ex-convicts get back on their feet—this included her husband, Billie Burke, who was a prisoner in Stockholm, Sweden. When he was released, he came back to live with her in Detroit and died in 1919.

NOTORIOUS THIEF DEAD
INTERNATIONAL CROOK CREDITED WITH BEING DIRECTOR OF MANY JEWELRY STORE ROBBERIES PASSES AWAY

DETROIT, MICH- Oct 25- William Burke, known as "Billy the Kid," or Billie Burke more familiarly, one of the most famous of international crooks and jewel thieves died Saturday Morning, Oct. 25 at the Boulevard sanitarium in this city. Sophie Lyons, his wife and former queen of confidence women was at his side when he died. Although never connected directly with any great jewelry store robbery

> in America, "Billie" Burke was known as the brains of many of the craftiest and boldest of jewelry store robberies. . . . His greatest robberies were abroad. Burke was arrested early in 1914 for complicity in the theft of $500,000 worth of diamonds from a broker in Alexandria, Egypt, but the charge was not proven. He took up with Sophie Lyons, then a noted leader of the underworld who has since reformed and made a fortune in real estate in Detroit.
>
> —*The Jewelers' Circular*, Vol. 79, 1919

Sophie tried to make amends with those she had exploited. According to Richard Bak and Neal Rubin, authors of *Detroitland*, "Sophie had sent a check to a down-on-her-luck actress to reimburse her for the jewelry she had stolen from her when times were flush." Sophie donated land that was worth $35,000 to build a home where young children could live while their parents were serving sentences in prison.

Despite her long and close relationship with Mandelbaum, in her book, *Why Crime Does Not Pay*, published in 1913, Lyons turned against her benefactor and mentor, portraying her as a criminal predator, someone who had coerced and seduced her into a life of crime.

> "For twenty-five years she [Mandelbaum] lived on the proceeds of other people's crimes. During that time she made many millions. But these millions slipped away for the most part in bribing, fixing, and silencing people. Still she was a very wealthy, fat, ugly old woman when the blow fell."
>
> —Sophie Lyons, *Why Crime Does Not Pay*, 1913

Mandelbaum did not live to see Sophie Lyons betray her but she wasn't the last to betray her trust. The beginning of the end for Mandelbaum's reign as "Queen among Thieves," began with betrayal, by Michael Kurtz, known as "Sheeny Mike," and James Hoey, criminals, like Sophie Lyons, who Mandelbaum had befriended and helped. The road leading to her end began not in a criminal proceeding, as one might have suspected it would, but in a civil suit brought against her in 1881 by a Boston merchant named James Scott.

PART III

MANDELBAUM'S FALL

7
NABBED

"All good things must come to an end."

—English proverb

What Mandelbaum was able to do outside the law was an amazing feat for anyone, no less an immigrant woman. She built a thriving, profitable business that had made her wealthy and powerful in an era in which most women struggled just to make ends meet. Her ethnicity played a significant role in this, at least in the eyes of both her supporters and her detractors. Based on the stereotypes held at that time, as a Jew, she was supposed to have a firm grasp of business. She was supposed to be shrewd, tight-fisted, and a haggler.

> The Jews have a monopoly of the pawn broking business in this city and many of them have acquired great wealth thereby. They are sharp and shrewd, always driving a hard bargain, whether dealing with the stylish and elegantly appearing pick-pocket or bargaining with the poor washerwoman who wants to borrow a few cents on her washtub. Nature and constant practice has made them as good judges of human nature as they are of the value of an article.
>
> —*The New York Times*, July 6, 1866

Mandelbaum fit many of the labels ascribed to Jews during this era. She was crafty, shrewd, and manipulative in matters pertaining to business. She was, after all, only engaging in practices that legitimate businessmen also participated in. Profit was not the exclusive domain of legitimate society. The growing industrialization of America during the Gilded Age did not offer as much advancement for women in legitimate enterprises as Mandelbaum found in her illegal activities. She encompassed the perceptions fostered by her immigrant cultural heritage, her ethnicity, and the long held stereotypes of her gender. She was a good wife, mother, businesswoman, and neighbor. It was these qualities, despite her criminal activities, that led her friends and neighbors to rally around her and protect her interests when necessary. It was also these many qualities that allowed them to turn a blind eye to her activities. She was a woman. She was successful. And she was charitable and generous. What more could anyone ask for in a person?

> [A Jew] is perhaps more inoculated with the love of money getting than is the average Christian and hence is a little keener and closer in his business transactions.
>
> —*Evening Telegram*, October 19, 1872

By the 1880s, things were changing, both for Mandelbaum as well as society in general. Many of her contemporaries were either dead or in prison. George Leslie was dead. Many of her best bank robbers were either in jail, on the lam, pursued vigorously by the police, or in the case of her favorite entertainer, Charlie Bullard, and Adam Worth, had moved on to greener pastures in Europe. The world was changing for Mandelbaum. Boss Tweed was dead and the chokehold he had on New York City's political establishment had loosened, giving way to more reform-minded elected officials. A unique, although not total, division had also occurred between the law enforcement system and the criminal underworld. There was still crime and corruption, but even within the criminal community, a dramatic shift in allegiances was occurring. Some of Mandelbaum's closest associates were discovering that playing ball with the police and prosecutors was more beneficial to them than remaining loyal to Mandelbaum. Pressed by reformers, the tide was turning and it did not bode well for her.

In 1881, a civil suit was brought against her. A Boston merchant named James Scott had managed, without any New York City police department assistance, to bring the suit against Mandelbaum. In his case *James Scott vs. Fredericka Mandelbaum,* he stated that back in January 1877, robbers had stolen twenty-six cashmere shawls worth $780 from his store on Washington Street in Boston. The thieves also absconded with two thousand yards of black silk worth approximately $4,000. Scott claimed that the merchandise ultimately ended up in the hands of Mandelbaum and that she was fully aware that the merchandise had been stolen from his store. He sued her for $6,000 including the cost of the stolen merchandise as well as associated legal fees and interest. The case was finally adjudicated three years later in January 1884, and Scott won a sizeable judgment against her.

Mandelbaum denied all the charges brought against her in the civil case. In her response to the complaint she claimed that she had no prior knowledge that the merchandise in question had been stolen, and further that she had no connection to the robbery at Scott's Boston store or with the men who were engaged in the theft. The civil case languished in the courts for several years but finally did make it to court after the original judge in the case, Charles Donohue, was replaced by Judge Hooper Van Vorst. Donohue was later investigated for his questionable legal behavior including the continued delay of cases that benefited favored defendants.

According to the newspapers, the courtroom during the civil trial resembled a who's who of the criminal underworld filled with an assortment of characters with nicknames like "Big Bill," "Sheeny Rosy," "Big French Louis," "Whitey Bob," "Tommy King." and "Red Leary," all known to authorities as thieves and burglars. They, according to a *New York Times* report, "sat alongside unprofessional citizens, looking as honest as anybody else."

The prosecution's case in the civil trial was primarily based on testimony from two of Mandelbaum's closest criminal associates, Michael Kurtz, known as "Sheeny Mike," and James Hoey. Kurtz gave testimony to James Scott's attorney in the case, Samuel A. Noyes, on twelve separate occasions from January 1882 until March 1883. Hoey made statements to Noyes on four separate occasions in 1883. Sarah Fox, "Sheeny Mike" Kurtz's sister, also gave statements to Noyes corroborating her brother's testimony. Mandelbaum sat in the courtroom along with her usual attorneys, William Howe and Abraham Hummel.

Attorney Noyes, on behalf of plaintiff James Scott, told the court that on the day of the robbery, Kurtz had expertly removed a lock from the outer door of Scott's Washington Street shop, taken it to a locksmith, had a key fitted for it and returned, replacing the lock undetected. That night, Sheeny Mike and two of his confederates returned to the store and let themselves in. They stole the 2,000 yards of silk and twenty-six cashmere shawls, placed them in a waiting carriage and drove off. When the plaintiff opened the shop the next day and discovered the theft, instead of notifying the Boston Police Department, he hired two private detectives. The detectives, working on a variety of leads, traced Sheeny Mike to Washington, D.C., where they apprehended him and started back to Boston with him in tow. On a stopover in Philadelphia, Sheeny Mike telegraphed Mandelbaum asking her to meet him in Jersey City. She met him there with a writ of habeas corpus for his release. The legal document through which a prisoner can be released from unlawful detention, however, was made out to be served on private detective Donald Wiggin. Ironically, Sheeny Mike was in the custody of and handcuffed to the other private detective, John Woods. Since the habeas corpus demanded the release of Sheeny Mike from Wiggin's custody and since Sheeny Mike was not in Wiggin's custody but Woods's, Detective Woods refused to release the prisoner.

Sheeny Mike was taken back to Boston, stood trial, was found guilty and sentenced to three years in prison. While in prison, Sheeny Mike became ill and was given a pardon, but not before he signed an affidavit confessing to the theft and maintaining that he had sold the stolen goods to Mandelbaum. According to the affidavit, he admitted to breaking into and stealing the merchandise from Scott's store in January 1877. The stolen silk and cashmere shawls were taken to his sister's home at 808 Sixth Street in New York. Mandelbaum came to view the merchandise where she agreed to pay seventy-five cents per yard for the silk and five dollars each for the cashmere shawls. The total cost of the transaction was $1,600. The silk was marked from $1.00 to $3.50 per yard and the shawls were marked from $25.00 to $45.00 each.

Mandelbaum was arrested on the charge of receiving stolen property. She posted $5,000 bail but by the time the case went to trial, Sheeny Mike had disappeared. Without his direct testimony there was no case against Mandelbaum, at least no criminal case. It was then that James Scott, seeing he could not make criminal charges stick against Mandelbaum, filed his civil suit against her. Although it held little credence in a criminal case, not without Sheeny Mike there to testify in person, Noyes was able to introduce Sheeny Mike's affidavit in the civil case. Next he called James Hoey, a once trusted confidant of Mandelbaum.

> Hoey is a good-looking man, with dark mustache and whiskers trimmed in the English style and gray and black mixed hair parted almost in the middle. He said he had been in Boston for 10 months past and before that lived in New York for 10 or 12 years. His relations with Mother Mandelbaum were at one time intimate and confidential.
>
> —*The New York Times*, January 24, 1884

Hoey informed the court that Mandelbaum sent a message with one of her shoplifters, Jeanette Clark, that she wanted to meet with him at her house. According to Hoey, Mandelbaum said that she had tried to get Sheeny Mike away from the private detectives and that at one point Kurtz told her to give back the stolen goods. According to Hoey's testimony, Mandelbaum reportedly said, "Now, what do you think of that sucker talking that way to me?"

Mandelbaum then asked Hoey to go to Boston to try to help Kurtz out of the mess. She gave him $500 and another $50 for expenses. Hoey claimed he went to Boston and offered Mr. Scott $1,500 in payment for the stolen loot. Scott refused. He wanted all the merchandise back or its full value and nothing less.

Hoey visited Sheeny Mike in jail. Sheeny reportedly asked Hoey why Mandelbaum wouldn't return the merchandise. Hoey informed him that Mandelbaum claimed that she had already sold the goods and couldn't get them back. Sheeny Mike called Mandelbaum a liar. Hoey said that when he returned to New York, Mandelbaum insisted again that she had sold all of the silk and cashmere shawls. She said she had paid $1,700 for them and made less than the $5,000 on the whole deal. It was of little solace to Sheeny Mike who was languishing in jail awaiting trial.

Mandelbaum's lawyer, William Howe, countered Noyes's argument with the frivolous claim that Mandelbaum was "the victim of a wicked conspiracy," one that set former colleagues against her in order for them to gain freedom in their own criminal cases. In an all-out effort to impugn the testimony of James Hoey, the defense called one of New York City's finest, Detective Sergeant Thomas Dusenbury, as its first witness. Dusenbury told the court he had known James Hoey and his wife for many years and that he would not believe anything they might say even under oath. Howe then called Jeannette Clark, who tried to discredit Hoey's testimony by insisting Mandelbaum never arranged any meeting between Hoey and Sheeny Mike.

Finally, Marm Mandelbaum took the stand in her own defense. She informed the court that she was a fifty-one-year-old widow with four children, and that she had gone to help Sheeny Mike as a favor to his mother Edna, whom she had known for some twenty years. She testified that she had heard that Sheeny Mike was a burglar but that she personally had no dealings with him. Her efforts were simply a gesture of kindness on behalf of Sheeny's dear mother. She completely denied any wrongdoing and testified that she had never in her life received stolen property from him or anyone else.

The jury decided for the plaintiff Scott in the amount of $6,666 plus court costs including $4,000 for the silk, $600 for the shawls and $2,066 in interest. Mandelbaum's attorneys immediately filed a motion for a new trial. Judge Van Vorst denied the motion and on January 25, 1884, Mandelbaum received the official order to pay James Scott a total of $7,267.75, including interest.

A ROBBED MERCHANT'S SUIT VERDICT AGAINST RECEIVER OF STOLEN GOODS GROWING OUT OF A ROBBERY IN BOSTON IN WHICH "SHEENY MIKE" WAS THE ACTOR WHERE THE GOODS WENT

> The suit was brought by Mr. Scott against Frederika Mandelbaum, better known among the thieving fraternity as "Mother Mandelbaum the fence," to who Sheeny Mike disposed of the plunder resulting from the robbery. . . . Judge Van Vorst told the jurymen that if the evidence satisfied them that the defendant received the goods she was responsible. . . .
>
> —*The New York Times,* January 24, 1884

With the civil matter behind her, Mandelbaum went back to business as usual. But even her best efforts to tighten up her operation could not forestall the inevitable, especially when Pinkerton detectives were called in to finally apprehend her. Robert Pinkerton, head of the Pinkerton Agency personally oversaw the operation. William and Robert Pinkerton succeeded their father and founder of the agency, Allan, in 1884 as co-principals of the business. William directed Pinkerton operations in the West from his office in Chicago. Robert maintained an office in New York and oversaw the East Coast operations.

Their father had founded the agency in 1850 in Chicago. According to Frank Horan, author of *The Pinkertons: The Detective Dynasty That Made History,* what was needed at that time "to fill the niche between the lack of rule of law and the incompetence of corrupt urban law-enforcement organizations, was a private police force that could move across local, county, and even state boundaries in the pursuit of criminals. This is what Pinkerton established."

During the mid-nineteenth and early twentieth centuries, the Pinkerton Detective Agency became celebrated for solving any number of sensational crimes, many involving the railroads, banks, and businesses. Although its primary area of concern in the beginning was the investigation of train robberies, Pinkerton's detectives also worked on cases involving forgery, counterfeiting, and even murder. Allan Pinkerton and his band of private detectives thwarted assassination attempts on presidents such as Abraham Lincoln, chased outlaws like Butch Cassidy across the American West, apprehended international thieves like Adam Worth, foiled train robbers like Jesse James, and broke up gangs of radicals like the Molly Maguires.

> "[The detective] should be hardy, tough, and capable of laboring, in season and out of season, to accomplish, unknown to those about him, a single absorbing object. . . . able to distinguish the real from the ideal moral obligation, and pierce the vail [sic] separating a supposed from an actual state of affairs."
>
> —Allan Pinkerton, *The Molly Maguires,* 1877

At his offices at 151 Fifth Avenue in Chicago, Allan Pinkerton hung a shingle and advertised his services in newspapers across the country. His trademark was the drawing of a large, unblinking eye with the slogan "We Never Sleep," which pledged the company's indefatigable pursuit of criminals. The axiom "private eye" actually comes from Pinkerton's trademark drawing.

Pinkerton set high standards for his detectives. In his book, *Allan Pinkerton – America's First Private Eye,* author Sigmund Lavine said, "In a day when many law enforcement officers openly associated with criminals and shared their illegal profits, Pinkerton's code reflected the honesty and integrity of the man."

According to Allan Pinkerton's code, his detectives were to have no "addiction to drink, smoking, card playing, low dives or slang." And to the public and his many clients he further vowed that his detectives would accept no bribes; never compromise with criminals; work closely with local law enforcement agencies, when necessary; refuse divorce cases or cases that might create a scandal for clients; investigate public officials, jurors, or political parties; turn down reward money; and never raise fees without informing clients and keep clients appraised on a regular basis. But most of all Allan Pinkerton promised results—and he readily delivered on this promise.

> "Allan Pinkerton was well known to the members of the 19th Century underworld. They knew he was incorruptible and so was his agency. They were also well acquainted with Pinkerton's tenacity; if necessary he would chase you to the end of the earth."
>
> —James Doran, *Desperate Men,* 1962

Besides establishing the nationally and internationally known premier detective agency, Allan Pinkerton served as a Union spy during the Civil War, established the American Secret Service, hired the first woman detective, Kate Warne, and was a prolific author. The men and women hired by the Pinkerton Agency were trained through crime simulations and taught how to assume disguises in the pursuit of criminals. Agents compiled and kept huge files on suspects and created a rogue's gallery of mug shots used to identify criminals. They broke open cases through scrupulous research, including frequently dangerous undercover work and in-depth surveillance. His agency accumulated a higher number of arrests for burglaries and murders than the official police department in Chicago. Pinkerton detectives quickly acquired a reputation for their stringent, careful, and seemingly relentless pursuit of criminals.

After the war, the agency focused on rounding up an assortment of thieves, bank robbers, swindlers, confidence men, and safecrackers. The agency developed a sophisticated filing system on criminals that was later adopted as a model for other law enforcement operations, including the FBI. It also became a model for many large city law enforcement departments. In the 1880s, the Pinkertons assembled a glossary of criminal colloquialisms including words like "ditched" (getting arrested), "jimmying a bull" (shooting a police officer), "gay cat" (someone who cases banks and towns for future jobs), "mouthpiece" (lawyer), "yegg" (a bandit leader), and "fence" (a receiver of stolen goods).

In the summer of 1884, Robert Pinkerton and undercover Pinkerton detective Gustav Frank were able to successfully "ditch" the biggest "yegg" and "fence" in New York City, and there was seemingly nothing her "mouthpiece" could do to get her off. Allan Pinkerton would have been proud.

> "For 25 years, Mrs. Mandelbaum has carried on a most successful business as a receiver of stolen goods —silks, diamonds, in fact she would buy the whole swag of a burglar. She is known, at least by name, to every thief and detective in the United States, and has received plunder from nearly every city in the country secured by traveling gangs of professional thieves."
>
> —Robert Pinkerton, July 24, 1884

Frank had been schooled in undercover work by the best—Robert Pinkerton. Pinkerton showed Frank how to conceal his identity through disguise and how to create for himself a completely fictitious biography when he was questioned by Mandelbaum, which he most certainly would be. Pinkerton drilled the phony background into Frank to the point where Frank probably believed it himself. He portrayed himself as an unscrupulous silk merchant looking for bargains at any price. Pinkerton also made it abundantly clear to Frank that he was to have nothing to do with any members of the New York City police department and was not to divulge his true identity to anyone, especially the police, since the whole operation was being conducted without the knowledge of the New York City authorities. Frank, with his scruffy appearance, unruly beard, and his ability to speak German, was the perfect match for Mandelbaum.

In 1884, the City of New York, or at least those reform-minded authorities who inhabited it, wanted to be rid of Mandelbaum. For twenty five years the New York City police department had claimed that they were unable to bring Mandelbaum to justice because they couldn't build a credible case against her. No one at any level of city government or law enforcement had reason to believe this excuse. If it was true, it spoke to the police department's ineptitude, but if it wasn't, according to *The New York Times*, "it was not imbecility but interest that prevented the making of a case against the woman." It was absolutely true: it was in the best interest of politicians, judges, and law enforcement officials to keep Mandelbaum in business since her bribes lined their pockets. But in the summer of 1884, all that came to an abrupt end.

In early March 1884, New York City District Attorney Peter Olney decided it was time to put an end to the career of the country's most infamous fence and he did it by bypassing local authorities. Olney had once been part of the corrupt Tammany Hall political empire but he had become one of its most ardent foes. Olney ran for district attorney on the Tammany Hall ticket and lost. Governor Grover Cleveland appointed Olney as District Attorney in December 1883, following the resignation of District Attorney Wheeler Peckham, who resigned after less than a week in office, citing ill health. Peckham had gained notoriety when he prosecuted Tammany Hall leader, William "Boss" Tweed.

During his swearing-in ceremony in Supreme Court Chambers, Olney told reporters, "I enter upon the discharge of my duties untrammeled and without prejudices. I intend to faithfully perform every duty of the office to the satisfaction of the public as far as I can, and to the satisfaction of my own sense of what is right."

What Olney thought was right from the start was that Fredericka Mandelbaum should be put out of business once and for all.

> "Mr. Olney undoubtedly took the utmost aggressive interest in 'Mother' Mandelbaum's affairs. If his private utterances are to be believed, and there has never been, among respectable persons, a doubt in this regard, he thought that the existence of a woman who by various means had been enabled to control the most dangerous and wealthy criminal interests of America, was a burning shame. He employed the Pinkerton agency, in order to discover a plan by which either the woman might be brought to justice or her business broken up."
>
> —George Washington Walling, *Recollections of a New York Chief of Police,* 1887

Less than three months into his term, District Attorney Olney set in motion plans to at long last apprehend one of the country's most successful criminals. Mandelbaum became the prime trophy of a far-reaching reform movement in New York City that was dedicated to eliminating political corruption, crime and vice. In order to do it, Olney bypassed the New York City police department and went directly to the Pinkerton Detective Agency for help. On July 22, 1884, Mandelbaum was arrested for receiving stolen property. It was a slap in the face to her, considering her many connections and the amount of money she paid for police protection. But in fact, Mandelbaum's end didn't start with a slap in the face; it began with a punch in the nose.

> The prosperous career for twenty years of the woman MANDELBAUM as a notorious receiver of stolen goods has itself been an indictment of the police force.
>
> —*The New York Times*, July 24, 1884

On July 22, 1884, a clean-shaven Pinkerton detective, Gustav Frank, with an arrest warrant in hand, approached the carriage in front of Fredericka Mandelbaum's haberdashery shop. Inside the carriage were Mandelbaum, her twenty-four-year-old son Julius, and her most trusted confidant, Herman Stoude. Detective Frank had spent the last five months working undercover to catch Mandelbaum red-handed receiving stolen merchandise, and his efforts had paid off handsomely. He had disguised himself by growing a thick, dark beard and maintaining a slovenly appearance, one most often associated with Mandelbaum's usual criminal clientele. Stepping into the carriage flanked by a cadre of Pinkerton detectives, Frank looked nothing like the man Mandelbaum had been doing business with over the past five months, but she recognized him immediately, not as a Pinkerton detective, but as Joseph Stein, a disreputable dealer in stolen merchandise—most notably silk—Mandelbaum's favorite commodity.

"You are caught this time, and the best thing that you can do is to make a clean breast of it," Frank told Mandelbaum waving the arrest warrant in her face.

"So you are the one who is at the bottom of this, you wretch you!" Mandelbaum snapped and without the slightest pause, she reached out and punched Frank in the face, bloodying his nose. The other detectives had to restrain her from striking him again.

Mandelbaum and the two men sitting in the carriage with her, Julius and Stoude, were served with the warrant for their arrest as well. Under guard, they were all transported to the Harlem Police Court, nearly a dozen miles away on the other side of Manhattan. It was a long way, but Mandelbaum had traveled a lot further in her lifetime in both time and distance.

> Her own hands, of course, remained unsullied; she cracked no safes, picked no locks, dodged no bullets. A student of the law, she understood that uncorroborated testimony meant little, and so took care to deal with one crook at a time."
>
> —Karen Abbott, "The Life and Crimes of 'Old Mother' Mandelbaum"

In February 1884, a scruffy looking man with an unruly beard entered Marm Mandelbaum's shop and asked about purchasing silk. He introduced himself as "Joseph Stein." He was, in fact, undercover Pinkerton agent Gustav Frank, who had been working undercover trying to infiltrate Mandelbaum's organization since January. Mandelbaum had kept him at bay for nearly five months. Initially, she didn't like the idea of doing business with strangers. Mandelbaum had always surrounded herself with a bevy of talented crooks and she prided herself on being a good judge of character, especially when it came to criminals, but her association with Stein turned out to be a fatal mistake. By July 1884, when he finally arrested her, Frank had compiled enough evidence to put her away for a long time.

Before approaching Mandelbaum, Frank wanted to be fully prepared. Knowing Mandelbaum's fondness for silk, he spent several weeks with legitimate silk merchants going over bolts of silks, reacquainting himself with the silk trade and the going rates. Working with several merchants, he was shown how they devised new, hard-to-locate marks on their merchandise that could be used to identify the owner, should the property be stolen. Many legitimate silk merchants adopted this process of concealing identification into their bolts of fabric. Once he felt knowledgeable enough, he made his move. He and several other Pinkerton detectives rented rooms in an apartment across the street from Mandelbaum's shop. For more than a month, Frank and his operatives spied on the comings and goings at the shop and quickly came to the conclusion that Mandelbaum was well-liked and protected by her neighbors. On several occasions the

Pinkerton detectives saw neighbors warn Mandelbaum about police in the neighborhood and several times they witnessed police officers scuttling in and out of Mandelbaum's shop. But no one was wise to the Pinkerton operation.

Frank's surveillance of Mandelbaum's business paid off. He and his operatives discovered that no one could stand on the street near Mandelbaum's place for very long before being tailed by one of Mandelbaum's minions. The bystander would be followed until his or her identity could be uncovered and the information reported back to Mandelbaum. Someone kept watch at the front door of her shop day and night, keeping track of the comings and goings of people in the neighborhood. Thieves doing business with her never used the front door. They slipped inside her shop through a side door. Mandelbaum would only do business with thieves she knew and only they were privy to use the side door. There was another entrance to her store through a small saloon located on Rivington Street. Those wanting to do business with her were shown behind the bar and out the back door to a yard that abutted the back of Marm's haberdashery shop. There they could enter Mandelbaum's inner sanctum. Everyone in the underworld knew the routine and took their plunder to Marm either through the side entrance or the back. But it wasn't just thieves who came to Mandelbaum. Legitimate businessmen from everywhere came to her shop to buy merchandise, even though they knew they were receiving stolen goods. Mandelbaum sold her goods cheaply to dressmakers and shopkeepers all over New York, including Albany and Buffalo, and as far away as Trenton, New Jersey, and Cincinnati, Ohio.

Mandelbaum was cautious, and Frank needed to take his time to build up her confidence in him. As time went on, Mandelbaum expanded her expertise to include knowing at a glance the worth of stolen jewelry, furniture, paintings, securities, gold, silver, and any other of the spoils that her criminal clients were able to get their hands on. Besides knowing her business, Mandelbaum was a ruthless businesswoman. For stolen merchandise, she paid about 20 percent of the true price. On silks worth $3 a yard, she paid 65 cents. For camel hair shawls worth $1,000 she paid a mere $100. None of it seemed to bother her many criminal suppliers. They all knew Mandelbaum drove a hard bargain, but they also knew she had cash on hand to pay. Unloading their stolen loot to Mandelbaum was the fastest and safest way to get rid of their plunder. Some people who tried to outsmart her found out the hard way that no one was going to get the best of her in any deal.

When Gustav Frank first approached Mandelbaum he gave her the false name of Stein. He told her he wanted to buy cheap silks—very cheap. She sent him away but he came back again and again. Still, every time he asked to buy silks she refused to do business with him. None of this dissuaded Frank. His persistency finally paid off when, in the early spring of 1884, Mandelbaum decided to put Frank to the test. In June he was summoned to Mandelbaum's shop. He arrived on time as he'd been requested. Mandelbaum and her son, Julius, were going over several bolts of silk that were lying on the counter. As Frank waited, Julius suddenly exclaimed, "Hold on, Mother. This piece is marked!" He showed her where the owner's secret mark appeared on one of the bolts. She took out a pair of scissors to cut off the marking. Frank beat her to the punch by taking out his jack-knife and offered to cut off the marked strip of silk. Although he tried to cut off the marking, his knife was dull and he couldn't sever the incriminating mark. Mandelbaum cut off the strip of silk with her scissors and handed the marked portion to Frank.

"Burn it up. Don't leave it about," she told Frank. Frank excused himself and went outside. When he returned he informed Mandelbaum that he had taken care of the marked piece of silk. In fact, Frank had simply placed the marked strip of silk in his pocket. Mandelbaum still refused to do business with him, but he had passed her little test. She asked him to return later and he did. Less than a week after, Mandelbaum offered to sell Frank several bolts of silk at an outrageous price. This time it was Frank's turn to test Mandelbaum. He refused to pay the exorbitant amount, telling Mandelbaum what he thought the fabric was really worth. This seemed to impress her. He had demonstrated a keen understanding of the business, something she was sure no undercover police officer would know. Besides, given her many connections within the police force, Mandelbaum surely could easily have checked with her inside sources to find out if the authorities were engaged in some sort of sting operation. None of her police sources knew anything, and for good reason because Frank's undercover operation had not been sanctioned by the New York City Police Department. It could not be jeopardized by leaks. New York District Attorney Peter Olney had bypassed the police department, knowing that there were many officers, as well as other authorities, including judges and politicians, who had long been on Mandelbaum's payroll. Olney went directly to the Pinkertons to get the job done.

> The peculiarity and the disgrace of this case is that in New York only has the receiving and sale of stolen goods been carried on for many years as openly as if it were a legitimate industry. Mrs. MANDELBAUM'S business has been as much under the protection of the law as the business of any one of the firms whose stolen goods constituted her stock in trade. The woman's character has been known during all these years to every detective and to every police magistrate in New York . . . her intimacy with the detectives of the police force was only less close and confidential than her intimacy with the thieves . . .
>
> —*The New York Times*, July 24, 1884

Frank was eventually allowed to buy a few rolls of silk from Mandelbaum. When these disappeared without any repercussions, Mandelbaum welcomed Frank's business. He took another risky step by confiding to Mandelbaum that he was a thief and that he wanted to buy stolen goods. This obviously set well with her. She warned him about selling various bolts of fabric in New York since they had been stolen in the city and might be recognized. "Don't sell this piece in New York," Mandelbaum told her him, "because it came from one of the big stores here." Over the next month, with Frank now in Mandelbaum's confidence, he was able to buy approximately 12,000 yards of stolen silk. Pinkerton detectives were able to trace much of it back to its original owners, using the secret marks that had been hidden on the silk.

On June 16, 1884, Frank purchased five bolts of silk that were secretly marked; three belonging to the silk merchant Simpson, Crawford & Simpson, and two belonging to James A. Hearn & Son. Frank claimed he would be selling them out of state. Instead, he took them to the Pinkerton offices for examination. Henry B. Porter, a purchasing agent for Simpson, Crawford & Simpson, identified the three rolls of silk Frank had in his possession as stock belonging to his company. Porter told Pinkerton detectives that the bolts of silk had been stolen by shoplifters in June. Upon careful examination, George A. Hearn, of James A. Hearn & Son, claimed the two other bolts belonged to his company and that they too had been stolen.

Enormous amounts of silk were stolen from legitimate merchants throughout the city, Simpson and Hearn among them. According to *The New York Times*, "Some large dealers suffer a loss annually in this way from the silk department alone of $5,000 or $6,000."

With hard evidence in hand and witnesses willing to testify in court, the Pinkerton detectives applied for an arrest warrant from Justice Henry Murray at the Harlem Police Court. Murray gladly issued the warrant as well as a search warrant for Mandelbaum's shop. Following a search of her premises, where even more bolts of stolen silk were recovered, Pinkerton detectives made their arrest of Mandelbaum, her son Julius and Herman Stoude. The three defendants were whisked away to the Harlem Police Court where the bail hearing was held before Judge Murray, the justice who had initially signed the arrest warrants. The newspapers had a field day. Mandelbaum, of course, maintained her innocence. Word of Mandelbaum's arrest spread like wildfire throughout the city.

8
DISORDER IN THE COURTS

> "I have never, never stolen in my life. I feel that these charges are brought out against me for spite. I have never bribed the police or had their protection. I never gave money to any person whatsoever to bribe or influence any officials so help me God."
>
> Fredericka Mandelbaum, July 1884

Mandelbaum's indignation was clear—she was a law-abiding citizen wrongly accused, or so she claimed. Word spread quickly through the city that the notorious Marm Mandelbaum had at long last been arrested and charged, and crowds of people from the lowliest pickpocket to established citizenry flocked to court, albeit the wrong courthouse, to see for themselves. Instead of taking Mandelbaum, Julius, and Stoude to the Manhattan district court, Pinkerton agents intentionally transported the trio to the Harlem Police Court nearly a dozen miles away to appear before Judge Murray. District Attorney Olney and the agents had chosen Murray specifically because he appeared to be one of the few uncorrupted judges in the city. Several months earlier, Murray had publicly lambasted the New York City police department's widespread corruption. "Police affairs in this City were never more rotten than at present," Murray said. "Vice flaunts defiance in the public eye, and it could not become such a shame to the city if no dues were paid for its protection." Without naming names, he went on to charge that New York City police captains "upon a salary of $2,000 a year live extravagantly and become rich."

It was enough for Olney and the Pinkertons. Judge Murray was their man and they not only filed for the arrest warrants for Mandelbaum and her co-conspirators with Murray, but made it clear that she and her gang were to be taken directly to Murray's court in Harlem where Mandelbaum exercised no influence. It was well-known throughout the city that Mandelbaum's payroll included any number of judges and police officers in Manhattan. Having her taken to the Manhattan Court would have proved as futile as having the New York Police Department conduct the investigation. Olney wanted the entire investigation taken out of the hands of anyone remotely connected to either the police department or the courts. With the Pinkertons he had secured investigators who were beyond reproach and with Murray he landed a judge who could not be bribed. Justice would be done at long last. Olney's decisions, however, would not be made without controversy from the highest places.

> Mr. S. A. Noyes, an attorney of No. 64 Cedar Street, who was counsel for Mr. Scott, of Boston, in his suit last Winter against Mrs. Mandelbaum to recover the value of stolen goods received by her, which resulted in a verdict of $6,666 and costs, expressed some decided opinions yesterday as to why she had enjoyed 20 years' immunity from Prosecution. He intimated plainly that she had enjoyed protection from the police and for that reason Mr. Pinkerton was called in in the present case. "The District Attorney didn't employ Pinkerton from love of him," said Mr. Noyes. "I have an affidavit here showing that a number of detectives have visited her place for years and that they extorted money from shoplifters there."
>
> —*The New York Times*, July 24, 1884

At the Harlem Police Court, Judge Murray arraigned Mandelbaum's son Julius and Henry Stoude on charges of grand larceny. In her statement to the court, Mandelbaum said, "My arrest and detention on these charges is an outrage. I claim that the war on the police is the cause of my arrest and has created a prejudice against me of which I am the victim." She continued to take the position that she was an innocent victim in the hopes that her powerful pronouncements would activate her powerful protectors.

Mandelbaum's attorneys, the infamous William Howe and Abraham Hummel, were notified of her arrest and rushed to the Harlem Police Court. Howe, the tall, burly and more flamboyant of the partners, tendered pleas of not guilty and demanded a bail examination. Bail was set by Judge Murray at $30,000 for all three of the defendants. According to the *New York Herald,* Howe was at his sartorial best. He was bejeweled from head to toe, wearing a white vest with a rolling high collar, buttoned with a large glittering diamond below which ran a series of smaller diamond studs. Hanging from his vest was a large gold chain with a giant gold pocket-watch also encrusted with glittering diamonds. On the index finger of one hand he wore a huge diamond ring and on the other hand a Masonic ring set with diamonds. The cuffs of his shirt were buttoned with two enormous solid gold cufflinks. He wore a long dove-colored top coat with tails and carried on his arm a bright blue umbrella. The lawyer blazed and sparkled from head to foot with jeweled splendor. Hummel, who stayed in the background, was short, thin, and dour looking. He was wearing his usual drab, dark suit. He let his partner do all the sparkling and most of the talking.

A QUEEN AMONG THIEVES
MOTHER MANDELBAUM'S VAST BUSINESS.
BUYING STOLEN SILKS BY THE THOUSAND YARDS—
DEPOTS IN MANY CITIES—
BLACKMAILING DETECTIVES.

In New York City there are not over eight or nine men and women who are known as professional receivers of stolen

> goods. First in the list and standing at the head of the country as the largest dealer was Mrs. Fredericka Mandelbaum, who kept a small dry goods store on the corner of Clinton and Rivington streets, and occupied the two houses adjoining on Clinton street, and whose arrest by Pinkerton detectives on Tuesday has already been reported ... she was a remarkably shrewd business woman, so that when her husband died about nine years ago, she took charge of the business and had carried it on with marked pecuniary gain until her arrest. She has accumulated a fortune, and is the owner of several tenements . . . All the noted thieves —burglars, sneak thieves, shoplifters, second story climbers —have been connected with her at one time or another —that is, all first class thieves in their branches . . . Professional thieves held her in high estimation owing to the power she claimed to posses with the authorities.
>
> —*The New York Times*, July 24, 1884

Howe argued that the value of the silk goods, five bolts of silk in all, in the complaints against Marm, Julius and Stoude equaled only $300. Murray had set bail at $2,000 per charge, totally $10,000 per defendant. This, Howe maintained, was out and out prejudicial against his clients. He went on to cite to the judge cases involving a client charged with murder who was given a bail of a mere $500, supporting his claim that his clients were being treated differently from others and worse than murderers. "A good deal has been said against this woman. She has never been indicted," Howe contended. "Her arrest was accomplished by conspiracy. She is not imprisoned upon the evidence of the police but upon the word of a detective about whom there are rumors that he was her accomplice. It is a violation of the Constitution to demand that such excessive bail shall be given for the release of this woman, who I think, we will show, has done nothing wrong," Howe argued.

Howe dramatically asserted that the entire arrest and bail hearing was highly unusual. He complained that the district attorney had used private detectives instead of the city police force to entrap his clients and that District Attorney Olney had the warrant sworn out in Harlem Police Court, rather than in Mandelbaum's own district on the Lower East Side. Howe pointed out that Judge Murray's position on the case appeared to reflect that of the district attorney's. The case was moved to Harlem "because it was cool up here," Murray said. Still, Howe maintained that the entire proceedings were unfair including the arrest, the locale, and the high bail. Howe's argument appeared to fall on deaf ears. Mandelbaum was a special case—it had taken authorities twenty years to finally get her charged before the courts, and she was, in the mind of both the judge and the prosecutor, a flight risk. Murray denied he had done anything irregular, although Howe had a point about the proceedings being held in Harlem and the amount of the bail far exceeding the severity of the crime. Ultimately Murray set bail at $5,000 for Julius Mandelbaum and Herman Stoude and $10,000 for Fredericka.

CRIME AND THE POLICE

> It is hoped that the arrest of the woman MANDELBAUM will secure the ending of a scandal which has for years been a reproach to this city, and especially to the police force. The woman has really been for more than twenty years the nucleus and centre of the whole organization of crime in New-York. She is believed to have furnished the capital without which extensive enterprises even of theft cannot be carried on. . . . It will, however, have a very wholesome effect upon malefactors of the same class as Mother MANDELBAUM in admonishing them that they are not entirely secure from justice, even after they have arranged for police protection."
>
> —*New York Times* editorial, July 24, 1884

Despite the reduction in bail, Howe still maintained it was an incredibly high amount considering the facts and the facts, as far as Howe articulated them to the court were that Mrs. Mandelbaum had never been indicted on any crime previously and that the charges against her were not predicated on any police investigation but based "upon the word of a detective about whom there are rumors that he was her accomplice." Murray, however, would not be swayed.

Howe turned his attention next to Mandelbaum's son, Julius. According to Howe, receiving stolen goods was not an offense under the law if there was no knowledge that they were stolen. He argued that Julius was simply doing what his mother asked of him as any good son would. Howe called for all the charges against Julius to be tossed out. "There is no evidence to show that he had possession of the property. It was his mother who owned it," Howe said. "The poor boy was simply doing what his Mama asked."

Assistant District Attorney Leroy Gove jumped to his feet to protest. "He's hardly a boy," Gove proclaimed loudly.

"Why, you're a boy," Howe retorted, winking at Gove, "an old boy."

According to Howe, Julius Mandelbaum was an upstanding, hardworking young man, and he pressed the judge to release him. Gove again objected and told the judge that it was an insult to the courts that Howe would suggest such a motion. Howe tore into the prosecutor with his usual dramatic flair. "As long as I live and have my faculties, I shall never deem it an insult to an intelligent man to submit a proposition of law which my mind tells me is correct," he told the court. "There is not a judge on the Supreme Bench who would not think as I do," he went on. "It is not an offense to receive stolen goods. It is a common mistake to think that it is. Receiving stolen goods is not an offense until you show a guilty knowledge of their having been stolen. Indeed, under the law this was true, and that was one of the reasons that the district attorney had hired the Pinkertons in the first place and why they had instituted a sting, to catch Mandelbaum red-handed and with knowledge that the goods were stolen."

Again, Murray was not swayed, although he remained amused by Howe's antics. Murray reminded Howe that the proceedings in the Harlem Police Court were only to set bail and decide whether Mandelbaum and her cohorts should be brought to trial. It did not escape anyone that the mere fact that she was in court facing charges was a colossal situation, not only for Mandelbaum but for the system that had sheltered her from arrest for decades.

"Your Honor's experience must tell you that the son in the house of his mother will always do her bidding. He is but an instrument, this boy," Howe argued to the court.

Recognizing that Judge Murray would not be swayed, Howe tried another tactic. He told the court that Mrs. Mandelbaum would post bail for her son.

"I don't think I could accept that," Murray said. "I don't think it is proper to take one of the defendants as bail for the other."

Howe protested, wanting to know on what grounds the judge was refusing Mandelbaum's bail for her son. "She is as good bail as ever you took," he informed Murray. "She will never disappear, rest assured, till her case is disposed."

Still Murray refused.

"On what principle should bail be refused if her property satisfies you?" Howe clamored. "Has she been guilty of any offense? She has been charged with one. I tell your Honor that she is worth $30,000 in real estate in this city. All you ought to desire is the security of his attendance. Anything beyond that is persecution," he said.

Murray remained steadfast. He declined to release Julius or allow his mother to pay his bail. By then Howe was red-faced, rocking impatiently back onto his heels, his voice booming. "The question is whether the security is sufficient. It is immaterial by whom it is offered," Howe bellowed. "If Mr. Jay Gould or some of these Wall-street magnates—some of those at least who have been committing frauds which have hurt the community more than a thousand Fredericka Mandelbaums—I say, if they can go bail for anybody, on what ground can you refuse Mrs. Mandelbaum? I tell you Judge Murray, I want your clerk to record it on your papers that I offered $30,000 on good property. It doesn't matter whether it is Mrs. Mandelbaum or Jay Gould who is the bailor. Constitutional rights cannot be infringed. In God's name let us have equal justice!"

"There is an indecent look about it," Murray informed him. "It is not customary."

"Property cannot be bail," Gove said rising to his feet, "except in one instance where the money itself is placed in the hands of the Chamberlain."

"Please wait a moment," Howe cutting Gove off with a dramatic flourish.

"I won't wait," Gove shot back.

"Then I suspect the court will make you wait," Howe said dismissing the young attorney.

"Gentlemen, don't get excited," Murray said. He allowed Gove to argue his point.

Howe removed himself to the table where his clients sat and with his legendary flair, he made it a point to disregard anything the prosecution had to say. Sitting at the defense table, Howe snapped open a newspaper as if he were reading it without even the mildest interest in what Gove had to say.

Gove, however, would not be rattled by Howe's theatrics and proceeded to give the judge his interpretation of the bail matter. "Bail is simply this," he said. "Instead of the prisoner being put in jail he is handed over to the custody of his surety, who stands to the law in the place of jailor, and is the jailor of the prisoner, and may haul him round as though he had him attached by a string which he could pull when he chose. Your Honor can refuse bail to anyone who is not competent to act as custodian, no matter what that person's wealth may be. You have a right to reject Mrs. Mandelbaum."

An elderly gentleman named Jonas Briggs, who claimed to be a retired merchant, asked to approach the bench. Briggs offered to put up the bail for Julius Mandelbaum. He claimed to the judge that although he did not know the Mandelbaums, as a good Christian, he was offering to pay the bail out of the goodness of his heart. Although Gove protested, Murray could do nothing but accept the bail money from Mr. Briggs. Several other people came forward offering to pay the bail for both Mrs. Mandelbaum as well as Herman Stoude. Judge Murray questioned all of them including a Mrs. Catherine Dupont and her daughter Susan Chambetta, two respectable women who lived in the Lower East Side who had offered to put up the bail, perhaps put up to it by Mandelbaum. Mrs. Dupont only spoke French so her daughter had to interpret for her. She claimed her home was worth more than $25,000, but Murray still refused to accept her offer. Her daughter explained that she and her mother would put up their combined property as bail claiming that together the properties were worth $50,000, surely enough to cover the bail amount. Murray asked the two women to produce the deeds to their properties. An irate Howe could hardly contain himself. "Better bail than Mrs. Dupont was never offered," he blustered. "It does creep out that there is something different in this case from anything in any other case."

Ultimately Judge Murray accepted bail in the amount of $15,000 for the release of Mrs. Mandelbaum and Herman Stoude from George Speckhardt, a baker whose shop was located in Mandelbaum's neighborhood. Murray continued the case to July 25.

HER SON JULIUS BAILED MRS. MANDELBAUM REFUSED AS SURETY BY THE JUSTICE MR. BRIGGS ACTS ON AN IMPULSE AND THE YOUNG HOPEFUL IS RELEASED—THE OLD LADY AFRAID OF THE ARTISTS

When Mrs. Fredericka Mandelbaum, the alleged "mother" of professional thieves, walked slowly into the room her

> every step awakening an echo. The woman's face was pale and her remarkably large sensual features with their high cheek bones and big protruding under lip, were shown off conspicuously by a jaunty black bonnet, the feathers of which stood erect like quills upon the fretful porcupine.... She was deeply embarrassed owing to the attempts which a number of energetic sketchers outside had made to take her portrait and kept her face averted during the examination, occasionally putting a handkerchief before her eyes. On the seat beside her was a youth of 24 years of age who wore green trousers, a brown coat and a small moustache. This was Julius Mandelbaum, his mother's assistant....
>
> —*The New York Times*, July 26, 1884

Although they were eventually bailed, Mandelbaum, her son, and Stoude were not off the hook for long. They were scheduled to appear in court on July 25 for a hearing on whether the case should go to trial. The decision that needed to be made was whether the district attorney's office case was strong enough to be transferred to the Court of General Sessions, where felony charges, like those lodged against Mandelbaum, were heard. The defendants were facing seven counts of second-degree grand larceny, and one of receiving stolen merchandise. The fate of the case would be determined by Judge Henry Murray alone. There was no jury.

The Harlem Police Court where Murray presided was one of seven police courts in the city where a variety of minor misdemeanor cases were heard. Under normal circumstances the judge would call on the prosecuting police officer to state the charges against the defendant and then allow the defendant to respond. These charges typically included public drunkenness, vagrancy, and petty theft. The judge would then make a decision to either sign over the defendant to jail, issue him a fine, or release him. This process usually took a matter of minutes. If the police officer making the arrest was not present to make his case against the defendant, the defendant would be released automatically. The judge would then move quickly on to the next case. If the judge was not able to get through the long list of defendants appearing before him during a particular session, the prisoners would be summarily led away to spend the night in the Tombs and brought back before the judge the next day. According to author Cait Murphy's in *Scoundrels in Law,* "Given the volume of cases, multitasking was common. Judges might be hearing evidence, signing over a prisoner to jail, and tossing off vulgar comments pretty much simultaneously—all this in a room crowded with the ill-behaved, and often drunk, effluvia of urban life."

But Mandelbaum's hearing was not a typical case in any respect. First, testimony in the case took two full days. Secondly, the courtroom was like a three-ring circus, packed with a colorful collection of spectators, not the least of which was Mandelbaum's larger-than-life attorney, William Howe. *The New York Times* described the infamous attorney as "a Maypole of more than ordinary circumference." On this day in July, Howe was wearing a bright green suit with a blue sash wrapped around his considerable waist, and a green, checked shirt adorned with an array of glittering diamond shirt studs of different sizes. Spectators included an array of legitimate business owners and merchants representing everyone from second-hand clothing dealers to more prominent upscale clothing enterprises, dry goods proprietors, wine merchants, newspaper reporters, police officers, and, of course, a collection of seedy, small-time thugs and thieves. It was a packed house. Detective Gustav Frank and his boss, Robert Pinkerton, sat near Assistant District Attorney Leroy Gove, while Mandelbaum, her son, and Stoude sat at the defendant's table beside her attorneys, Howe and Hummel.

BULLDOZING THE COURT MRS. MANDELBAUM'S LAWYER REBUKED BY JUDGE MURRAY THE QUEEN OF FENCES HELD FOR TRIAL AND HER DEFENSE OF THE POLICE FORCE STRICKEN FROM THE RECORD

> The solemn silence which had been brooding for fully a half and hour over the motley crowd in the Harlem Police Court was suddenly dissipated at 3 o'clock yesterday afternoon. All the figurants in the Mandelbaum case were in their accustomed places, and had ceased to attract more than casual attention, when Mr. Howe made his appearance upon the scene. Then it was that a titter was heard at the back of the room, which was gradually extended until it reached the judicial bench, where it would go no further. The cause of this slight ripple of mirth was Mr. Howe's personal appearance, or, in other words, his "get up."
>
> —*The New York Times*, July 31, 1884

The flashily dressed Howe wasted no time attacking the prosecution's case and laying the groundwork for his defense—that Mrs. Mandelbaum was an honest shopkeeper who was caught in the middle of an ongoing battle between the district attorney's office and the police. Howe began by reading into evidence Mandelbaum's signed statement:

"My name is Frederika Mandelbaum and I am 52 years old. I am a widow and live at No. 79 Clinton-street, New York City. I have resided there with my children for 20 years. I keep a dry good store and have done so for 20 years past. I buy and sell dry goods as other dry goods people do. I have never knowingly bought stolen goods, neither did my son Julius." At this point, it was reported, Attorney Howe managed to conjure up tears in his eyes.

"I and my son are innocent of these charges preferred against us," he read aloud. "I never knew that any one piece of the silk was stolen, nor do I believe it was. I got the property now produced—the subjects of these charges—in an honest and business-like way. I insist on being discharged. Herman Stoude was my employee, and was in no way responsible for the buying or selling of anything in my store. He was simply a clerk to open and close the store, arrange the goods, wait on the customers, and obey my orders. My arrest and detention on these charges is an outrage. I claim that the war on the police is the cause of my arrest, and has created a prejudice against me, of which I am the victim. I say that in many respects the testimony of the witness Frank is false, and he knows it to be so. I say that I will not be the cat's paw to suffer because there is a feud and a fight against the police and other officers. I am innocent of the crimes charged against me, and say that they are preferred simply to attack the police. There are, I believe, very many retail dry goods dealers who innocently purchase goods which may be stolen."

When Howe stopped he noticed the court stenographer had stopped writing down the statement and was sitting back in his chair with his pencil resting behind his ear.

"I'll have that taken down word for word," Howe bellowed at the stenographer. "If you doubt my right to do so I'll refer you to section 198 of the Criminal Code."

Judge Murray chimed in, "What have the police to do with this lady's statement?"

"She made her defense according to the statute. If she has to bring the President of the United States, she has a right to do it in her own defense," Howe shot back.

Judge Murray wasn't buying it. He refused to direct the stenographer to resume writing.

"This is the reply she gives and which the magistrate must take down in answer to the question, what she has to say. She may say anything she thinks proper according to the statute," Howe imperiously instructed the judge.

"I don't think it was ever meant that a person could make a slanderous statement in her defense. When she says there is a feud existing between herself and other officials, I say that it is not true," Murray argued.

Howe was furious. "How do you know?" he roared at the judge.

"As far as this case is concerned, it is not true," Murray responded calmly. "I say so."

"You say it is not true?" Howe grilled the judge. "Does your Honor undertake to know what is going on out of court?"

"No," Murray snapped. "I mean as regards the evidence in court. You cannot introduce irrelevant and outside matters."

"Bring in the Criminal Code," Howe demanded.

"Bring it in," Judge Murray said unperturbed.

"Now, here it is. Section 198 Criminal Code," Howe said holding the law book in one hand, raising aloft his other hand, and gesturing dramatically as he read aloud. "If the witness chooses to make a statement the magistrate must proceed to take it in writing, without oath, and must put to the witness the following questions only: What is your name and age? Where were you born? Where do you reside? What is your business or profession? Give any explanation you think proper."

"I think that means only on the charges," Murray said.

"What do you think doesn't matter?" Howe asked.

"I won't have it taken down, except so far as it bears upon this case," Murray said.

"You will take it down or be liable for impeachment!" Howe bellowed.

The court went dead silent. All eyes were on Judge Murray, anticipating his response to Howe's threat.

"I am willing to take down any statement she might make in relation to the case against her, but I am not willing and will not permit any statement to be taken down in relation to another subject which there is no evidence at all," Murray said, his voice barely above a whisper.

"How do you know whether we are not going to give evidence?" Howe shot back at the judge.

"Give it then," Murray advised him.

"I make this motion, and I desire that the stenographer take it down," Howe railed. "I move that the defendant, pursuant to section 198 of the Code of Criminal Procedure, be permitted to make to each charge against her the explanation she thinks proper of the circumstances bearing on the testimony against her and to state any fact which she thinks will tend to her exculpation."

"*Any* fact," Murray said emphasizing the words.

"Yes, sir," Howe said glowing in triumph. His triumph, however, was short-lived.

"The motion is denied," Murray said.

"You deny it?" a startled Howe asked.

"I do," Murray said.

"You refuse to let her make it?"

"I refuse to let her make a stump speech," Murray said.

"You must not speak like that to me," Howe stammered, his face glowing red with anger and frustration. "In a court room it is improper."

"I say it," Murray replied steadfastly.

"It is very disgusting, very indecent, very injudicious," Howe shouted at the judge.

"I say it and I shall not take it back," Murray said.

A slight twitter moved through the crowd of spectators. Howe had finally been put in his place by the soft-spoken judge. It was a rare occurrence in the lawyer's career.

"It shall go on the record," Howe said softening his tone.

"Let it go where it ought," Murray responded, this time his voice rising. "Any statement that his defendant desires to make, either herself or through her counsel, she is at liberty to make. I shall not allow her to bring public matters, which have no relation whatever with the complaint, into her defense."

"Do you mean that she shall give some answers and some statements, and that the portion which is disagreeable to the court shall be expunged?" Howe asked.

"She must confine herself to the evidence given in court," Murray said and ordered the statement to be read again.

"Now, is the stenographer ready?" Howe taunted the judge and the anxious stenographer.

Howe read Mandelbaum's statement through a second time, uninterrupted until he came to the words, "I never bribed the police."

Murray ordered the words stricken form the court record.

"I never needed their protection," Howe read aloud.

"Strike it out," Murray ordered.

"I never gave to any person any money," Howe read.

"Strike it out," Murray said.

"I claim the war on the police is the cause of my arrest," Howe read.

"Strike it out."

"The Justice desires that to be stricken out?" exclaimed Howe.

"It shall be stricken out," Murray replied sternly.

"For the present you mean?" Howe asked slyly.

"At least as far as I'm concerned," Murray said.

"Very well put," Howe said flippantly. "There is another court." Howe went back to reading before the judge could respond. "It has created a prejudice against me of which I am the victim."

"Strike it out," Murray replied.

"Is that to be stricken out? Poor victim!" Howe said playing to the crowd. Laughter erupted in the court.

Howe continued reading the statement aloud until Murray again stopped him.

"Now, strike out from the word cat's-paw to police," Murray ordered.

"Very well," Howe said shrugging his massive shoulders. "I wish we could get hold of the cat's-paw in this case. We will do so before we're through." The phrase "cat's-paw" originated from the "The Monkey and the Cat" written by French fabulist and seventeenth-century poet Jean de La Fontaine. It refers to the unwitting use of one person by another person to accomplish his own goal.

The courtroom again burst into a smattering of laughter and slight applause over Howe's courtroom performance. It was not just through Mandelbaum's signed statement that Howe tried to plant the seeds of doubt concerning a feud between the district attorney's office and the police. During his questioning of Pinkerton detective Gustav Frank, Howe rifled off a series of incriminating questions.

"Were you ever told that it was necessary to get Mrs. Mandelbaum arrested in order that Inspector Byrnes and the Police Commissioners might be attacked?" he quizzed Frank, not giving the detective a chance to answer. "Did the DA's office tell you there was a feud with Inspector Byrnes?" he asked. "Did you ever see any of the municipal police at Mrs. Mandelbaum's?" he continued to badger the witness. At the heart of the attack on the police department, aside from what everyone knew already, were the comments made by Mandelbaum herself in court. Following the bail hearing, Mandelbaum, Julius, and Stoude, were released. After returning home to take care of her business and other household responsibilities, Mandelbaum met with her attorneys to plot their legal defense. Although she had no reason to believe that her arrest was anything more than a minor inconvenience and would be taken care of as everything had been in the past, her second attorney Abraham Hummel was less optimistic. His concern was that unlike previous attempts to apprehend Mandelbaum, this time the New York police department hadn't been involved, which meant whomever she had on her payroll in the department couldn't help her. Besides that, there was a public uproar, fed by the newspapers, demanding her arrest and conviction. More so, the newspapers kept a steady drum beat attacking the police department for either sheer incompetence or corruption. In either case, Hummel was right in assuming that this time, unlike the past, things would be different. Even with several judges on her payroll, Mandelbaum might not be able to squirm out of the charges, since District Attorney Olney had seen to it that Mandelbaum's case would not be heard by any of the judges in her debt but by judges like Murray, who were seemingly incorruptible.

CRIME AND THE POLICE

> Mrs. MANDELBAUM'S business has been as much under the protection of the law as the business of any one of the firms whose stolen goods constituted her stock and trade. . . . this woman's store was the recognized exchange of stolen goods . . . her intimacy with the detectives of the police force was only less close and confidential than her intimacy with the thieves.
>
> —*The New York Times*, July 24, 1884

If Hummel had a feeling of apprehension about the case, it did not rub off on his more colorful partner, William Howe. Howe maintained his usual prideful demeanor, asserting that he could beat the rap, like all the cases he had previously handled for Mandelbaum. In fact, he had already devised what he felt was a surefire defense. By depicting his client as a mere pawn in an ongoing political battle between the district attorney's office and the police department, he would be able to shift the attention off Mandelbaum and onto Olney and the police, although Judge Murray was able to dilute Howe's attacks by striking much of Mandelbaum's testimony from the record.

> "Here's how!
> And there's Hummel!"
>
> —An amusing toast, frequently uttered in drinking establishments during the late 1800s

Howe's line of defense was that Mandelbaum was a legitimate business woman with no criminal record and a pillar of the business community, as hundreds of shopkeepers would testify, who had been dragged into this turf battle between the district attorney and the police. According to Howe, the politically ambitious Olney was merely trying to show up the police department and in doing so, feather his own political nest. The district attorney's office had already played right into Howe's hand by both privately and publicly insinuating that the police force was riddled with corrupt officers, from the cop on the beat to some of the highest officials. The police department fired back that Olney's office was filled with political hacks intent on achieving higher office at any price. Even Robert Pinkerton got into the act by leaking an affidavit to the newspapers taken from Mollie Hoey, the sister of James Hoey, who had acted as a go-between for Mandelbaum in the civil case filed by Boston shopkeeper James Scott and who later testified against Mandelbaum during the civil matter. The affidavit maintained that a detective sergeant named Dusenbury was a frequent visitor to Mandelbaum's shop and that he was even involved in standing watch during the transportation and sale of stolen goods within the place. According to Hoey's affidavit, during one occurrence, Dusenbury informed Mandelbaum that his wife needed some black silk. Hoey reportedly told Dusenbury that she knew that Mandelbaum didn't have any on hand at the time. When Dusenbury was informed of the situation, he demanded that Hoey get her hands on some. When she told the officer that there was no way of getting it without stealing it, Dusenbury reportedly said he didn't care how she got it. According to Hoey's affidavit, Dusenbury got the silk his wife wanted and took it free of charge, even after being told that it had been stolen. Howe's plan of pitting the district attorney's office against the much maligned police department was starting to look like it would work—almost.

> "All the official detectives were better known by sight to professional thieves and their accomplices than they were to the Police Commissioners."
>
> —Seth Hawley, Esq., Chief Clerk, July 29, 1884

If Howe's attack on the district attorney's office and the police didn't sway the judge, it did rile the police department who responded publicly to the charges of corruption. The arrest of Mandelbaum by Pinkerton detectives was an embarrassment to the New York City police department. According to the *New York World*, it was "the most effective snub which the municipal police have probably ever received. It shows that the District Attorney had no confidence in them." The case opened up a Pandora's Box in the relationship between the police and the district attorney's office and what followed was a very public mudslinging battle between them.

9
MUDSLINGING

"Really, none of the attacks upon the police are more injurious to it than these official defenses."

—*The New York Times*, July 29, 1884

In an opening salvo between the police department and the district attorney's office the New York City Police Commissioners fired off a letter to the district attorney's office a day after the hearing, demanding to know what if any evidence the DA had that somehow implicated the police department in wrongdoing. The letter was addressed to District Attorney Peter Olney.

> DEAR SIR: It appears by publication in the newspapers that charges injurious to the Police Department are made concerning improper and scandalous transactions between members of the police force, who are not named, and Mrs. Mandelbaum. It is alleged that there are in your possession of affidavits or written statements which corroborate the statements in the newspapers. This board would be much obliged if you would send copies, or would allow us to take copies, of such affidavits to enable it to take immediate proceedings against any and all members who may be charged with such reprehensible proceedings. The board trusts that you will be willing to this extent to aid in bringing to . . . punishment any member of the force who may be found to be guilty. Please advise the board at your earliest convenience whether you will furnish copies of such papers and statements or allow this department to cause them to be copied in your office.

By order of the Board of Police.
S. C. HAWLEY, Chief Clerk.

THE POLICE WROUGHT UP INSPECTOR BYRNES ORDERED TO INVESTIGATE THE CHARGES AGAINST THEM

In reply to the letter sent on Friday to the District Attorney's office with reference to certain accusations made against the detective force in connection with the arrest of Mrs. Mandelbaum for receiving stolen goods the following communication was received by the Commissioners yesterday:

July 25, 1884

S.C. Hawley, Esq. Chief Clerk of the Board of Police:

SIR: I have the honor to acknowledge the receipt of your communication of this date addressed to the Hon. Peter B. Olney, District Attorney. In reply I beg leave to state that, in the absence of Mr. Olney, who is at present out of the city, I am unable to give you any information on the subject therein referred to. On his return I shall submit the letter to him, and have no doubt that an early reply will be forwarded to your department. Truly yours,

EDWARD L. PARRIS
Acting District Attorney
—*The New York Times*, July 27, 1884

A spokesman for the district attorney's office reported that although they had in their possession a statement explaining fully why the police department was not used in the arrest of Marm Mandelbaum, they asserted that the document could not be released until Olney returned. The spokesman, responding to the letter sent by the Police Commissioners, told reporters that in reference to calling in Pinkerton detectives rather than relying on the police department, even Police Superintendent George Walling had said at one time that the police had not been able to prove a case against Mandelbaum in the course of some twenty years. The statement only further added fuel to a very public and nasty fight between District Attorney Olney's office and the police department.

It was hoped by reformers in the city that the arrest of Mandelbaum would at long last put an end to not only her role as the "Queen among Thieves," but it would lay bare the scandal regarding the police department's ongoing behavior toward Mandelbaum and many other known criminals who had haunted the city for so long. The police commissioners responded quickly to Mandelbaum's charges on July 27, adopting a resolution that was sent immediately to the district attorney's office. The resolution read:

> *Whereas,* It appears by newspaper reports that certain charges and allegations have been made against members of the police force connected with the Detective Bureau; and
>
> *Whereas,* This Board is desirous that any and all members of the force shall be tried, and, if found guilty, to be dismissed from the force or otherwise punished, The Board, on the 25th instant, addressed a letter to the District Attorney asking for information, to which a reply was received Now, therefore, for the purposes of obtaining full information in relation to the subject matter, it is
>
> *Resolved,* That the Inspector in charge of the Detective Bureau be and is hereby directed to report in writing at an early day all the acts and proceeding within his knowledge, which may enable the Board of Police to decide to what extent, if any, the force under his command is censurable for the acts done or committed in the case referred to; and that he also investigate and report in relation to the character and

source of the embarrassments which attend the performance of detective duties, to the end that the Board may take any measures as shall be deemed proper to encourage and protect the members of the force in all cases in the prompt and vigorous discharge of their responsible duties, and punish such as shall fail to properly discharge such duties.

A NUT FOR THE POLICE COMMISSIONERS

District Attorney Olney yesterday sent the following communication to the Board of Police Commissioners in reply to their note requesting information as to the charges against the police in the Mandelbaum case:

DEAR SIR: Your note addressed to me by direction of the Board of Police, was received at this office, and its receipt acknowledged by my assistant Mr. Parris in my absence. I am now, and shall be at all times, desirous to aid in the correction of any abuses which may exist in the police force in any of its branches. But, in view of the proceedings and investigation still pending, it is my judgment, as prosecuting officer charged with the conduct of these matters, that the public interests would suffer should I at the present time comply with the request contained in your note. I am yours,

PETER B. OLNEY
District Attorney

—*The New York Times*, August 2, 1884

The investigation into the alleged police corruption fell to Chief Inspector Thomas Byrnes. Byrnes immediately called together several police captains and officers and conducted a series of interviews with them. When asked by a *New York Times* reporter, "Is the district attorney's office one of the embarrassments besetting the performance of the detective duties?" Byrnes responded cryptically, "We will find out now. We want to get at what is the matter."

Police Commissioner James Mathews was more forthcoming regarding the charges and ongoing investigation. The charges of police corruption, according to Mathews, who had been appointed commissioner in 1881, were "groundless, but we will do our best to find out." Mathews told reporters, "I think the District Attorney ought not to be hasty in condemning a department on the evidence of a convicted felon. He ought to be slow to cast discredit on men who have charge of the property and lives of the citizens of a great city like this. On the contrary, he ought to aid the police to the extent of his ability, and whenever they are derelict, report the facts to this Board, that they may be punished or dismissed from the force. I very much mistake the character for fairness of Mr. Olney, if he does not at an early day publicly correct, as far as his office is concerned, any charge reflecting upon the efficiency of the detective force. Disaster to the public interests must follow unless the arresting and prosecuting authorities concur and act together."

Byrnes filed a report with the police commissioners saying that he had found no wrongdoing on behalf of the police department.

NEW YORK OFFICIALS AT WAR
INSPECTOR BYRNES'S SCATHING PRESENTMENT OF THE DISTRICT ATTORNEY'S OFFICE

Relating to the charges alleged against the Detective Police force in New York by the District Attorney, especially in reference to the Mother Mandelbaum case, Inspector Byrnes made the following report to the Police Board yesterday:

GENTLEMEN—I have the honor to submit herewith a report in response to your resolution of July 26, a portion of which calls for an investigation and report in relation to the character of the embarrassments in which attend

> the performance of detective duty in this city. In describing some of the difficulties connected with the proper administration of the Detective Bureau, it is desirable that the misstatements and misrepresentations recently published should be corrected, and also that the District Attorney, Peter P. Olney, and his assistant, Henry G. Allen, are not only antagonistic to the Detective Bureau and the Police Department, but in their official capacity are enemies of the public good. . . .
>
> —*Brooklyn Eagle*, August 3, 1884

No one expected anything less from Byrnes's report, although no one expected his report to be so openly hostile toward the district attorney's office. William Howe had succeeded in turning the tables on both the police and the district attorney. Instead of focusing on Mandelbaum, they were at each other's throats. Byrnes's report went on to call into question the district attorney's relationship with "disreputable lawyers and convicted felons," for the sole purpose of "defaming the character of honest, trustworthy and efficient officers." According to Byrnes the ongoing hostility toward the police department by Olney and his offices only contributed to the "defeat of the ends of justice . . ."

Byrnes reiterated the claim that Olney's office had been reluctant or unable to produce sufficient evidence to support his claim that police officers and detectives acted inappropriately in the Mandelbaum case. "From the time I was assigned to the command of the Detective Bureau in March 1880, the house of Mrs. Mandelbaum has been constantly under surveillance," Byrnes claimed. He went on to charge that Assistant District Attorney Allen had been protecting known criminals. According to Byrnes, during his interrogation of a well-known robber, who confessed to doing business with Mandelbaum, the robber stated to him that he was protected by police prosecution by his friend Allen from the district attorney's office and that he never did any business except under the advice of Allen. He confessed to

Byrnes that Allen always removed any legal obstructions and that he always consulted Allen before engaging in any criminal activity making sure to get Allen's blessing beforehand.

MR. OLNEY'S BOOMERANG INSPECTOR BYRNES ON THE DISTRICT ATTORNEY'S OFFICE MR. ALLEN'S SHADY FRIENDS—THE WAY HE ASSISTED (?) JUSTICE—HOW THE HOEY AFFIDAVITS WERE OBTAINED

I [Byrnes] first learned Mollie Hoey had made statements against members of the department through the boasting of her consort, "Jimmy" Hoey, in various disreputable places which are the resort of thieves. He claimed that the District Attorney had promised her immunity from punishment if she would make certain statements against police officers and other officials. He also stated that at the request of Mr. Allen he should corroborate what she said.... Next day (Sunday) a disreputable lawyer, Samuel A. Noyes, of No. 62 Cedar-street, and Mr. Jordan, a stenographer attached to the District Attorney's office went to her and obtained statements from her against detective officers and others . . . Samuel Noyes once tried unsuccessfully to compromise a case of a bank robber, Jordan, with Inspector Byrnes. "It is only recently," continues the Inspector, "that Daniel Noyes (the brother of Samuel Noyes) met a gentleman at Long Branch and asked him if he had the New-York papers on our detective force. He replied that he had. Noyes said: Well they brought it all on themselves. My brother had a suit against a woman named Mandelbaum for $6,666, and the detectives could have made her "settle" if they felt so disposed. They did not do so and now he's getting even.... You have been a long while in the Police Department and ought to know better than to insist on having a case tried when we don't want it tried, and the

> best thing you can do is to have nothing more to say about it . . ."
>
> —*The New York Times*, August 3, 1884

According to Byrnes, Olney's condemnation of the detective bureau and himself had to do with politics—Olney was a Democrat and he (Byrnes) was a Republican who had not agreed to help Olney during a past election. "That the District Attorney may have a personal dislike for me I can readily understand, for at one time he discovered that he could not use me in my official capacity for his own political advancement," Byrnes said. All told, it was a damning indictment against the district attorney's office but the more Byrnes and the police department attacked the district attorney's office, without providing a reasonable explanation why Fredericka Mandelbaum was able to conduct her illegal operations for twenty years without prosecution, the more public sympathy shifted away from Mandelbaum. Neither the public nor the newspapers, fed up with what they saw as police corruption, bought into Byrnes's attack and soon both Byrnes and the police department found themselves on the defensive.

> Mr. HAWLEY 'did not know why it was that the District Attorney's office acted in a way to evince hostility.' And yet there is a plausible explanation. It is that a District Attorney may sometimes be an eccentric person who honestly means to do his duty and enforce the laws. It would be interesting to know how such a person could fail to 'evince hostility' toward the Police Department."
>
> —*The New York Times*, July 29, 1884

Olney's public response to Byrnes's charges was swift, thorough, and damning. He began by dispelling any charge of wrong-doing as far as Mollie Hoey was concerned. According to Olney no application for a pardon had been sought for Hoey as compensation for her testimony against either Mandelbaum or the police department. "I was informed that both Mollie Hoey and her husband, James Hoey, were both willing to give me all the information in their power relative to the Mandelbaum woman and her methods and ways of carrying on her criminal practices," Olney said. He then did his best to debunk Byrne's charges against him. "The Inspector makes some other allegations against me which are not only trashy in their nature, but untrue," Olney said. "I never asked him at that or any other time to do anything in any manner improper. The question of his politics has nothing to do with this matter." According to Olney, "I always understood that he was a Republican, though the question of his politics has nothing to do with this matter."

He went on to say that regarding the charges Byrnes made against Deputy Assistant Henry C. Allen that, "and other matters in the office which occurred prior to my becoming its chief, Mr. Allen, who is of age, can speak for himself." Olney went on to defend Allen, however, by saying he'd been told by many sources that "Mr. Allen was more accomplished and learned in the criminal law than any man . . . at the Bar in the city. . . . I have found Mr. Allen at all times energetic, industrious, intelligent and zealous in the discharge of his duties."

GIVING THE LIE DIRECT MR. OLNEY'S ANSWER TO INSPECTOR BYRNES WHY HE DID NOT EMPLOY THE POLICE—THE PERSECUTION OF MOLLIE HOEY—WHITEWASHING MR. ALLEN

"The Inspector inquires whether it is in accordance with my ideas of justice and public policy that public officers should be charged in the press with atrocious crimes and not have the opportunity of refuting the charge. My answer to that is, those charges have been made in the public press in considerable detail, and if the Police Board is anxious to investigate them, why don't they do so? They would seem to be of a sufficiently serious nature to demand their attention."

—*The New York Times*, August 5, 1884

Perhaps most damning to the police department was Olney's explanation why he had hired Pinkerton detectives rather than go to the police in his effort to finally apprehend Mandelbaum. According to Olney he had many reasons. First and foremost it was because of Superintendent Walling's statement that the police had been unable to arrest Mandelbaum. And if that wasn't enough, according to Olney, there was the incident involving James Hoey. Hoey had been threatened by the police before the civil trial against Mandelbaum. Hoey was told that if he testified against Mrs. Mandelbaum that his wife, Mollie, who was then incarcerated in Boston on other charges, would be brought back to New York to be tried on more serious charges. After Hoey did testify in the case where the jury found Mandelbaum guilty, unbeknownst to Olney, a detective was sent by direction of the Detective Bureau to Boston to extradite Mollie Hoey to New York. The police department's ineptitude in arresting Mandelbaum over the years, their overt hostility toward the district attorney's office, and the department's behavior toward Hoey and his wife were all good enough reasons, Olney maintained, to circumvent the usual police channels in apprehending Mandelbaum.

Without consulting with the district attorney's office, the police department had decided unilaterally to transport Mollie Hoey from Boston back to New York City where she was incarcerated. The police reportedly wished to send Mollie Hoey to Riker's Island located in the East River between Queens and the Bronx. Women prisoners were held at Riker's. The island was bought by New York City from the Riker family in 1884 for $180,000. According to Olney, the police had taken steps against Mollie Hoey in retaliation for her husband's testimony against Mandelbaum in the previous civil case.

> The confession of Superintendent Walling that twenty-five years had been spent by the police in an effort to convict this notorious receiver in chief of stolen goods, recently made in print, furnishes Inspector Byrnes with a stumbling block in his attack against the public prosecutor that the latter is not slow to avail himself of. That one shrewd woman at the head of an organization of criminals—a class notoriously deficient in intellect —should defy the combined wisdom, enterprise, ingenuity and authority of a police force for twenty-five years is a fact that does not at once seem to establish beyond a doubt the claim that it is the finest, most intelligently and most honestly administered force in the world.
>
> —*Brooklyn Eagle*, August 3, 1884

Byrnes was slinging mud at the district attorney's office at an alarming rate. Olney had to strike back hard. He challenged Byrnes and the New York City Police Department to undertake a full investigation based on the recent May 15, 1884, findings of the Roosevelt Committee which had been charged by the state legislature to investigate years of reported corruption within the New York City Police Department. Freshman Assemblyman Theodore Roosevelt served as the chairman of the committee, hence its name. "If they (the Police Department) are really anxious to investigate, why not take up the charges made by the Roosevelt Committee in May last?" Olney had asked.

According to Roosevelt's report, "there are graver instances of wrong doings where the Commissioners have failed and seemingly willfully failed to do their duty as required by law." The Roosevelt Committee charged "that a large amount of the vice, drunkenness and misery which exist in the City of New York is due to the failure of the Board of Police Commissioners to discharge their duties relative to the enforcement of the laws."

It was a stinging indictment.

"I have never yet heard that the Police Department made any investigations or made any reform or changes in the administration of their department in consequence of this report," Olney fired back at Byrnes and the police department. "Counsel for the Mandelbaum woman have already prevailed upon their client to say in court that the prosecution against her was a prosecution against the police, thus seeking to confuse the real issue, and one of her counsel has said that in such a fight he was with Inspector Byrnes," Olney charged. "And am I to suppose that in a fight of the people against Mandelbaum the Inspector is to be on her side?" he charged.

And that wasn't the end of it. Assistant District Attorney Allen also took a potshot at Byrnes and the police in the papers.

ANOTHER SHOT AT BYRNES THE WAR BETWEEN THE POLICE AND THE DISTRICT ATTORNEY ASSISTANT ALLEN THROWS HIS HANDFUL OF MUD AND REPEATS THE CHARGES AGAINST THE DETECTIVES

> Assistant District Attorney Allen made a very long reply to the charges of Inspector Byrnes in his communication to the Board of Police on Saturday last. Mr. Allen characterized them as most wanton, vile and malicious.
>
> —*The New York Times*, August 8, 1884

Henry Allen had been with the distinct attorney's office since 1858. In his own estimation, he was "very conversant with the nature of the peculiar relations which exist between the police and criminals." According to Allen, despite Byrnes's claim that Mandelbaum's operations had been ended because of the outstanding efforts of the New York City Police Department, during the period of time her shop was under the surveillance of Pinkerton detectives, nearly 15,000 yards of stolen silk alone were bought and sold at her premises, and during this same period, known shoplifters, pickpockets, and sneak thieves were constantly entering her establishment day and night. Allen also took umbrage over Byrnes's accusation that he had somehow betrayed the district attorney's office by protecting various criminals from prosecution. Allen claimed, "if he has enjoyed any reputation at all in connection with that department it has been that of the most bitter enemy of crime and criminals of every grade and description."Allen charged that every assertion Byrnes made about his relationship with Mollie Hoey was utterly untrue.

> "The efficiency of this bureau during the four years that it has been under my charge has been publicly recognized by the Judges and officers of almost every court in this city. In strong contrast appears the condemnation and strictures in open court against the gross stupidity, carelessness, neglect, if nothing worse, of the officials in the District Attorney's office for improperly preparing the cases for trials and thereby frustrating the ends of justice."
>
> —Chief Inspector Thomas Byrnes, August 3, 1884

This public display of mudslinging went on for several days in the newspapers. It was ugly and nasty and benefited no one except Mandelbaum and her attorneys. Knowing that the hostility between the district attorney's office and the police department would only play right into Mandelbaum's hands, Olney decided to offer an olive branch. He needed the hostility to end so he could get on with the prosecution of the Mandelbaum case.

"I would like to say this further, that I cheerfully bear testimony to the courage, zeal and efficiency of the majority of the rank and file of the police force as I have had occasion to witness them since I have held this office. I am glad and proud to be associated with such as collaborators in the common cause of detecting and punishing crime," Olney told reporters. Assistant District Attorney Allen joined Olney in trying to put an end to the dispute. According to a *New York Times* article dated August 8,

"Mr. Allen, in conclusion, joins Mr. Olney in his commendation of the rank and file of the Police department, the body of men composing this department having shown themselves to be as a rule good men."

The reputations of those connected with the District Attorney's office and the Police Department were being irreparably damaged while Mandelbaum's astute attorney William Howe gleefully stood by and watched. According to *Scoundrels in Law* by Cait Murphy, "Wisely, the two sides stopped after a couple of free and frank exchanges of views. No good to their reputations could come of this circular firing squad. They needed each other." And so, the battle between them ended, with both sides forced to refrain from their public attacks and withdraw to lick their wounds. It was a foregone conclusion in just about every intelligent person's mind that the New York City Police Department was riddled with corruption from the top, beginning with its four-member Board of Commissioners, down through precinct Captains, detectives, straight down to patrolmen who walked a beat. They were all on the take, some to a lesser degree than others and some on a much grander scale. The issue wasn't determining if it existed—there was never any doubt of that and a plethora of hearsay evidence to substantiate it—but how to fix it. And more so, how to get any credible witnesses to testify against the police. New York State Assemblyman Theodore Roosevelt's investigating committee of 1884 was not the first attempt at reigning in vice and corruption within the department. As early as 1840 there had been investigations but little had been accomplished.

It would not be until March 1894, when the Lexow Committee, chaired by state senator Clarence Lexow, that any real change occurred. By then Roosevelt had been appointed head the Board of Police Commissioners by the city's newly elected, reform-minded mayor, William L. Strong. Once again, Roosevelt ran headlong into an array of his previous foes, including Inspector Byrnes, now Superintendent of the police department. This time, however, the results were much different than the 1884 investigation. The Lexow Committee was able to do what the 1884 Roosevelt Committee could not —it uncovered a reliable witness to testify about police corruption from the inside. That witness was Police Captain Max Schmittberger. He testified before the Lexow Committee that small vice shops paid $20 a month, for police protection although, he said, some monthly fees went as high as $200 a month for some of the more lucrative gambling dens or successful brothels. According to Schmittberger each police officer took a 20 percent cut from the bribes as the money made its way from the police to Tammany Hall. Schmittberger's testimony before the Lexow Committee helped lead to the hiring of reform-minded Theodore Roosevelt as the New York City Police Commissioner in 1895. The Lexow Committee handed out approximately 70 indictments against various police officers, two former police commissioners, 20 police captains and three police inspectors. Although many of these men were convicted, the verdict against them was overturned in a higher court, which was overseen by hand-picked Tammany Hall judicial appointees. Many of those indicted were reinstated on the police force. Although the indictments didn't stick, the city's reform-minded citizenry forced out the Tammany Hall mayoral candidate in the city's 1894 election. William L. Strong, a reform-minded Republican, was elected mayor and came into office with the clear and abiding mandate to reform the city's police department. One of Mayor Strong's first acts as the newly elected head of the city was to get rid of all the Tammany Hall–appointed Police Commissioners and appoint his own men to the positions. In 1896, Strong named the thirty-six-year-old Theodore Roosevelt as president of the newly organized Police Commission. One of Roosevelt's first orders of business was to get rid of the upper echelon of the police department including Superintendent Thomas Byrnes. Byrnes resigned before Roosevelt could press charges against him.

> "An earlier inquiry into the policing of the city had reported as long ago as 1840; another had sat in 1875; and a third (led by none other than Theodore Roosevelt) in 1884.
>
> Each committee had found vice flourishing in the city, and each concluded that New York's police abetted it. Firm evidence of wrongdoing, admittedly was scanty, and none of the commissions produced credible witnesses who could describe the inner workings of the system. Even so, accumulated testimony demonstrated that some senior officers had been pocketing $10,000 a year from graft as early as 1839."
>
> —Mike Dash, *Satan's Circus*, 2007

Although the immediate impact of the Roosevelt Committee's findings appeared futile, it managed to lay the foundation for further investigations which ultimately led to a variety of civil service reforms, including the forced resignation of Thomas Byrnes. The 1884 report by the committee laid out ten areas of concern that needed to be addressed along with a list of changes that needed to be made in order for the police department to rid itself of ongoing corruption. Among the committee's recommendations was a call to disband the existing four-member Board of Police Commissioners, who were appointed by the mayor, and replace it with a single Commissioner, "either appointed to hold during good behavior or else who should take and leave office with the Mayor appointing him." According to the report, "With a many-headed commission, moreover, the long-termed system works badly . . ." The Committee also called for police officers to be appointed through a civil service process rather than purely as political appointments. "The constant disregard of their own rules by the Commissioners, though very properly exposing them to severe criticism, is still an evil that can be in great part reached by legislation, for instance, by including the department within the provisions of the Civil Service Reform bill."

The Committee identified gambling and prostitution as two of the main vices allowed to operate openly in New York City with seemingly no police interference. "Down to within the last two years the lottery policy business and kindred forms of gambling were conducted in New-York in the most open and defiant manner and to an extent which it was absolutely unpardonable of the police authorities to permit," the report noted. The Committee further indicated that the matter of open gambling had been brought to the attention of the police department and its Commissioners again and again without any action being taken. It was further stated that the closure of illegal gambling businesses would not have occurred if it weren't for the efforts of various public organizations and societies and the use of Pinkerton detectives. "Outside societies and private individuals with the help of Pinkerton detectives were able to put an end to it in many places . . ."

Roosevelt's Committee also brought to light damning evidence of police payoffs by gambling establishments, including account books taken by Pinkerton detectives during their raids showing "numerous entries of expenses (amounting in the aggregate to thousands of dollars annually) under the head of "Police Moneys . . ." and in many of these instances these entries were accompanied by the name or the abbreviation of the name of the Captain in whose precinct the policy shop was." According to the Committee far more arrests and convictions of known gamblers and the proprietors of gambling house enterprises had been made by Pinkerton detectives than the police.

According to the Committee's report, "In a less degree, these remarks apply to the laws against prostitution. This is a vice that can probably never be eradicated, but the evils resulting from it can be minimized and at least such flagrant and offensive exhibitions of indecency as prevail in certain streets of the city can be prevented."

The work of the Roosevelt Committee was long and laborious and although it did little at the time to stem the tide of police corruption it served as notice to the Police Commissioners and the department that they were being watched and that there would be changes coming. The Police Commissioners and men like Chief Inspector Thomas Byrnes were hard-pressed to heed these warnings and instead spent their time defending the status quo of the department.

MR. BYRNES GETS EXCITED THE INSPECTOR'S ENERGETIC DEFENSE OF THE POLICE WHY DETECTIVES MUST ASSOCIATE WITH THIEVES AND GAMBLERS—COMMISSIONER CAUFIELD ON THE STAND

> The Inspector called for a glass of water and sat down with the remark that he had been in the Police Department 21 years and any reflections on it were a great measure reflections on him. "Mr. Allen," he added "always wanted me to cooperate with private detectives and I declined to do so."
>
> "Mr. Byrnes," said Mr. Russell, "something has been said about police detectives associating with thieves. Is it apart of their duty?"
>
> "Yes," was the answer, "it is the first duty of a detective to make himself familiar with all kinds of criminals, expert cracksmen, their haunts and their methods. Without the knowledge thus gained he would be almost useless. Therein lies his power. Then, when anything happens he knows whom to ask for information, where to look and how to act. I myself daily spend two hours out of the 24 in the company of criminals. Oh no not because it's a pleasure to me," said the Inspector, when the committee laughed, "but because it's my duty—my education."
>
> —*The New York Times*, May 13, 1884

The department was not without its supporters which included judges and former Commissioners. In light of the facts and in the face of historical evidence, their undying support seems ludicrous.

IN PRAISE OF THE POLICE THREE JUDGES SPEAK HIGHLY OF THE FORCE CAPTAINS AFRAID TO DO THEIR DUTY, ACCORDING TO MR. VOORHIS

The Assembly investigating committee devoted itself yesterday to listening to the defense offered by the Police Department to the many charges which have been made against it . . . Dock Commissioner Voorhis was the first witness called. He was cross-examined by Col. Bliss. He said that he thought that some of the Police Commissioners during his term of office were indifferent on the question of shutting up houses of prostitution but he did not know that any Commissioners had taken any money from these places . . . Judge Rufus B. Cowing of the City Court was the next witness called. On the examination by ex-Judge Russell the Judge said that he knew every Police Captain on the force and many of the police force. "During the past five years," said Judge Cowing, "from what I have seen of the police I unhesitatingly say that they are efficient and trustworthy. Capt. Williams from my observation is a very brave and efficient officer. I believe that he is a man of strict integrity and I take no stock in the rumors that have been circulated against him . . ." Judge Henry A. Gildersleeve, of the Court of the general Sessions was called by Mr. Russell. He said that in his judgment the police force was exceedingly efficient, very trustworthy and one of which the city should be proud. The Judge said that the condition of the city so far as crime was concerned was improving all the time . . .

—*The New York Times*, August 11, 1884

10

SHE WENT THAT-A-WAY

"Thank God we are rid of the villain!"
—District Attorney Peter B. Olney, December 5, 1884

The newspapers were not kind to Mandelbaum when she appeared in court. According to a January 1884 *New York Times* article, she was described as "a gross woman, a German Jewess, with heavy, almost masculine features, restless black eyes, and a dark, unhealthy looking complexion. Her stout figure was incased in a rich sealskin cloak, below which appeared the folds of a silk dress. On her big hands were brown kid gloves and in her lap a handbag rested. There were diamonds in her ears, and her collar was confined by a pin set thick with pearls. On her head rested a black bonnet trimmed with beads and bright colored feathers."

It did not matter what Mandelbaum looked like; there was no doubt that despite her capture by Pinkerton detectives and the subsequent hearing before Judge Murray, Mandelbaum still had friends in high places from whom she might solicit help. Murray had his worries about what she and her lawyers might do to get out of the charges, who she might call some favor from and when. Murray proceeded cautiously, waiting for the other shoe to drop.

The hearing to determine whether there was enough evidence for the case to be transferred to the Court of General Sessions which would hear the felony charges against Mandelbaum, her son, and Stoude, took two full days. Howe's defense tactics were a wonder to behold. First he tried to position his client as a victim in an ongoing battle between the district attorney's office and the police, a ruse that seemed to work perfectly when the two departments engaged each other in a battle of name-calling in the newspapers. His second move was to call into question the reliability and character of the prosecution's chief witness, Pinkerton detective Gustav Frank. In the Roosevelt Committee's report in 1884, the report that District Attorney Olney had used against the Board of Police Commissioners, Frank had been named. According to the report, Frank had been instrumental as an undercover agent in bringing down several of the gambling establishments in the city. New York police therefore knew of Frank long before his undercover work on the Mandelbaum case. Frank's citation in the report was made even more interesting when William Howe's next line of defense was to personally discredit the Pinkerton agent.

According to *The New York Times,* Frank was dressed conservatively when he was called to the stand. "He wore a very glossy black suit, white tie and a jaundiced-looking countenance. In his mouth was a gumdrop which apparently declined to melt as he chewed it so persistently that Mr. Howe scowled," *The New York Times* reported.

Howe began his questioning. "Please tell us everything that was said to you by the prisoner Stoude on each of the occasions you visited Mrs. Mandelbaum."

Assistant District Attorney Gove jumped to his feet and protested Howe's line of questioning. It wasn't Frank who was on trial. Little did Gove suspect that, in fact, it was exactly Howe's intention to put Frank's character on trial.

"I have a right to test this man on everything that has happened to him from his cradle up to the present moment," Howe blustered. He again asked the question of Frank. This time Gove sat passively by.

Frank testified that Stoude had told him that Mrs. Mandelbaum would not do business with just anyone who came along. He was asked whether Stoude ever mentioned anything about stolen goods. Frank testified he hadn't.

"Go on, tell us everything, if it takes you a year," Howe said goading the witness.

Murray interrupted him. "Were these conversations always in regard to stolen goods?" he asked of Frank.

Howe fumed. "That's a very leading question," he protested. "And one which I would not allow the District Attorney to ask."

Frank continued with his testimony. He told the court that he had purchased some silk from Mandelbaum after she got to know him and seemed comfortable with him. He said that it had been Stoude who delivered the silk to him.

At this point, Howe motioned to have Stoude released since by Frank's own testimony all Stoude did was deliver goods and never once spoke of any of the goods Frank purchased as being stolen. Hence Stoude obviously knew nothing about where the silk came from and was merely a delivery man, according to Howe.

Gove protested saying that Stoude had worked for Mandelbaum for over a dozen years and therefore had to know what kind of criminal activity she was engaged in.

"Law is just like laudanum. It is far more easy to use it as a quack than applying it as a physician and I say that my friend is giving you a dose of quackery," Howe said waving his arm dramatically at the assistant district attorney. "Do you decide this case upon inference? Please let me have justice," he shouted at Gove.

"The case is here and shall be treated legally," Murray countered. "It has been shown that Stoude was the confidential man of Mrs. Mandelbaum and his relations to the business have been explained. The whole thing appears to me strong and so strong that it would be absurd to discharge him."

The examination of Frank continued. He testified that when he had purchased the silk from Mrs. Mandelbaum, she had told him not to dispose of it in the city. She told him it was because that's where the silk had come from. Howe asked Frank whether he had ever been connected to any of the gambling dens in the city as a detective. Frank testified that he had. Howe asked if he had ever received any money directly from any of them.

"Not a cent," Frank testified.

"Who paid you then?" Howe asked.

"Pinkerton," Frank said.

Howe feigned astonishment. "You mean you were employed by the gambling institution and received no payment from them?" But before Frank has a chance to answer, Howe fired another question at him. "Was Mr. Pinkerton the only person to whom you made a statement of what you did at Mrs. Mandelbaum's store?" he asked.

"Mr. Pinkerton and his Superintendent," Frank said.

"Did you ever go to the District Attorney's office?"

"No, sir," Frank said.

The questioning was fast and pointed. Howe asked where Frank had written his affidavits for the case against Mandelbaum. "Was it in Mr. Gove's office?" he asked.

"I don't know," Frank sputtered. "I can ask him if you like."

"Was Judge Murray there?"

"Yes," Murray chimed in.

Howe went for the jugular. "Were you ever told that it was necessary to get Mrs. Mandelbaum arrested in order that Inspector Byrnes and the Police Commissioners might be attacked?" Howe asked.

Gove jumped to his feet again objecting vehemently to Howe's line of questioning.

This didn't deter Howe. He continued to grill Frank. "Did the DA's office tell you there was a feud with Inspector Byrnes? Did you ever see any of the municipal police at Mrs. Mandelbaum's?"

Frank refused to answer.

The district attorney protested even louder.

"This slander upon the Police Department is unfounded," Howe said calmly in the face of Gove's temper tantrum.

"Well, upon my soul," a frustrated Gove blurted out.

"Upon your soul," Howe said contemptuously. "Don't be indecent." He was through with Frank for the time being. He called the four merchants whose silk had been identified previously as having been stolen. He questioned them again. He wasn't able to elicit any new facts regarding the merchandise, but still he pressed on. Each time the witnesses were unable to positively identify the silk belonging to them, but they also contended they were fairly certain they had been stolen from their stores. Howe motioned to have the charges against Mandelbaum dismissed. If they couldn't identify their own merchandise, how on earth could Mandelbaum know it was stolen if they didn't?

Each time Howe motioned for dismissal, Murray turned him down. "I should like to add that I am getting tired of those repeated queries. Are we to have fair play? It is getting monotonous," Murray said after dismissing Howe's final motion to dismiss.

"Well, I don't mean any disrespect to you," Howe said, smiling at the judge. "I am getting weary myself."

Following Howe's last motion to dismiss all charges against his clients and each motion summarily overruled by Murray, the judge gaveled the hearing closed. He had, he explained, taken all the testimony under advisement and was convinced that there was enough evidence for the case to go to trial in the Court of General Sessions. Mandelbaum, her son Julius, and Herman Stoude were charged with seven counts of second degree grand larceny and one of receiving stolen goods. The trial would be scheduled without delay.

MRS. MANDELBAUM'S CASE JUSTICE MOVING ON ITS COURSE SOMEWHAT SLOWLY THE PRISONERS' DISCHARGE REFUSED—LIVELY SPARRING BETWEEN COUNSEL

[Mandelbaum] with the ferocious bunch of ostrich feathers in her bonnet, betook herself into the holy sanctity of the Harlem Police Court where she was at once recognized… The woman was greeted by her smiling counsel, Messrs. Howe & Hummel, who scintillated in the court room and

> talked in vulgar parlance...Assistant District Attorney Leroy S. Gove, in a shabby genteel suit of clothes, represented the intangible crowd, thirsting for justice, known as "the people."
>
> —*The New York Times*, July 29, 1884

On August 14, Murray issued the official indictment papers charging all three defendants with grand larceny in the second degree and receiving stolen goods. Mandelbaum's case was placed on the docket and scheduled to be heard in the Court of General Sessions on September 22, 1884. Yet William Howe wasn't done with Gustav Frank. Howe filed a motion to have Frank's character investigated and suggested that a commission be appointed to examine a letter purportedly received from the Crown Prosecutor of Rhenish, Prussia, Frank's hometown, that implied that Frank was a fugitive from justice. According to Howe he had received a letter on September 6 from the prosecutor that was written in German and that according to Howe's translation, Frank had absconded from Germany fifteen years ago and was wanted in connection with both bankruptcy and forgery charges. According to Howe's translation, the German prosecutor wrote: "On the telegraphic message of the 19th of this month (August) I have the honor to inform you that the present prosecuting Attorney acted against Gustav Frank since 1867 without accomplishing anything. The present Directors of the Police also made inquiries concerning Frank which were fruitless." The message was cryptic at best. The court wasn't about to let Howe's translation go untested and had the letter translated by two German speaking translators. Their translation of the letter was very different than Howe's: "I have the honor to answer your communication by telegraph of the 19th of this month, that there were no documents to be found in the office of the District Attorney of this city against Gustav Frank since 1837. Also an inquiry at the Police Direction of this city about Frank was without result."

Howe's contention from the beginning was that any testimony Frank had given regarding Mandelbaum was tainted by the fact that Frank himself was a criminal at large. No one was buying it.

Still, Howe persevered. He submitted an affidavit to the court that claimed Frank was in business in Croch, near Cleves, in Germany until 1865. He went bankrupt, failed to pay his debtors, and became a forger. Howe claimed that a proclamation for his arrest had been issued and was still outstanding. Howe demanded that a special commission travel to Germany to interview firsthand the German prosecutor and police regarding Frank's criminal charges. In Howe's opinion to the court, Frank was unworthy of belief as the principal witness against his client.

Frank, of course, disputed every part of Howe's accusation. According to Frank, he had never been in business in Croch, Germany, and had in fact never heard of the place. The charges must be against another man with the same name. He testified to the court that he left Cologne in July 1863, when he was twenty-three years old and came to America. In 1864, he enlisted with the Fourth Massachusetts Regiment where he served during the war. After his discharge he said he'd been working for the Pinkerton Detective Agency. The Pinkerton Agency also filed an affidavit with the court claiming that Frank had been working for them since 1865. He left the agency for a time but returned in 1881 and had been working as a detective ever since. His character and honesty were unimpeachable according to the Pinkertons.

The district attorney's office filed a motion opposing Howe's call for a special commission claiming that Mandelbaum's case did not hinge solely on the testimony of Frank. The court ruled against Howe's motion.

IS DETECTIVE FRANK ON TRIAL?
MOTHER MANDELBAUM'S COUNSEL TRYING TO PROVE HIM A FORGER

In the Court of General Sessions yesterday counsel for Mme. Frederika Mandelbaum, the notorious "fence' was heard on a motion that a commission be appointed to take testimony as to the character of Detective Gustav Frank,

> the Pinkerton detective whose testimony secured Mother Mandelbaum's indictment.
>
> —*The New York Times*, September 16, 1884

When the Frank ploy didn't work, Howe switched to another tactic—delay. Howe argued that the case should be heard in another court, the Court of Oyer and Terminer. The court was made up of a Supreme Court Justice and two or more judges of the Court of Common Pleas with jurisdiction to hear all felony cases including those punishable by life imprisonment or death. Howe's motion to remove the case to Court of Oyer and Terminer was pure rubbish as far as District Attorney Olney was concerned. The only reason Howe wanted a change of venues was to delay the case in the hopes that several of the witnesses against Mandelbaum might change their minds. Luckily for William Howe his motion to move the case was heard by Judge Charles Donahue, a more sympathetic judge. In actuality, Donahue was more than sympathetic. He was beholden to Mandelbaum and was later investigated by the New York City Bar Association and censured for his conduct in a variety of criminal cases, including Mandelbaum's. A new trial date was set for December 2, 1884.

As far as Olney was concerned it was only a delay. He had Mandelbaum right where he wanted her, and she wasn't going to wiggle out of the charges no matter what legal maneuvers her legal counsel made. He had fourteen witnesses ready to testify against her, including Gustav Frank's damning testimony. But William Howe still had several tricks up his copious sleeve. The indictment against Mandelbaum, Julius, and Stoude had two felony charges on it: grand larceny and receiving stolen goods. The law required that only one charge be issued in any one indictment. Olney was out maneuvered again. He had to withdraw the original indictment and reissue it this time with separate indictments for each of the charges as the law required. It was another setback for Olney, but the biggest one of all was just around the corner.

MOTHER MANDELBAUM'S STRUGGLES

> "Mother" Mandelbaum's big and little lawyers applied to Judge Donohue in Supreme Court Chambers yesterday for an order removing her case from the Court of General Sessions to the Court of Oyer and Terminer and for the continuance of an order staying her trail in the former court . . . District Attorney Olney opposed the motions arguing that the application for removal was tantamount to saying that the Court of General Sessions, presided over by Recorder Smyth, was not competent to try an ordinary case of grand larceny in the second degree.
>
> —*The New York Times*, September 20, 1884

Despite all of Howe's legal maneuverings, District Attorney Olney believed steadfastly that he had Mandelbaum right where he wanted her and that a conviction would strike a blow not only on the criminal underworld but bring to light the incompetent and corrupt police department shenanigans. Even though Mandelbaum's lawyers did their utmost to get the charges against her dropped, all they managed to accomplish was to get the case continued. Mandelbaum was out on bail awaiting trial, as were her son Julius and Herman Stoude. During this time Pinkerton detectives were on around-the-clock surveillance of Mandelbaum's home. They had set up stakeouts around her Clinton and Rivington Streets shop, keeping tabs on her every move. Mandelbaum kept a low profile. She met several times at her attorney's office, taking a carriage from her home to Howe and Hummel's lavish offices at 89 Center Street to discuss the upcoming case and to make some real estate transactions that would later come under legal scrutiny. Pinkerton detectives followed her there and everywhere she went. Two or three detectives were not far from her sight at any one time. Mandelbaum was well aware that her every move was being followed, and she made elaborate gestures to keep the detectives aware of her various jaunts. Coming out of her home, dressed in black as she usually was, with her small feathered hat perched on the top of her large head, made her an easily recognizable target. She meant to have it that way. With her enormous girth and feathered hat, she was easy to spot. She never just slipped into her waiting carriage when she made her trips to the law offices. She would circle the carriage to give the watching detectives a good look at her, and then she would ask for the footman's help in getting into the carriage. Sometimes she would wave as the carriage rode away. If there was a game of cat and mouse going on, little did the Pinkerton detectives surmise that it was they who were the mice.

It became clear to Mandelbaum that despite all the legal wrangling by her lawyers and the calling in of every political favor she was owed, nothing could be done to stop the case from going to court in December. As the trial date neared, she made a decision about her future—and it didn't include spending time in a jail cell. There was no way she was about to let anyone take away everything she had struggled so hard to achieve—the wealth, the power, the lifestyle she had become accustomed to. So, subsequently, this "no way" became "a-way."

On December 2, 1884, the day the trial was scheduled to begin, District Attorney Olney sauntered into the courtroom bursting with determination and armed with enough evidence and testimony to finally put an end to Mandelbaum's reign as "Queen among Thieves." Her attorneys were present in the courtroom but Mandelbaum, Julius, and Stoude were not. Howe filed a motion to once again postpone the case. Olney immediately and vehemently objected. Howe argued that there were still details in the case that he needed time to clarify. Olney argued that Howe had been given enough time during the many delays to prepare for the case. Howe promised that everything he needed to have worked out would be taken care of in a matter of days. The judge granted Howe's motion to continue the case, but only to December 4, and held that there would be no further continuances. Howe assured him there would be no need to delay the case after December 4. The judge adjourned the matter until the new date. Howe was exponentially pleased with himself and the delay. Olney was left fuming.

THE CASE OF MRS. MANDELBAUM

> District Attorney Olney came into the Court of Oyer and Terminer with 14 witnesses yesterday morning prepared to terminate the professional career of Frederika Mandelbaum, the eminent "fence," with the assistance of seven indictments and two Assistant District Attorneys. Frederika, however, was not in the court to be terminated and her counsel secured an adjournment of her case until tomorrow morning. Mr. Olney strenuously opposed the adjournment . . .
>
> —*The New York Times*, December 3, 1884

On December 4, 1884, the morning the trial was to begin, the Court of Oyer and Terminer was packed with reporters, police, merchants, a slew of known and unknown criminals, and the just plain curious, all of them come to witness the proceedings. It was standing room only. People jostled for front row seats. The beaming district attorney sat at the prosecution table flanked by his fourteen witnesses and assistants including Robert Pinkerton and Gustav Frank. No one more than District Attorney Olney could wait to get the case that would finally end the career of New York City's most notorious fence underway. Judge Barrett, the presiding justice, adorned in his best dark robes, took the bench. "All rise," the clerk of courts bellowed loudly above the din, silencing the noisy crowd with his familiar "Hear yea. Hear yea." When the clerk ordered that everyone in the courtroom be seated, it became glaringly apparent that everyone was there except one very important person—Marm Mandelbaum. Julius and Stoude were also not seated at the defense table. Heads began to spin around the courtroom looking for the errant defendants. A buzz hummed through the crowd. At exactly 11 o'clock, the clerk called the names of the defendants—Fredericka Mandelbaum, Julius Mandelbaum, and Herman Stoude. There was no response. The buzz in the courtroom grew louder. The judge banged his gavel. Again the names of the defendants were called and again there was no response. The names of the defendants were called a third and final time.

William Howe, seated at the defense table and dressed in his finest attire—a dove grey waistcoat, striped trousers, gold vest studded with diamonds, billowing purple bow tie, and matching handkerchief flowing from the breast pocket of his coat—did not appear disturbed. His partner, the dour Abe Hummel, dressed in his usual charcoal grey suit and dark tie, sat in the chair beside Howe and quietly hummed what sounded like a show tune. When the clerk of courts had called Mandelbaum's name for the third and last time, Howe slowly lumbered to his feet and facing the bench, calmly told the court, in an almost singsong voice, "If your honor please, my clients are not in court. They were each notified to be at my office at 10 o'clock this morning, but they did not come, and are not here now."

Pandemonium broke out in the courtroom. Several people cheered.

"The District Attorney must, in the words of Shakespeare, 'have the due and forfeit of his bond.' Mrs. Mandelbaum is not here," Howe advised the court.

District Attorney Olney's jaw dropped. He was momentarily speechless. He looked at Robert Pinkerton quizzically. Pinkerton looked as dismayed and confused as Olney. His detectives had been shadowing Mandelbaum and the other defendants day and night. They had last reported to him that yesterday she made a visit to Howe's Center Street offices by carriage where she stayed for a time and then returned to her home where she remained for the evening. She had not been reported seen that morning.

Olney tried to recover his composure. He jumped to his feet. "I move, your honor, that the bonds of the defendants be forfeited, and a bench warrant be issued for the defendants," he said.

Judge Barrett slammed his gavel accepting Olney's motion, and the clerk of courts ordered that all bail be forfeited in the case. But this would be easier said than done. Not only had Mandelbaum fled, but she had seen to it that the bail money that had been put up for her, Julius, and Stoude could not be claimed by the district attorney's office. She had arranged to have the deed to the two properties that had been put up as bail legally transferred first to her daughter and then summarily back to relatives of the various bondsmen. She had done so for all of the bail money, which meant that the property put up by various bondsmen could no longer be attached. No property, no bail money. This included the bail posted by several citizens including

John Briggs who posted bail for Julius Mandelbaum in the amount of $5,000, using his house at 105 West Twenty-Fifth Street as collateral, and Conrad Petri, who had posted bail using his property at 421 East Houston Street as collateral. Mandelbaum had outsmarted Olney's office yet again.

"Like the defendants, the bail had vanished."

—Cait Murphy, *Scoundrels in Law*, 2010

William Howe, still standing before the bench and in no apparent hurry to leave the limelight said, "I believe Mrs. Mandelbaum acted upon Mark Twain's theory that absence of body is often better than presence of mind." Neither the judge nor District Attorney Olney were amused; still it didn't dampen Howe or Hummel's apparent joy. Abe Hummel mused admiringly, "Ah, Fredericka the Great."

When questioned, Howe said he had no idea where his clients had gone and even if he did, he wasn't about to divulge it. Finding them was up to the district attorney's office and of course the illustrious Pinkerton detectives, he said winking at a flummoxed

Robert Pinkerton. Howe was questioned by a reporter about his fees. Hadn't Mandelbaum's escape cost him, too? William Howe rocked back on the heels of his well-shined and expensive shoes, looked up at the ceiling, and began to whistle. Sticking his hands deep into the pockets of his trousers he tossed the coins in his pockets dramatically and said no more. Later he explained to reporters that his firm always secured fees in advance up to and including the cost of an appeal.

"If our client is hanged before the appeal is made, he will never need the money, and we might as well have it," Howe said. "We look very far ahead—much farther, I would remark, than the District Attorney."

Mandelbaum, Julius, and Stoude were gone and nowhere to be found, at least not in New York City. A flurry of legal activity had transpired on the day before the trial in the offices of Howe & Hummel, much of it real estate transfers. Not only did Mandelbaum see to it that none of the property put up as collateral as bail could be taken by the authorities, she did the same for her own real estate holdings, deeding them over to her daughters. The only real question left was how did she do all this given the fact that she had been under constant surveillance by Pinkerton detectives? The answer lay in the cat and mouse game she had been perpetuating on the detectives all along.

MRS. MANDELBAUM MISSING THE NOTORIOUS RECEIVER FLIES FROM THE CITY NEITHER HERSELF, HER SON, OR HER CLERK TO BE FOUND—TRANSFERS OF PROPERTY BY THEIR BONDSMEN AND THE WOMAN HERSELF

Judge Barrett was in his seat at 11 o'clock yesterday prepared to listen to Mrs. Mandelbaum's trial. District Attorney Olney sat, sternly imposing, just in front of the judicial seat. He stroked his black mustache with anything but a gentle hand. He was evidently resolved to put an end

> to Mrs. Mandelbaum, professionally speaking . . . Mr. Howe was plumbly serene and ponderously gracious . . . "I have been told," he [Olney] said to Judge Barrett, "that they have left the city and fled the state."
>
> —*The New York Times*, December 5, 1884

Olney tried to put on his best show despite the escape of Mandelbaum. "I suspected it," he said. "As I said in court, though it was not absolutely necessary for her to be present last Tuesday, it was strange that she could not be, and I called attention to that," he said. "Since then—in fact before that time—I took steps to have the matter looked into . . . It seems to me that if there can be any doubt as to the guilt of the woman, this performance must satisfy anybody. Flight is evidence of guilt and could be used against her as such. I thought all along that she could never face trial . . ." Olney told reporters that he had Mandelbaum's house watched continuously. "They have gone to Canada, that refuge for the oppressed—without doubt," he said. "Thank God we are rid of the villain!" he proclaimed, almost triumphantly despite the situation. "The number of criminals from this country who visit Canada is simply shocking. The old girl was so awfully cocky. She had been in business so long that she positively thought it was improper for us to arrest her," Olney opined.

Howe remained his bemused self. He told reporters he had been greatly delighted when he learned that Judge Barrett would be hearing the case in the Court of Oyer and Terminer. "There was no judge there before whom I would sooner have argued than Judge Barrett," Howe gushed enthusiastically. When asked by reporters if he could account for the disappearance of Mandelbaum and the others, he said that she had been to his offices on the Friday before to make certain arrangements and go over the case. When asked what arrangements, Howe blathered on, ignoring the pointed question. It was obvious to everyone that the arrangements had to do with securing her bondsmen's bail and her own properties in the city. "I think her absence is to be accounted for by impulsive mania. She was the victim of it and skipped on the spur of the moment," he said, winking at his partner Abe Hummel. Hummel laughed heartily.

Attention turned immediately to Robert Pinkerton. It had been his detectives who had been assigned to shadow Mandelbaum. How could she have slipped through his fingers, he was asked? "I had no right to touch Mrs. Mandelbaum. She was on bail. She could go wherever she pleased and it had nothing to do with me. Until she had forfeited her bonds, not a soul had a right to touch her," Pinkerton told reporters in an effort to evade the question. He claimed that when his men had been watching her house on Friday, she must have already made her escape. "The neighbors are all friends of hers and think a great deal of her so they wouldn't help us out," he said. According to Pinkerton, despite her disappearance, "it is a victory enough to have got rid of her and we ought to be thankful for the redemption."

Reporters raced from the courthouse to Mandelbaum's store. They were met there by one of Mandelbaum's daughters who let a crowd of them inside. She stood behind the counter.

"If smartness be written on any face it was indelibly traced upon the countenance of Fredericka's daughter. Her features were sharp and her manners sharper," wrote a *Times* reporter.

"What do you know about your mother?" she was questioned.

"Nothing," she said. "Nothing. Nothing," she repeated, as if she liked the sound of it. "Don't come to me for information. You'll get none," she said.

"Have you no idea when your mother left?" she was asked.

"I know nothing," she said.

"Could you not guess at her whereabouts?" another reporter asked.

"I tell you I know nothing," she said calmly.

"The detectives are worrying themselves terribly," she was told.

"Let them worry," she laughed. "Let them go on worrying, poor things. That's what they've got to do. I'm very glad to have seen you. Come again when you have time. I shall be delighted," she said finally dismissing them all. She showed the reporters out of the shop closing the door tightly behind her after they had left.

MOTHER MANDELBAUM

> The police have at last been too powerful for the district Attorney and his private detectives. That, at least, will be the explanation generally accepted of the escape of "Mother Mandelbaum."
>
> It is a pity that Mr. OLNEY should not have been able to complete his excellent work in this case by securing the conviction and imprisonment of the woman who for so many years has been at the centre of the organization of crime in New York.
>
> —*The New York Times*, December 5, 1884

Mandelbaum's escape from the authorities, despite being shadowed by Pinkerton detectives day and night, was another testament to her cunning. On the Friday before the trial was to begin, she closed the trap on the cat and mouse game she had been playing with Pinkerton detectives who were following her. As she usually did, she came out of her house, dressed all in black, the feather plumes on her small hat bobbing in front of her face. She waved to the detectives, who by now had come to acknowledge their cover had been blown, and climbed into the carriage with the help of the footman and rode off. The detectives followed close behind. They followed her to her lawyers' office at 89 Centre Street. She exited the carriage and went inside. She had made several trips to visit her lawyers during the time she was out on bail and there was nothing unusual about it. She stayed for a time, came back out, waved and was helped back into the carriage that took her directly home. It was always the same and the Pinkerton detectives had gotten used to the routine.

This day was no different. They waited outside of her lawyers' office until she exited. Only this time, it hadn't been Marm Mandelbaum who exited the law offices. It was a maid who worked for Mandelbaum dressed like Mandelbaum in a black dress and long cape and dark gloves. The plumes from her tiny hat had for a time concealed her face. Still, she waved and climbed into the carriage and the detectives, thinking it was Mandelbaum, followed the imposter's carriage back to her home. After it was determined that the coast was clear, the real Mandelbaum exited the law offices and boarded a waiting carriage, making a clean getaway. The carriage took her to New Rochelle where she boarded a train to Chatham Four Corners, New York. There she boarded another train bound for Canada. She arrived in Toronto sometime on December 5, 1884. Her son Julius and Herman Stoude met her there. They all escaped, leaving the Pinkerton detectives in the lurch.

MRS. MANDELBAUM IN CANADA

> TORONTO, Dec. 5. —On Wednesday morning there arrived by the Great Western Railway from the Suspension Bridge a woman of fine stature, weighing about 200 pounds and handsomely attired in a rich sealskin cloak and cape. A young man supposed to be her son accompanied her. The two refused all offers of the hotel agents and calling a hack immediately drove away . . . "Well if they're in Canada," said Mr. Olney, when spoken to about this matter, "the detectives tell me that since I first prosecuted the woman she has done no illicit trade and absolutely stopped her stolen goods transactions. I think we effectively floored the old girl and broke her business up into fragments."
>
> —*The New York Times*, December 6, 1884

The how of Mandelbaum's escape was clear—she had outsmarted the Pinkerton detectives using a decoy, but the why of it all would always remain a mystery. For a woman of Mandelbaum's wealth and power who had operated openly for some twenty-five years and who had established deep roots in both the legitimate and illegitimate communities to pull up stakes and flee to Canada remained puzzling. Being a shrewd businesswoman, perhaps she came to the conclusion that her heyday was behind her and that no matter how many tricks her legal counsel tried to pull she would not escape conviction. Clearly if she thought she could, she would have stayed, but the tides had turned against her and all the legal and political wrangling in the world couldn't save her.

According to Rona Holub, "She [Mandelbaum] decided her only recourse was escape, a painful decision to say the least. Her Lower East Side, Kleindeutschland was home . . . The Lower East Side had been her business partner, providing an environment in which she used her skills and intelligence to unearth great riches. Here, she raised her family, lost her husband, made friends and created a life of abundance for herself, her family, and associates."

Mandelbaum held the neighborhood close to her heart. Once she decided to flee she had put into a place an elaborate plan to secret her son and Stoude out of the country and secure her properties and those of her bondsmen from the authorities by transferring their ownership and raise as much capital as she could. Altogether it was estimated that Mandelbaum escaped with approximately $1 million in cash and jewelry. She had been wise enough to realize that her days were numbered in New York City, not just because of the efforts of the tireless prosecutor, District Attorney Peter Olney, and the detective work of the Pinkertons, but because the social, cultural, and political tides had turned against her. William Howe had not been far off the mark when he claimed his client was caught in the middle of a battle between two opposing forces—the district attorney's office and the police. But it was not just the two law enforcement entities that were at odds; it was the entire political system with reformers battling for the control of city government and the old guard struggling to hold on. Boss Tweed was dead and gone and although the

Tammany Hall politicians still had some control over patronage and construction throughout the city, it was in a constant state of flux.

Edward Cooper, the only son of New York City industrialist Peter Cooper, had been elected Mayor in 1879. Cooper, a Democrat, established his political credentials via the brief, reform-minded political organization Irving Hall that fought to make a clean sweep of political corruption in the city at the hands of the tainted Tammany Hall crowd. His tenure as mayor was followed by the 1881 election of another reform-minded mayor, William Russell Grace, who battled the Tammany Hall Ring relentlessly. And in 1883, Franklin Edson, a vehemently anti–Tammany Hall Democrat, was elected mayor and continued the battle against political corruption.

Mandelbaum's vast network of crime had flourished under the corruption of Tammany Hall and the likes of Fernando Wood and Boss Tweed. They had a particular and favorable understanding about her business, as long, of course, as they received a piece of the action. It had a political domino effect on her criminal enterprise. Without the support of corrupt politicians, she lost her ability to bribe police and judges. And without their support, she could no longer afford the luxury of operating her lucrative business openly and without fear of prosecution. Peter Olney's pursuit of her was a clear enough indication that the political tides had turned against her. A rising and more organized attack on crime in the city beset her ability to buy her way out of trouble as she always had been able to do in the past.

And there were far-reaching economic reasons to put Mandelbaum out of business as well. Many high-end dry goods wholesale merchants wanted her out of business because she was able to undercut them by offering goods at greatly reduced prices. She was diminishing their profits and if truth be told, circumventing the established capitalist protocol. There was nothing wrong with making a profit, but they thought it should be a legitimate one, or at least a profit at the expense of the buyer, not the seller. Other retail establishments wanted her gone because her vast network of shoplifters was costing them huge sums of money each year—another of Mandelbaum's blows against the established capitalistic, profit-making system. While she was in business, it was estimated that stores were losing between 5 and 10 percent of their potential profits each year from Mandelbaum's shoplifting enterprises.

And there was another reason. When once she could depend on the loyalty of her many cohorts because she was able to provide them with protection from prosecution, she now found herself in the position where some of her oldest partners in crime—"Sheeney Mike" Kurtz, Jimmy Hoey and his wife, Mollie, among them—were now testifying against her. If her own "little chicks" were turning against her, what hope was there?

Political reformers and law enforcement officials like Olney knew she was well-connected to the city's police department and judiciary, and city officials and had used bribes at every level to secure favors. It no doubt crossed their minds that if they could bring Mandelbaum down, they could bring down the hundreds of other city officials that she had infected with her bribes. Mandelbaum's escape from justice not only deprived the reformers of their biggest catch ever, it ended any dreams they ever had of tracing Mandelbaum's bribery back to police officers, judges, and politicians. Mandelbaum's arrest and conviction would have also given the city's reformers a three-for-one trophy. Mandelbaum was a criminal, she was a woman succeeding in a male-dominated world, and she was a Jewish immigrant from the lower class—everything the white, male, Protestant, bourgeois class despised. Although District Attorney Olney's plan had not succeeded as much as he had hoped, he had in essence, put the successful fence out of business in New York City. Even though she had escaped prosecution by fleeing the city, the effect was the same—she was out of business once and for all.

11
O'CANADA

"The name of the place is enough to sicken me."
—Fredericka Mandelbaum, November 12, 1885

Despite their flight to Canada, Mandelbaum, Julius, and Stoude were still not out of the woods. She and her entourage stopped at a hotel in Hamilton, Canada. It was a second-rate hotel located near the Grand Trunk Railway station. The news of Mandelbaum's escape from justice had been published throughout Canada along with descriptions of the three fugitives. At the hotel, they kept to themselves. Mandelbaum stayed most of the time in her room. Julius and Stoude also kept out of view, but they often had dinner in the hotel's dining room even then they ate at separate tables pretending not to know each other. Mandelbaum was not sure that they had secured their escape so she wanted everyone to keep a low profile. On the morning of December 9, 1884, Hamilton police officers and detectives who had been alerted to Mandelbaum's whereabouts, arrested the three while they sat down for breakfast together. They were charged with bringing stolen property across the border. Old habits died hard for Mandelbaum, and her first reaction to the police was to try to bribe them to let her go. The police refused the bribe and arrested them all. The offenses they had been charged with in the United States did not fall under any existing extradition treaty between the United States and Canada, so New York City authorities had no jurisdiction over the matter. Distinct Attorney Olney didn't even bother to send anyone up to the Hamilton Court to testify.

Mandelbaum's arrest in Hamilton was based on information—that she has smuggled stolen diamonds across the border—which the Hamilton police had received from an unnamed source, most likely Olney's office, although he subsequently denied it. According to the Canadian police, the diamonds, valued at approximately $4,000 and found in Mandelbaum's possession, had been stolen in 1883 from the Troy, New York, jewelry company Marks & Sons.

> "It is said that the diamonds found on her were part of the goods stolen by Billy Porter and 'Sheeny Mike' in a burglary committed by them in Troy some time since, and two weeks after Porter was acquitted of killing Jack Walsh in Shang Draper's saloon. She can be tried for carrying stolen goods into Canada."
>
> —District Attorney Peter Olney, December 10, 1884

The police summonsed Fred Marks, the company's owner to Hamilton to examine the diamonds. Although Marks told police that they resembled the diamonds that had been stolen from his store, he could not positively identify them. A Canadian customs inspector confiscated the diamonds and held them in his custody until after the hearing. The hearing was held on December 9, at the Hamilton Police Court. It attracted a huge crowd of curiosity seekers as well as newspaper reporters. The trio was assigned a Canadian defense attorney but Mandelbaum wired Howe and Hummel. Abe Hummel wired back that he was on the way and would serve as a consultant in the case. The defense attorney for Mandelbaum requested a one-day delay to allow Hummel to get there and the delay was granted. No bail was set because the three fugitives were considered extreme flight risks. They were held overnight in the Hamilton jail.

"MARM" MANDELBAUM ARRESTED
CAUGHT IN A HOTEL IN HAMILTON, CANADA
BY LOCAL POLICE

TORONTO, Dec. 8—For some days past the detectives here have been endeavoring to locate Mme. Mandelbaum, her son Julius and Herman Stoude, her confidential clerk... This morning Chief Stewart and Detective Castell surprised Mrs. Mandelbaum and her son in the ladies' parlor by saluting them by their proper names... When shown their pictures, the fugitives acknowledged their identity and offered to pay for their release. They will be arranged before the police magistrate upon a charge of bringing stolen property into Canada.

—*The New York Times*, December 9, 1884

On the day of the hearing, December 10, the Canadian prosecutor told the court that he had wired District Attorney Olney's office in New York City asking him to send a representative to testify in the case and for a continuance until Olney's representative could arrive. Abe Hummel, who had come to Hamilton to advise Mandelbaum's Canadian defense attorney, laughed out loud when asked what his strategy would be now that Olney was sending someone up to testify. He told Canadian reporters that Mrs. Mandelbaum could not be extradited in any case and that he was doubtful that Olney would ever send anyone. He was right. Olney refused the request. The case was continued until December 12.

All the defendants pled not guilty on all charges on the day of the hearing in the Hamilton Police Court. No witnesses appeared from the district attorney's office in New York City. Fred Marks, the owner of the jewelry store in Troy where the diamonds were allegedly stolen failed to identify the diamonds as his. The prosecution had no case. The case was dropped and the defendants were released.

MRS. MANDELBAUM RELEASED

The charge against her was the bringing of certain specified articles of jewelry into Canada knowing the same to have

> been stolen. The County Crown Attorney stated that in the absence of witnesses from the United States he would not press the case and the prisoners were accordingly acquitted.
>
> —*The New York Times*, December 13, 1884

Finally, Mandelbaum was free. She had once again outsmarted the authorities. And, in the end, not only had the charges against her, Julius, and Stoude been dropped, she petitioned for and received her diamonds back from the Canadian customs office after paying a duty charge of $614. She was now ready to settle down and she bought a small two-story, whitewashed house located along the main street in Hamilton and joined the local synagogue. Sometime in 1886, she opened a small dry goods store. Her younger children, Anne and Gustav, moved to Hamilton, as well as her married daughter Sarah (Weill) who stayed for a time before returning to New York City. Once again, Mandelbaum was surrounded by the things she loved the most—her loving family and a new retail enterprise.

She sent a letter to friends in New York City announcing her new store:

> I beg to announce to you that I have opened my new emporium, in every respect the equal of my late New York establishment. I shall be pleased to continue our former pleasant business relations, promising not alone to pay the best prices for the articles which you may have for sale, but also in carefully protecting all my customers, no matter at what expense. With my present facilities, I am able to dispose of all commodities forwarded to me with dispatch and security. Trusting to hear from you soon and assuring you that a renewal of past favors will be greatly appreciated.
>
> I am, yours faithfully, F. Mandelbaum

According to a *National Police Gazette* article published in September 1886, when a reporter went to Hamilton to call on Mandelbaum at her dry goods store, he was surprised to discover that all the merchandise in her store came from New York and was selling at incredibly low prices. When he took a perusal of some of the goods, he found there were no identifying labels on any of the merchandise.

Mandelbaum began a new life in Canada carrying on much as she had in New York City. She and her family lived more or less uneventful lives in Hamilton, and although her whereabouts were known to authorities, she was never hampered in any of her new endeavors. For almost a year, from the time she fled New York in late 1884 until late 1885, hardly a word surfaced about her. But in November 1885, the sudden and tragic death of her eighteen-year-old daughter, Annie, brought her back to New York. Annie, who had been living in Hamilton with her mother, two brothers, Julius and Gustav, and Herman Stoude, traveled back to New York City to visit friends. There she visited with her married sister, Sarah Weill. While visiting, she came down with a cold that worsened to pneumonia. On November 10, 1885, within a week of her arrival, she died. Overcome with grief, Mandelbaum made plans to travel back to New York City to say goodbye to her daughter, whatever the cost. Mandelbaum and Julius took the train to Buffalo and then on to New York City. They arrived at Grand Central Station where they were met by a carriage that took them to a friend's home at 99 Clinton Street not far from the home Mandelbaum had occupied for nearly twenty-five years. The home now belonged to a Mrs. Marx, with whom Annie had been staying when she died. Mandelbaum and Julius slipped into the house to pay their last respects. Mandelbaum became so overwhelmed with grief that she fainted. Afraid that she might be seen, friends escorted Mandelbaum out of the house where she stayed in a home just across the street. There was a brief discussion about giving Annie a Christian burial so the ceremony would not be noticed by the authorities but Mandelbaum objected. She wanted Annie buried in a Jewish service.

The service was held the next day. Word had spread through the close-knit neighborhood, and crowds gathered not so much to pay their respects to the dead girl as to catch a glimpse of Mandelbaum, who it was reported was in the city in defiance of the indictments hanging over her head. The scene at the service was gut-wrenching. Mandelbaum sobbed uncontrollably and had to be escorted away. A crowd gathered outside the house where the service was being held, and, ironically it was only through a burly policeman who was stationed at the front door that anyone could get in. Many of the visitors who had come to pay their last respects at the service were old friends of Mandelbaum's and included a plethora of known criminals, burglars, bank thieves, and pickpockets, all of whom had at one time or another worked for her. Mandelbaum, who would have been hard-pressed to conceal her looks, was dressed all in black with a veil covering her face. Julius had taken some pains to conceal his identity by shaving off his beard and hair. According to a *Times*' account of the affair, "Mother Mandelbaum was unchanged and undisguised, and any person who had ever seen her before could distinguish her features."

Following the service the coffin was transported by hearse to be interred in the Union Field Cemetery in a grave next to Wolf Mandelbaum. The hearse was followed by a dozen or more coaches. Neither Julius nor his mother made the trip out to the cemetery. They were later secreted to the train station where they took a coach back to Hamilton.

MRS. MANDELBAUM'S VISIT HER FAVORITE DAUGHTER'S DEATH BRINGS HER HERE VISITING THE BODY AT NIGHT WITH HER SON JULIUS—TIRED OF CANADA, BUT ON HER WAY BACK THERE

> "Mother" Mandelbaum, the noted receiver of stolen goods, and her son Julius, over who indictments are hanging, have been in this city for the past two days, and they left for Canada yesterday afternoon, without having been detected by the police . . . The thought of having her favorite child buried without taking a last look at her face touched a tender chord in the heart of the hardened criminal and to gratify her wish she took the chance of falling into the hands of the police and passing her remaining days in prison . . . She showered kiss after kiss on the cheeks of the dead girl and her piteous cries brought tears to the eyes of the persons who witnessed the scene. Several times she attempted to leave the room but she kept returning to the coffin and finally had to be almost carried away . . .
>
> —*The New York Times*, November 12, 1885

Whether or not District Attorney Olney, Pinkerton detectives, or the police took pity on Mandelbaum's situation is undetermined, but surely her presence in the city for her daughter's funeral was widely known. That a police officer was hired to stand at the front door and that newspaper reporters were able to interview her both attest to that fact.

Mandelbaum was asked by a reporter if she planned to ever return to New York City.

"I don't know. I've often thought of coming back, delivering myself up and standing trial. I am sorry I ever left New York. I should have faced the music," she said.

"Have overtures ever been made to you by police officials?" she was asked.

"That's a question I don't like to answer," she said. "But I will say that if I spent $10,000 I could come back to New York and be a free woman."

"How did this strike you?" she was asked.

"It didn't strike me at all. I'm sick and tired of putting up money to square things and I don't intend to do it anymore. The more money you produce, the more they want. If I hadn't been so free with my money I wouldn't have got in this scrape."

She was asked how she liked living in Canada.

"The name of the place is enough to sicken me. I'm tired of it," she said.

> "Since her flight from New York Mrs. Mandelbaum has lived quietly in Canada. Her exile has been cheered by frequent visits from emissaries of her council and saddened by the intelligence of the death of her younger daughter . . . she would gladly forfeit every penny of her wealth in order to once more breathe freely the atmosphere of the Thirteenth Ward . . ."
>
> —George Washington Walling, *Recollections of a New York Chief of Police*, 1887

Following her foray back to New York for her daughter's funeral, Mandelbaum returned to Hamilton where she maintained her livelihood at the small haberdashery shop she had opened on John Street in downtown Hamilton. From the shop she reportedly sold ladies' goods and apparel. She advertised in the local papers and her shop became quite successful, if not for the simple reason that people were curious to meet and be waited on by the notorious Mrs. Mandelbaum. Julius and Herman Stoude remained in her employ, but there were no reports concerning any possible criminal endeavors. Whether she had decided to forgo her criminal enterprises in Canada and turn legit or whether she simply became better at concealing her illegal activities is unknown. What is known is that she had no problems with the Canadian authorities. She reportedly told customers that her stock of merchandise came legitimately through customs from America and that she was able to sell it at reduced prices because her suppliers in America bought only from pawnshops and auctions at cost and not from high-end wholesalers. None of this, of course, could be verified. It is more likely that Mandelbaum was able to have the vast amounts of stolen merchandise she had secreted away in many of her warehouses in New York sent to her. Because of her various real estate maneuverings before running off to Canada, the New York authorities were unable to confiscate the property or the merchandise stored in these various warehouses.

Much as she had done in New York City, Mandelbaum became a visibly active member of the Hamilton community, offering help and charity whenever possible and became known for her kindness and generosity. She became an active member of the local synagogue and was seen attending services as part of An she Shalom Hebrew congregation regularly. Although Canada, because of its lax extradition laws, had become a refuge for many American criminals, there are no records of Mandelbaum's name being in any way associated with any of them. Once again, either she had decided on walking the straight and narrow, or she had learned from her mistakes in New York and did not openly associate with criminal types.

Despite her exile in Canada, Mandelbaum remained a popular topic of concern especially in regard to the relationship between America and Canada. Her escape intertwined with Canada's seemingly unwillingness to cooperate with the United States when it came to extraditing American criminals. Reformers in New York City and elsewhere in the country demanded a change in Canada's stance, pushing for Canadian officials to either refuse refuge to criminals like Mandelbaum or agree to extradite them if they were found to be living there. As was the case with Mandelbaum, existing extradition laws prohibited any legal efforts to return the suspect to the United States. For Mandelbaum and other criminals like her, Canada became a safe refuge from the long, although weak, arm of the American law. There were many people in New York City, with District Attorney Peter Olney at the top of that list, who thought that obtaining a conviction for Mandelbaum would have led to a vast exposé of corruption in the city when Mandelbaum turned state's evidence in return for a pardon.

MARY HOEY PARDONED HER REWARD FOR BETRAYING MOTHER MANDELBAUM TO JUSTICE

> ALBANY, Jan. 5—The notorious "Mother" Mandelbaum figures in the pardon granted today by Gov. Cleveland. At the request of ex-District Attorney Olney, of New York, he has extended Executive clemency to one of her former associates, Mary Hoey.... She and her husband have since that time furnished the authorities in New York such information and evidence as led to the finding of a number of indictments against Mrs. Mandelbaum....
>
> —*The New York Times*, January 6, 1885

With Mandelbaum safe in Canada, there was no chance of that, to the relief of many in the police department and judicial system with whom she had done business. That was one theory that percolated beneath the surface of Mandelbaum's sudden departure and her subsequent ability to return untouched to New York to attend her daughter's funeral–the police were in on it. Whatever the case, Mandelbaum served as a living, breathing symbol of everything that was wrong with the extradition laws between Canada and America.

It would be more than eighty years before a treaty of extradition between the United States and Canada was signed in Washington on December 3, 1971. The treaty was amended in 1974 and was finally fully ratified by the United State Senate in 1975.

> "She receives the results of robberies and embezzlements, in the United States, takes criminals to her bosom and protects them . . . When the strong arm of the United States law reaches after the thieves, Canada leans gently over the boundary line and says, I have them and you can't get them."
>
> –*Puck Magazine,* June 17, 1885

The speculation that surrounded Mandelbaum was overwhelming for a time. She was reportedly seen from time to time in various parts of the country. *The New York Times* had to squelch one rumor that was widely circulated concerning Mandelbaum as having been sighted in Paterson, New Jersey, and then slipping into New York City. A New York City detective was sent to investigate the rumor but he proclaimed it to be false.

NOT MRS. MANDELBAUM

> A rumor was current in this city yesterday that Mrs. Mandelbaum had returned from her trip to Canada, wither she had gone to evade trial for receiving stolen goods and had been seen in New York . . . There does not appear to be any truth in the story which seems to have originated in the fact that a woman resembling Mrs. Mandelbaum had been seen in Jersey City where she crossed over to this city on the ferry boat. Detective Sergeant Richard King said last night that he had investigated the rumor and had discovered who the woman was who was mistaken for Mrs. Mandelbaum. He is satisfied that the latter woman is still in Canada.
>
> —*The New York Times*, January 30, 1885

In early December 1885, there was another Mandelbaum sighting, this time in Trenton, New Jersey, where authorities claimed she was seen selling fine laces, silk, and jewelry door-to-door to wealthy patrons at their homes. According to the Trenton police chief, it was believed that it was none other than Mandelbaum and he subsequently contacted Inspector Byrnes in New York about the sighting. Byrnes was nonchalant about the report.

"I would be pleased to effect the arrest of Mother Mandelbaum. If there is a woman in your city who looks like Mother Mandelbaum and she is peddling laces, she is the wife of David Mandelbaum, and not wanted," Byrnes wired the Trenton police chief. This would be the wife of Wolf Mandelbaum's younger brother.

> The peddler who was here today wore a long dark circular, under which she carried a satchel containing laces. She had on also a pair of eye glasses which she had not been known to wear before . . . The local police are puzzled."
>
> —*The New York Times*, December 10, 1885

Mandelbaum's name, although not her presence, was referenced once again in the newspapers about a minor civil matter before the courts regarding her daughter, Sarah Weill. Weill was found guilty by default of abandoning and not paying rent on property in Brooklyn. Despite the fact that the case was relatively minor, the newspaper headline was more sensational, conjuring up the ghost of the once powerful fence.

> MOTHER MANDELBAUM'S DAUGHTER
> SHE IS A DEFENDANT IN THE CITY COURT
> AND LOSES HER CASE BY DEFAULT
>
> —*Brooklyn Eagle*, March 3, 1885

It was not just the New York and New Jersey newspapers and magazines that kept Mandelbaum's name alive. In 1887, nearly three years after Mandelbaum's flight to Canada, the *Washington Post* ran a satirical article aimed at poking fun at criminal celebrity sightings. In it, the *Post* lumped Mandelbaum in with a host of the country's most despicable and notorious (and mostly dead) criminals who had on one occasion or another been reportedly sighted alive and well. Mandelbaum's name continued to turn up in a variety of magazines, newspapers, and books during the last ten years of her life. She remained a legendary criminal.

> Jesse James, the outlaw who was killed by Ford, his pal, has come to life and was recently seen in the wilds of Arizona.

> Of course. Eminent rascals always come to life this way. Madame Restell, who committed suicide in her bath-tub in New York, is in Canada with Mandelbaum; Wilkes Booth's death was a ruse—he is at this moment an Australian miner; Boss Tweed is a grandee in Spain; Capt. Kydd is probably masquerading as Jay Gould, and Benedict Arnold and Judas Iscariot are perhaps living on obscure claims in Montana . . .
>
> —*Washington Post*, January 30, 1887

In June 1888, Julius Mandelbaum had a change of heart. Either that or his mother decided it for him. In either case, he surrendered himself to the district attorney in New York City, asking for the mercy of the court. Peter Olney, the man who had charged Julius and his mother, was no longer district attorney. The case against Julius was dropped and he returned to Canada for a time. He later returned to New York City and became the principal in a company that manufactured and distributed various medicines.

During the ensuing years, whether because of her daughter's sudden death, or homesickness for her old New York neighborhood or just plain old age, Mandelbaum was besieged by a series of illnesses. Although she remained active in her adopted Canadian community she was seen less and less in public. The operations of her shop were turned over to Julius and Herman Stoude and later Stoude when Julius returned to America. On February 26, 1894, Fredericka Mandelbaum died at her home in Hamilton surrounded by her family and Stoude. The cause of death was reported as Bright's Disease, described in modern medicine as a chronic form of nephritis or kidney disease. She was sixty-five years old. Although the obituary notice that appeared in the *Hamilton Spectator* took note of her criminal past, it called her "a woman of kindly disposition, broad sympathies, and large intelligence."

Her body was returned to New York City for burial at the family plot in Union Fields Cemetery of Congregation Rodeph Sholom in Queens, New York. A huge crowd of mourners turned out for her funeral. The crowd included neighbors and friends, legitimate businessmen, police, politicians, judges, newspaper reporters, curiosity seekers, and a score of well-known criminals. They all turned out to pay their last respects to the "Queen of Thieves." Ironically, following Mandelbaum's graveside service at Union Fields Cemetery in Queens, New York, several of the mourners reported to police that their pockets had been picked.

DEATH ENDS HER TROUBLES MRS. FREDERICK A MANDELBAUM DIED THIS MORNING SHE HAD A CHECKERED AND EXCITING HISTORY BUTFOR NEARLY TEN YEARS SHE LIVED AN UNOBTRUSIVE AND UNEVENTFUL LIFE IN HAMILTON—TO BE BURIED IN NEW YORK

—*Hamilton Spectator*, February 27, 1894

OLD "MOTHER" MANDELBAUM IS DEAD SHE WAS A FAMOUS "FENCE" WELL KNOWN TO THE POLICE OF THIS CITY

HAMILTON, Ontario, Feb. 26—Mrs. Fredericka Mandelbaum, known in New York City as a notorious "fence" and who did a profitable business there in that line for a number of years, died here this morning. She came here about ten years ago when the New York authorities began proceedings against her and her convictions seemed probable. A legal fight ensued for her extradition, but with the assistance of Howe & Hummel, the criminal lawyers of New York, she was enabled to remain in Canada . . . Her body will be taken to New York tomorrow afternoon for interment there Wednesday morning . . .For nearly a quarter of a century she prospered. Her success was in a great measure due to her friendship for and her loyalty to the thieves with whom she did business. She never betrayed her clients, and when they got into trouble she procured bail for them and

> befriended them to the extent of her power ... It is said that professional jealousy of her success as a receiver of stolen goods, and a quarrel with a clique of detectives who had long been her friends, led to her downfall. Pinkerton detectives were employed to secure her arrest. A trap was laid for her, and the shrewd woman was caught. This happened in July, 1884, when several pieces of black silk, which had been marked, were taken by a "stool pigeon" from a Broadway dry-goods store and sold to Mrs. Mandelbaum.
>
> —*The New York Times,* February 27, 1894

Newspapers throughout the country ran the story of Mandelbaum's death and several ran longer than average reports. The *Boston Globe* reported that "there is not a thief of note in the land to whom her name is not as familiar as his own." The *Washington Post* reported she had amassed a substantial fortune working "as a go-between for thieves and crooks, and as the receiver of stolen goods in New York." The German newspaper, *The New York Staats-Zeitung,* proclaimed that "With her stiffening body, a piece of New York the way we know it will be taken to the grave." Fredericka Mandelbaum had aroused the imagination of many people during her career, and continued to do so even after her death. There was a claim that Mandelbaum had faked her own death so that she could return to New York City and take up where she left off in her criminal activities. New York City police officials called the story a "ridiculous yarn." Still, rumors of her continued to persist.

MOTHER MANDELBAUM SAID TO BE ALIVE OUT IN COLUMBUS, OHIO, THEY THINK—HER REPORTED DEATH A RUSE

> COLUMBUS, Ohio, Aug. 27.—A story is published here that Mother Mandelbaum, the notorious "fence," who lived for a long time in New-York and who was reported to have died recently in Montreal, is not dead.

> The reported death, according to this story, was for the purpose of concealing her further movements. A coffin filled with stones is said to have been shipped to New-York as one containing her body . . . Inspector McLaughlin said yesterday that he did not credit the statement that Mother Mandelbaum was alive. He declared the entire story to be a "ridiculous yarn . . ." Others however are inclined to think that Mother Mandelbaum may really be alive . . . the casket which was said to contain her body was not opened . . .
>
> —*The New York Times*, August 28, 1894

Whatever the reason, the dichotomy of Fredericka Mandelbaum's life—her cunning ability to acquire wealth and power in ways unheard of by any woman—served for many poor immigrants as a glorious tale of achievement, providing them with the hope and possibility of achieving the American dream despite great odds. Her power was celebrated by the powerless. For others, she was a symbol of all that was wrong with the workings of government and law enforcement. Her role in society was not to be emulated, but stopped. During her lifetime, that was all but impossible. After her death, one way or another, she was destined for legendary status. Mandelbaum's 1884 obituary in the *New York Volkszeitung,* a German language daily labor newspaper, referred to her as "honorable and reliable" in business dealings and asserted that "her word was as good as gold." The newspaper advocated that a plaque in her name be erected in her Lower East Side neighborhood. This would have greatly pleased Mandelbaum, who probably would have asked who she had to pay off in order to get the plaque erected.

> "Mother Mandelbaum was the smartest fence in America."
>
> —Charles S. Frost, *Brooklyn Eagle,* June 27, 1897
>
> (Frost was a New York City detective for forty years)

AFTERWORD

"Out, out, brief candle! Life's but a walking shadow."

—William Shakespeare, *Macbeth*

Among Mandelbaum's mentors in the fencing business, Joe Erich died in 1865. No mention of him was made in the press. Ephraim Snow reportedly died in 1868. Abe Greenthal died in 1889 at the age of sixty-three years old. His criminal career was written up in *The New York Times*.

END OF A CRIMINAL CAREER
OLD ABE GREENTHAL DIES OF OLD AGE—
HIS LIFE STORY

> He was the head of a gang of clever pickpockets and shoplifters, and when he was not actually engaged in thefts he was instrumental in disposing of plunder. In this connection he once had close "business" relations with "Mother" Mandelbaum . . . He fell into the hands of the police many times but managed almost invariably by the lavish use of money and the peculiar influence he could make use of, to escape conviction . . .
>
> —*The New York Times*, November 20, 1889

Mandelbaum's archrival in the fencing business, John "Traveling Mike" Grady, died in 1880.

BANKER OF THE BURGLARS
DEATH OF JOHN D. GRADY, RECEIVER
OF STOLEN GOODS

> No man was better known to the Police, not only of New York but every large city in the United States, and to criminals of high grade, especially bank burglars, than John D. Grady, whose ostensible calling was that of a diamond broker. . . . Many Police officers asserted—and Grady never denied it—that the diamond broker was not only a receiver of stolen goods, but the banker of many first-class criminals. . . . Grady, Police officials say, arranged the details of the Manhattan Bank burglary, and spent $10,000 on the preliminary attempts. . . .
>
> — *The New York Times,* October 4, 1880

Fernando Wood, considered New York City's most corrupt mayor, went on to serve as a Congressman from New York from 1863 to 1865 and 1867 to 1881. He died in Hot Springs, Arkansas, in 1881 at the age of sixty-nine years old.

William Marcy "Boss" Tweed, the archetypal big city political boss, never left the confines of his Ludlow Street Jail cell where he was sent in 1876 and died on April 12, 1878, from severe pneumonia.

Kitty Flynn, the beautiful wife of bank burglar and safecracker Piano Charlie Bullard, who died in a Belgium prison in 1892, and was the paramour of international thief Adam Worth, died in 1894.

MRS. KATE LOUISE TERRY DEAD HEIRESS TO A $1,000,000 FORTUNE AND HER DAUGHTER TO GET $5,000,000

> Mrs. Kate Louise Terry, the widow of Juan P. Terry, died last week and was privately buried. She had been before her second marriage, Mrs. Kate Flynn and had lived in Brooklyn. She married some years ago, Charles Bullard, alias "Piano Charlie" the bank burglar, but when she found out his true character and also that he had another wife living, she left

> him and resumed her maiden name . . . Juan Pedro Terry was the son of Tomas Terry, a millionaire sugar planter. In 1887 he died leaving $1,000,000 to his wife, and $5,000,000 in trust for Juanita Teresita, her baby daughter.
>
> —*The New York Times*, March 22, 1894

Adam Worth died on January 8, 1902, and was buried in Highgate Cemetery in London. Perhaps one of the most compelling ironies of all was that Worth's son, Harry Raymond Jr., grew up to become a Pinkerton detective.

WORTH STOLE THE GAINSBOROUGH
DETAILS AS TO THE THEFT AND RETURN OF THE PICTURE MADE PUBLIC

> CHICAGO, Feb. 6—With the announcement of Adam Worth's death to-day all the details of the recovery of the celebrated Gainsborough painting were made public here . . . it was here in London that Worth conceived of the idea of carrying off the picture . . . Assisted by his partner he climbed into the Agnew galleries one night, cut the painting from its canvas and carried it away . . . he took the picture to Paris and finally brought it to America where it was conciliated for fifteen years. In the meantime Worth was arrested in Belgium and forced to serve seven years . . .
>
> —*The New York Times*, February 7, 1902

Sophie Lyons, who rose to the heights of criminal infamy under Mandelbaum's tutelage becoming known as the "Princess of Crime," and who in later life disavowed her life of crime, died in May 1924. Living in Detroit and working to rehabilitate convicts, her life came to a tragic end when thieves she had been trying to reform visited her home and demanded money and jewels. When she refused, they pistol whipped her. She died of head injuries at the age of seventy-five years old. She was cremated and her ashes were placed in her son's grave at the Woodmere Cemetery in Detroit.

ONCE QUEEN OF CROOKS, DIES A PHILANTHROPIST SOPHIE LYONS, WHOM INSPECTOR BYRNES CALLED THE WORLD'S MOST DANGEROUS WOMAN, FINISHED HER DAYS AS A PEACEABLE CITIZEN AND A PROPERTY OWNER

> MRS. SOPHIE BURKE, property owner, is dead in Detroit . . . leaving to charity a fortune (including jewelry) worth anywhere from $200,000 up—some say $1,000,000. That is the end of Sophie Lyons.
>
> —*The New York Times*, May 18, 1924

Thomas Byrnes, New York City's top cop resigned from office after being investigated for corrupt practices by then New York City Police Commissioner Theodore Roosevelt.

Byrnes denied any wrongdoing and the committee never presented any evidence otherwise, but rather than face public scrutiny Byrnes retired. He became an insurance investigator, opening a detective agency on Wall Street. He died in 1910 of stomach cancer.

Robert Pinkerton, co-director along with his twin brother William of the celebrated private security firm the Pinkerton National Detective Agency died in 1907. His brother died in 1923.

Allan Pinkerton, founder of the detective agency died at age 64 on July 1, 1884, a month before his son Robert was able to apprehend the infamous Fredericka Mandelbaum. He slipped and fell onto the pavement of a Chicago street and bit his tongue. His death resulted from gangrene.

Mandelbaum's nemisis, Peter B. Olney, ran for re-election for the office of District Attorney in 1884 but lost. He died on February 9, 1922. He was seventy-eight years old. His attempt at prosecuting Mandelbaum was not mentioned in his lengthy obituary.

PETER BUTLER OLNEY DIES OF PNEUMONIA EX-DISTRICT ATTORNEY SUCCUMBS SUDDENLY AT HIS CEDARHURST HOME AT 78 YEARS

Peter Butler Olney, District Attorney for New York Country from 1883 to 1885 and younger brother of the late Richard Olney, Secretary of State in Cleveland's second Administration, died suddenly yesterday of pneumonia at his home in Cedarhurst, L.I . . . In 1897 he established a new firm, Olney & Comstock, of which he continued as senior partner until his death . . .

—*The New York Times*, February 10, 1922

William Howe, half of Mandelbaum's notorious legal team of Howe & Hummel, died in 1902 of a heart attack.

WILLIAM F. HOWE, DEAN OF CRIMINAL BAR, DEAD NOTED LAWYER STRICKEN WITH HEART DISEASE WHILE IN BED

William F. Howe, senior member of the law firm of Howe & Hummel, was found dead in bed at his home . . . Mr. Howe was one of the most picturesque figures at the American bar. In the course of his fifty years of practice in this city he had defended six hundred men in homicide cases and a very remarkable percentage of those men enjoyed almost miraculous escapes from sentences of death through the ingenious tactics of their counsel . . . Mr. Howe was spectacular from whatever view he was regarded. He was only 5 feet 7 inches high, yet he weighed nearly 250 pounds . . . Mr. Howe had been married three times . . .

—*The New York Times*, September 3, 1902

In 1907, five years after Howe's death, his partner, Abraham Hummel, was convicted of persuading a witness to commit perjury, disbarred, and sent to prison for a year. The company of Howe & Hummel was dissolved. After his release from prison, Hummel moved to Paris and later to London where he died in 1926 at the age of 75.

BIBLIOGRAPHY

Abbott, Karen. "The Life and Crimes of 'Old Mother' Mandelbaum." *Smithsonian.com,* 2004.

"Allan Pinkerton's Death . . ." *New York Times,* July 2, 1884.

"Another Bank Robbery . . ." *New York Times,* April, 1870.

"Another Shot at Byrnes . . ." *New York Times*, August 8, 1884.

Asbury, Herbert. *The Gangs of New York: An Informal History of the Underworld,* Thunder's Mouth Press, 2001 (reprint of 1928 edition).

___. *All Around the Town,* Basic Books, 2003.

Anbinder, Tyler. *Five Points: The 19th-Century Neighborhood that Invented Tap Dance, Stole Elections, and Became the World's Most Notorious Slum.* New York: The Free Press, 2002

Atkins, Gordon. *Health, Housing and Poverty in New York City, 1865–1898.* Ann Arbor, MI: Edwards Brothers, 1947.

Abelson, Elaine S. *When Women Go A-Thieving: Middle-Class Shoplifters in the Victorian Department Store.* Oxford: Oxford University Press, 1992.

"Adroit Larceny of $2,600. . ."*New York Times,* December 4, 1870.

Bak, Richard and Neal Rubin. *Detroitland: A Collection of Movers, Shakers, Souls and History Makers from Detroit's Past.* Wayne State University Press, 2011.

Bak, Richard. "From Rogue to Reformer."*Hour Story*. November 2009.

"Bank Burglars Captured . . ."*New York Times,* April 30, 1880.

"Bank Heist," The National Night Stick: Crime, Eccentricity and 19th-Century America, April 3, 2011, no author cited, online journal.

"Banker of the Burglars . . ." *New York Times,* October 4, 1880.

Barnes, David. *The Draft Riots in New York.* New York: Baker & Godwin, 1863.

Bird, Caroline. *Enterprising Women.* New York: W. W. Norton & Company, Inc., 1976.

"Bold Attempt at Burglary . . ." *Brooklyn Eagle,* February 29, 1868.

"Bold Bank Robbery . . ." *New York Times,* August, 1870.

Bosak, Michael. quoted in David J. Krajicek, "A Look Back at Corrupt Cops," *The New York Daily News,* July 3, 2011.

Browne, Julius Henri. *The Great Metropolis: a Mirror of New York. A Complete History of Metropolitan Life and Society, with Sketches of Prominent Places, Persons and Things in the City as they Actually Exist.* Hartford, CT: American Publishing Company, 1869.

Bryk, William. "The Scams of Grandma Fence." *New York Press,* 2003.

"Bulldozing the Court . . ." *New York Times,* July 31, 1884.

Burrows, G. Edwin and Mike Wallace. *Gotham: A History of New York City to 1898.* New York: Oxford University Press, 1999.

Byrnes, Thomas. Professional Criminals in America (1896). Reprint, New York: Lyons Press, 2000.

Caldwell, Mark. *New York Night: The Mystique and Its History.* Simon and Schuster, 2005.

Callow, Alexander B. Jr. *The Tweed Ring,* Oxford University Press, 1966.

Campbell, Helen. *Darkness and Daylight: Lights and Shadows of New York Life.* Hartford: The Hartford Publishing Company, 1891. "The Case of Mrs. Mandelbaum . . ." *New York Times,* December 3, 1884.

Cashman, Sean Dennis. *America in the Gilded Age.* NYU Press, 1993.

"Chinese men sold candy and cigars . . ." *New York Magazine,* August 12, 1991.

Clinton, H. L. *Celebrated Trials.* New York: Harper & Brothers Publishers, 1897.

"Copy of Certificate of Inspectors Furnished . . ." *New York Times*, September 5, 1861.

Cordey, Stacy A. "Women in Industrializing America," *The Gilded Age: Perspectives on the Origins of Modern America*, Charles Eilliam Calhoun, editor, Rowman & Littlefield Publishers, 2006.

Costello, Augustine E. *Our Police Protectors: History of the New York Police from the Earliest Period to the Present Time*. New York: A. Costello, 1885.

Crapsey, Edward. *The Nether Side of New York or the Vice, Crime, and Poverty of the Great Metropolis*. New York: Sheldon & Company, 1872.

"Crime and the Police . . ." *New York Times*, July 24, 1884.

Dash, Mike. *Satan's Circus: Murder, Vice, Police Corruption, and New York's Trial of the Century*. New York: Three Rivers Press, 2007.

"Death Ends Her Troubles . . ." *Hamilton Spectator*, February 27, 1894.

Dickens, Charles. *American Notes for General Circulation*. London: Chapman and Hall, 1842.

Doran, James D. *Desperate Men*. New York: Doubleday & Co., 1962.

Dunlop, M. H. *Gilded City: Scandal and Sensation in Turn-of-the-Century New York*. New York: William Morrow, 2001.

Eldridge, Benjamin and William Watts. *Our Rival, the Rascal: A faithful Portrait of the Conflict Between the Criminals of this Age and the Defenders of Society*. Boston: Pemberton Publishing, 1897.

"End of a Criminal Career . . ." *New York Times*, November 20, 1889.

Ernst, Robert. *Immigrant Life in New York City*. New York: King's Crown, 1949.

"The Escape of Porter and Irving . . ." *New York Times*, July 25, 1879.

"The Express Robbery . . ." *New York Times*, January 9, 1869.

"A Fatal Riot . . ." *New York Times*, July 23, 1871.

The Finest to be Investigated . . ." *Brooklyn Eagle*, July 27, 1884.

Fried, Albert. *The Rise and Fall of the Jewish Gangster in America*. New York: Columbia University Press, 1993.

Francis, Mary. "Fair Financiers Who Have Fleeced Cautious Capitalists" *The Scrap Book*, Vol. 5, 1908.

"Funeral of the Victim . . ." *New York Times,* June 10, 1878.

Joseph Geringer, "Adam Worth: The World in His Pocket," (no date provided)

"Geo. L. Howard [Leslie] . . ." *Brooklyn Eagle,* March 10, 1879

Geringer, Joseph. "Adam Worth: The World in His Pocket" (no date given).

Gilfoyle, Timothy J. *A Pickpocket's Tale: The Underworld of Nineteenth Century*. New York, W. W. Norton & Company, 2007.

___. *City of Eros: New York City, Prostitution, and the Commercialization of Sex, 1790–1920*. New York: W. W. Norton & Company, 1994.

"Giving the Lie Direct . . ." *New York Times*, August 5, 1884.

"A Great Bank Robbery . . ." *New York Times,* October 28, 1878.

"The Greenthals, for many years have been known . . ." *New York Times*, November 24, 1874. Hartsfield, Larry K. *The American Response to Professional Crime, 1870 - 1917*. Westport: Greeenwood Press, 1985.

"Heavy Bank Robbery . . ." *New York Times,* August, 1872.

"Heavy Bank Robbery . . ." *New York Times,* October, 1876.

Heidensohn, Frances M. *Women and Crime*. New York: New York University Press, 1995.

Higham, John. "Anti-Semitism in the Gilded Age: A Reinterpretation." *The Mississippi Valley Historical Review,* Vol. 43, No. 4, 1957.

Horan, Frank. *The Pinkertons: The Detective Dynasty That Made History*, New York: Crown, 1968.

Holub, Rona. "Fredericka 'Marm' Mandelbaum 'Queen of the Fences:' The Rise and Fall of a Female Immigrant Criminal

Entrepreneur in Nineteenth-Century." New York: Columbia University doctoral dissertation, 2007.

"He (a Jew) is perhaps . . ." *Evening Telegram*, October 19,1872.

"Her Son Julius Bailed . . ." *New York Times*, July 26, 1884.

Holbrook, Stewart Hall. *The Age of the Moguls*. Garden City, New York: Doubleday & Co., 1953.

Howe, William F., and Abraham Hummel. *Danger: A True History of a Great City's Wiles and Temptations*. New York: Courier, 1886.

"If a Shoddy . . ." *Vanity Fair*, November, 1861.

"In Praise of the Police . . ." *New York Times*, May 11, 1884

"Inspector Byrnes and the District Attorney . . ." *Brooklyn Eagle*, August 3, 1884.

"Is Detective Frank on Trial . . ." *New York Times*, September 16, 1884.

"Jesse James, the outlaw . . ." *Washington Post*, January 30, 1887.

"The Jews have a monopoly . . ." *New York Times*, July 6, 1866.

"Jimmy Hope Dies . . ." *New York Times*, June 3, 1905.

Johnson, Marilynn S. *Street Justice: A History of Police Violence in New York City*. Boston: Beacon Press, 2004.

Josephson, Matthew. *The Robber Barons*. New York: Harcourt, 1934.

Kirchner, L. R. *Robbing Banks: An American History, 1831 –1999*. New York: Barnes & Noble Books, 2003.

Klockars, Carl B. *The Professional Fence*. New York: The Free Press, 1974.

Krajicek, David J. "A Look Back at Corrupt Cops," *The New York Daily News*, July 3, 2011.

Lardner, James and Thomas Reppetto. *NYPD: A City and Its Police*. New York: Henry Holt & Company, 2001.

Lavine, Sigmund A. *Allan Pinkerton –America's First Private Eye* NY: Dodd, Mead & Co., 1963.

"Leary's Capture and Escape . . ." *New York Times*, August 1877.

Lening, Gustav. *The Dark Side of New York, and Its Criminal Classes from Fifth Avenue Down to the Five Points. A Complete Narrative of the Mysteries of New York*. New York: Frederick Gerhard, 1873.

"The Life and Crimes of 'Old Mother' Mandelbaum," *Smithsonian*, 2011.

"Living Underground . . ." *New York Times*, December 5, 1869.

Long, Kat. *The Forbidden Apple: A Century of Sex & Sin in New York City*. New York: Ig Publishing, 2009.

Longstreet, Stephen, ed. *Nell Kimball: Her Life as an American Madam by Herself*. New York: The MacMillan Company, 1970.

Lyons, Sophie. *Why Crime Does Not Pay*. New York: J.S. Ogilvie Publishing Co., 1913.

Lynch, Denis Tilden. *Boss Tweed: The Story of a Grim Generation*. New York: Boni and Liveright, 1927.

Macintyre, Ben. *The Napoleon of Crime: The Life and Times of Adam Worth, Master Thief*, New York: Broadway, 2011.

McNamara, Joseph. *The Justice Story*. New York: Sports Publishing LLC, 2000.

Marcus, Jacob Rader. *United States Jewry, 1776-1985*. Wayne State University Press, 1989.

Marcuse, Maxwell F. *This Was New York! A Nostalgic Picture o/Gotham in the Gaslight Era*. New York: LIM Press, 1969.

"Marm Mandelbaum Arrested . . ." *New York Times*, December 9, 1884.

Martin, Edward Winslow. *The Secrets of the Great City: A Work Descriptive of the Virtues and the Vices, the Mysteries, Miseries and Crimes of New York City*. Philadelphia: Jones Brothers & Co., 1868.

Maurice, Arthur B. *Fifth Avenue*. New York: Dodd, Mead & Company, 1918.

"The Mob in New York . . ." *New York Times*, July 14, 1863.

Morton, James. *Gangland: The Early Years*. New York: Time Warner Paperbacks, 2004.

"Mother Mandelbaum . . ." *New York Times*, December 5, 1884.

Mother Mandelbaum's Daughter . . ." *Brooklyn Eagle*, March 3, 1885.

"Mother Mandelbaum's Escape . . ." *New York Times*, December 6, 1884.

"Mother Mandelbaum's Struggles . . ." *New York Times*, September 20, 1884.

"Mother Mandelbaum was the smartest fence in America. . ." Charles S. Frost, *Brooklyn Eagle,* June 27, 1897.

Moss, Frank. *The American Metropolis, From Knickerbocker Days to the Present Time; New York City Life in All Its Phases*. New York: P.F. Collier, 1897.

"Mr. Byrnes Gets Excited . . ." *New York Times*, May 13, 1884.

"Mr. Olney's Boomerang . . ." *New York Times*, August 3, 1884.

"Mrs. Kate Louise Terry Dead . . ."*New York Times*, March 22, 1894.

"Mrs. Mandelbaum Case . . ." *New York Times*, July 29, 1884.

"Mrs. Mandelbaum in Canada . . ." *New York Times*, December 6, 1884.

"Mrs. Mandelbaum is a German Jewess . . ." *New York Times*, July 24, 1884.

"Mrs. Mandelbaum Missing . . ." *New York Times*, December 5, 1884.

"Mrs. Mandelbaum Released . . ." *New York Times*, December 13, 1884.

"Mrs. Mandelbaum's Visit . . ." *New York Times*, November 12, 1885.

Murphy, Cait. *Scoundrels In Law: The Trials of Howe & Hummel, Lawyers to the Gangsters, Cops, Starlets, and Rakes Who Made the Gilded Age*. Washington D.C.: Smithsonian, 2010.

"Mysterious Escape of Express Robbers . . ." *New York Times*, April 6, 1869

Nadel, Stanley. *Little Germany: Ethnicity, Religion, and Class in New York City, 1845-80*. Urbana: University of Illinois Press, 1990.

Nash, Jay Robert. *Bloodletters and Badmen.* M. Evans, 1973.

Nevius, Michelle and James Nevius. *Inside the Apple: A Streetwise History of New York City.* Simon and Schuster, 2009.

"New York Officials at War . . ." *Brooklyn Eagle,* August 3, 1884.

Newton, Michael. *The Encyclopedia of Robberies, Heists, and Capers.* New York: Facts on File, 2002.

"The Northampton Bank Robbery . . ." *Brooklyn Eagle,* January 27, 1876.

"The Northampton Bank Robbery . . ." *Springfield Republican,* March 19, 1877.

"Not Mrs. Mandelbaum . . ." *New York Times,* January 30, 1885.

"The Notorious Shoplifter's Conviction . . ." *Brooklyn Eagle,* December 11, 1878.

"Notorious Thief Dead . . ." *The Jewelers' Circular,* Vol. 79, 1919.

"A Nut for the Police . . ." *New York Times,* August 2, 1884.

O'Connor, Richard. *Hell's Kitchen: The Roaring Days of New York's Wild West Side.* New York: J. B. Lippincott, 1958.

O'Kane, James M. *The Crooked Ladder: Gangsters, Ethnicity, and the American Dream.* Somerset, New Jersey: Transaction Publishers, 2003.

"Old Mother Mandelbaum Is Dead . . ." *New York Times,* February 27, 1894.

"Once Queen of Crooks . . ."*New York Times,* May 18, 1924.

Paine, Albert Bigelow. *Thomas Nast: His Period and His Pictures.* New York: Macmillan, 1904.

Patton, Clifford W. *The Battle for Municipal Reform: Mobilization and Attack, 1875–1900.* Washington, D.C.: American Council on Public Affairs,1940.

Peiss, Kathy. *Cheap Amusements: Working Women and Leisure in Turn-of-the-Century New York.* Philadelphia: Temple University Press, 1990.

Pietrusza, David. *Rothstein: The Life, Times, and Murder of the Criminal Genius Who Fixed the 1919 World Series.* New York: Carroll and Graf, 2004.

Pinkerton, Allen. *Criminal Reminiscences and Detective Sketches*. New York: Garrett Press, Inc., 1969 Reprint (1879).

___. *Professional Thieves and the Detective*. New York: G.W. Carleton & Co., Publishers, 1973 Reprint (1881).

___. *The Molly Maguires*, G.W. Dillingham, 1905, Copyright 1877.

___. *The Expressman and the Detective*, W.B. Keen, Cooke & Co., 1874.

"The Police Condemned . . ." *New York Times*, May 16, 1884.

"Police Reports . . ." *New York Times*, February 20, 1861.

"The Police Wrought Up . . ." *New York Times*, July 27, 1884.

"Porter and Irving Again Escape . . ." *New York Times*, July 24, 1879.

"A Queen Among Thieves . . ." *New York Times*, July 24, 1884.

"Recent Robberies . . ."*Brooklyn Eagle*, March 19, 1873.

"Receivers of Stolen Goods . . ." *New York Times*, July 18, 1873.

"The Responsibility for Yesterday's Bank Robbery . . ." *Brooklyn Eagle*, October 28, 1878.

Richardson, James F. *The New York Police: Colonial Times to 1901*. New York: Oxford University Press, 1970.

Riis, Jacob. *The Making of an American*. New York: Macmillan, 1901.

"A Robbed Merchant's Suit . . ." *New York Times*, January 24, 1884.

Rockoff, Hugh. "Great Fortunes of the Gilded Age."*National Bureau of Economic Research*, December, 2008.

"The Rogues Gallery . . ." *New York Times*, June 27 1875.

Rovere, Richard. *Howe and Hummel: Their True and Scandalous History*. New York: Farrar, Straus, 1947.

Sachar, Howard M. *A History of Jews in America*. New York: Alfred A. Knopf, 1992.

Sante, Luc. *Low Life: Lures and Snares of Old New York*. New York: Farrar, Straus and Giroux, 2003.

"She receives the results of robberies . . ." *Puck Magazine*, June 17, 1885.

"Sheeny Mike's Career . . ." *New York Times*, April 29, 1876.

"Shinburn Again Caught . . ." *New York Times*, June 30, 1895.

Smith, Matthew Hale. *Sunshine and Shadow in New York*. Hartford: J. B. Burr & Company, 1869.

Soodalter, Ron. "The Union's 'Shoddy' Aristocracy."*New York Times*, 2011.

Steffens, Lincoln. *Shame of the Cities*. New York: McClure, Phillips & Company, 1905.

Swierczynski, Duane. *This Here's A Stick-Up: The Big Bad Book of American Bank Robbery*. Indianapolis: Alpha Books, 2002.

"Tenement Houses . . ." *New York Times*, March 14, 1856.

Waldo, Gordon P. *Professional Theft*. Beverly Hills: Sage Publications, 1983.

Walling, George Washington. *Recollections of a New York Chief of Police*. New York: Caxton Book Concern, 1887.

Woodiwiss, Michael. *Organized Crime and American Power: A History*. Toronto: University of Toronto Press, 2001.

Wood, Sharon. *The Freedom of the Streets: Work, Citizenship, and Sexuality in a Gilded Age City*. Chapel Hill, North Carolina: University of North Carolina Press, 2005.

"Worth Stole the Gainsborough . . ." *New York Times*, February 7, 1902.

INDEX